Palgrave Studies in Religion, Politics, and Policy

Series Editors
Ted G. Jelen
Political Sciences
University of Nevada
Las Vegas, NV, USA

Mark J. Rozell
School of Policy
Government and International Affairs
George Mason University
Fairfax, VA, USA

A generation ago, many social scientists regarded religion as an anachronism, whose social, economic, and political importance would inevitably wane and disappear in the face of the inexorable forces of modernity. Of course, nothing of the sort has occurred; indeed, the public role of religion is resurgent in US domestic politics, in other nations, and in the international arena. Today, religion is widely acknowledged to be a key variable in candidate nominations, platforms, and elections; it is recognized as a major influence on domestic and foreign policies. National religious movements as diverse as the Christian Right in the United States and the Taliban in Afghanistan are important factors in the internal politics of particular nations. Moreover, such transnational religious actors as Al-Qaida, Falun Gong, and the Vatican have had important effects on the politics and policies of nations around the world.

Palgrave Studies in Religion, Politics, and Policy serves a growing niche in the discipline of political science. This subfield has proliferated rapidly during the past two decades, and has generated an enormous amount of scholarly studies and journalistic coverage. Five years ago, the journal Politics and Religion was created; in addition, works relating to religion and politics have been the subject of many articles in more general academic journals. The number of books and monographs on religion and politics has increased tremendously. In the past, many social scientists dismissed religion as a key variable in politics and government.

This series casts a broad net over the subfield, providing opportunities for scholars at all levels to publish their works with Palgrave. The series publishes monographs in all subfields of political science, including American Politics, Public Policy, Public Law, Comparative Politics, International Relations, and Political Theory.

The principal focus of the series is the public role of religion. "Religion" is construed broadly to include public opinion, religious institutions, and the legal frameworks under which religious politics are practiced. The "dependent variable" in which we are interested is politics, defined broadly to include analyses of the public sources and consequences of religious belief and behavior. These would include matters of public policy, as well as variations in the practice of political life. We welcome a diverse range of methodological perspectives, provided that the approaches taken are intellectually rigorous.

The series does not deal with works of theology, in that arguments about the validity or utility of religious beliefs are not a part of the series focus. Similarly, the authors of works about the private or personal consequences of religious belief and behavior, such as personal happiness, mental health, or family dysfunction, should seek other outlets for their writings. Although historical perspectives can often illuminate our understanding of modern political phenomena, our focus in the Religion, Politics, and Policy series is on the relationship between the sacred and the political in contemporary societies.

More information about this series at
http://www.springer.com/series/14594

We are dedicating this book to the new generations in Southeastern Europe.
A critical mind is the only way to freedom...

FOREWORD

Whether and how religious education is to be delivered in public schools largely depends on the relationship between the state and religious institutions (usually couched in terms of church-state relations) and the degree of religious liberty and human rights in specific societies. A basic typology of church-state relationships from the perspective of religious liberty can be formulated into four basic types.[1]

Type A: Ecclesiastical Absolutism. This type can also be seen as absolutist sacral monopoly in which one religious community monopolizes the religious space and dominates and suppresses all alternate interpretations of religion and reality. Minority religions, agnosticism, and atheism are stifled. Generally this type prevailed during the Middle Ages, but can still be detected in countries like Saudi Arabia, from which impulses are sometimes disseminated as far as the Balkans.

Type B: Religious Toleration. The state is benign toward religion in general, but tends to give preferential treatment to one or more religious communities. Religious minorities are tolerated but are often given unequal practical treatment. While freedom of religion and thought are often legally guaranteed, atheism and "cults" are denied equal treatment. This model was and is the prevalent arrangement in most European countries.

Type C: Secularistic Absolutism. This type consists of radical and sometimes even violent restrictions to public expressions of religiosity, driving religion into the private sphere under the guise of separation of church and state. Religious instructions are eliminated from the curriculum and atheism is vigorously promoted in education as it is in most areas of life. Communist countries implemented this model to various degrees. Former Yugoslavia initially practiced this model but gradually relaxed and modified its implementation up to the end of the 1980s.

Type D: Pluralistic Liberty. This social arrangement would promote the free, non-interventionist approach by a tolerant secular society that would indicate the full exercise in freedom to a variety of truth claims, both religious and non-religious. The state would be indifferent or neutral, yet benignly accept positive contributions of religious belief and practice for both individuals and society, but certainly refrain from discriminating against religious or atheist organizations and persons. This, in my view is the desired for social model of the future, toward which the evolution of a country like the former Yugoslavia should aim.

Few anticipated the rapidity of the formal collapse of the Communist system throughout Eastern Europe and the Soviet Union and even less the explosion of violence that characterized the transformation from communism to post-communism in Yugoslavia. During the tragic wars of the 1990s in the territories of former Yugoslavia, I traveled to better understand what was transpiring. I used the opportunity to inquire of those whom I interviewed, some of whom were important religious leaders, as to their preference for the type of church-state relations and their aspiration in regard to teaching religion in schools. My Orthodox interviewees quickly opted for a Greek model while my Catholic interviewees opted for an Austrian or Italian model (at the time I had few opportunities to interview Muslim leaders). Obviously they wished for a Type B model and quickly indicated their disinterest in the USA model which is probably closer to Type D. Their wishes have now largely been implemented throughout the region.

It is evident to me that their aspirations did come to fruition as is illustrated by the chapters in this book, edited by Gorana Ognjenović and Jasna Jozelić, *Education in Post-Conflict Transition: Politicization of Religion in School Textbooks*. Unsurprisingly, after the partition of Yugoslavia into seven separate countries, of which several have sharply contesting visions of their internal arrangement that may yet lead to further fragmentation, different proposals emerged as to how religion was going to be taught in the public school system. A novelty emerged in ex-Yugoslavia, namely that religious communities are permitted to operate their own schools in addition to those for the education of the clergy or professional leaders. That was a positive step toward expanding religious liberty.

More conflictual was the question of whether religion should be taught as a scholarly subject not controlled by the religious communities (to which many scholars educated in the previous system were inclined), or whether the control should be turned over to the faith communities to conduct a more or less catechetical form of instruction. Consensus was achieved relatively quickly on the need, in the words of Dragan Todorović, a professor at the University of Niš in Serbia, "for the democratization of our social reality and of the process of demarxization and deatheization of our educational system."[2] He pointed out several models proposed by well-known scholars from various areas of the former Yugoslavia, but soon other alternatives emerged as well. Some of the chapters in this book portray not only a general division of opinion regarding the desired alternative but this was the case even within the religious communities. The central role of the predominant church or religious community prevailed both due to the hugely increased social role of churches/religious communities both locally and regionally, and to overwhelming parental preference. The faith communities were generally legally mandated to provide instruction to children of their faith in the public schools. Let me provide an example from Croatia, which has its parallels in most of other successor states of Yugoslavia, "a whole set of other laws and regulations . . . enforce a nationalist agenda, and Catholicism largely determines who belongs to the nation. Religious catechism is introduced in schools, and Catholic priests sit in committees for approving history books with which they are enforcing their religious views. Religion, therefore, has a significant position in the religious education Croatian pupils receive, and the education is one-sided and nationalistic."[3] That, of course, left the question of minority children's position in the system, who either had to attend religious instruction in a faith not their own or had to be exempted from instruction and feel ostracized. However, this does not seem to deter the historically dominant religions, each in their own state. As Vjekoslav Perica noted, the Roman Catholic "Church has a role in the making of the new Croat nation and this project is unfinished and unarticulated like the other new ethno-confessional identity constructs in the post-Yugoslav space."[4]

To implement faith-based education was quite a challenge to the churches/religious communities. First, there was no precedent except the pre-World War II obsolete catechetical practice. Second, they had to rapidly train teachers and provide textbooks (Catholics had an advantage in regard to textbooks as they could adapt German and Austrian literature).

Third, they had to present this content with a contemporary pedagogy. Fourth, they faced a contradictory task to contribute to the integration of the new states consistent with the EU practices by educating children and young people for living in pluralistically diverse societies dealing with "others" in an ecumenical and interreligious spirit, while aiming to strengthen their own religious community. These were formidable tasks, particularly because many religious leaders and educators did not subscribe to the multicultural and multiconfessional approach of nurturing plurality of ideas and positions as these results in a loss of criteria of what is good or evil and what is useful or harmful, and thereby diminishes Christian values.[5]

The result of introducing ethnoreligiously based education was that in states like Bosnia and Herzegovina, a drastic bifurcation or trifurcation of curricula took place. Children of different faith traditions were often taught entirely different ethnoreligious content, even if they attended school in the same building. The positive side of it was that the near uniformity of the educational delivery in the Socialist Federal Republic of Yugoslavia was discontinued and a diversification of educational approaches was introduced. The near tragic side of the new educational programs was that children were now taught drastically different content in social sciences and literature as well as religion classes and, therefore, no longer shared a common understanding of their past and present. This is, of course, ominous in regard to the prospect of building a democratic, pluralistic, tolerant, and cooperative future in their common homeland, because the uniformity in which religious education is delivered "is a mere role-switching" with the dogmatic Marxist approaches in education.[6]

Churches and religious communities have experienced a massive realignment since the fall of communism. Under communism, former rival and competitive churches and religious communities faced a common controlling and dominant ideology that was hostile to the very existence of religion, which forced them to cooperate at least superficially. As a result, some fleeting experiences of ecumenism and interreligious dialog began manifesting themselves in their mutual relationships, with prospects of growing into genuine cooperation. But then the wars of the 1990s erupted and, as is well known, there was a religious, or more accurately an ethnoreligious factor to them that poisoned all previous cooperative efforts. Obviously it will take many years for the hatred and bitterness to subside.

Religious education trending toward learning, understanding, sharing, tolerance, mutual appreciation and cooperation, and respect for individual and collective rights can be subsumed under a genuine "deep dialog" coupled with learning critical thinking. It could go a long way toward building future post-conflict societies in the Balkans in which military conflict would really become part of the past. But if both the content and the methodology of religious instruction replicate the tensions of the past and paint the "others" as permanent and irreconcilable enemies, then the future will only confirm that the Balkans is *prokleta zemlja*, namely cursed and tormented land. I was hoping—as it turns out futilely—that the advantages of incipient ecumenical cooperation and dialog during the communist period would have demonstrated its advantage in good and bad times. But it wasn't to be. Insights by the authors of this book give us a *tračak nade*— a trace of hope—that the joint aspiration to join EU will result in a more scholarly delivery of religious education that would not be primarily indoctrination, but challenge the children with diverse religious backgrounds to learn to appreciate their own and each other's religion. That may be too much to hope for because at the current time, the opportunity to make up for all the lost opportunities to instruct children and young people of one's own religious tradition is too great a temptation to be able to resist it. It is clear that during and after the wars of the 1990s, a large number of people turned to religion, but probably more as an identity marker of ethnic belonging than a conviction based on the knowledge of teachings and practices of the religion, or even attendance at worship. Religious leaders are deeply desirous to deepen and expand the religious experience of their adherents and mandatory or optional/mandatory teaching promises to deliver their expectations. It would be tragic if they overreach their goal and use it for a narrow indoctrination of the traditional kind when they do have the alternative to train their teaching staff in contemporary pedagogy and provide content in doctrines/teachings, ethics, and ritual that will also recognize the values of their co-citizens, as well as global citizens whose religious or non-religious values differ from their own.

The value of the sociological studies of the impact of religious instruction in the successor states of the former Yugoslavia found in this book is that they can alert relevant opinion makers as well as the general public of the challenges, advantages, and disadvantages of the various approaches.

Paul Mojzes
Prof. Emeritus, Religious Studies and Humanities Department
Rosemont College
Pennsylvania
USA

Notes

1. These types were described in Paul Mojzes, *Religious Liberty in Eastern Europe and the U.S.S.R.: Before and After the Great Transformation* (Boulder, CO: East European Manuscripts, distributed by Columbia University Press, 1992), 7–10 and applied throughout the book.
2. Dragan Todorović, "Religious Education in Schools: Contribution or Not to Dialogue and Tolerance?" in *On Religion in the Balkans*. Ed. Dragoljub B. Djordjević (Niš and Sofia: Yugoslav Socity for the Scientific Study of Religion and "Ivan Hadjyiski" Institut for Social Values and Structures, 2013), 181.
3. Martina Topić, "Religion and the Education system in Croatia: A critique" in the *South Slav Journal*. 32: No. 1–2, (Spring 2013): 54.
4. Vjekoslav Perica, "Power, Corruption, and Dissent: Varieties of Contemporary Croatian Political Catholicism," *Occasional Papers on Religion in Eastern Europe*, XXXV, 4 (August 2015): 4–5.
5. Josip Šimunović, "Vjeroučitelj i izazovi Hrvatskog suvremenog društva i Hrvatske suvremene škole" [Religion teacher and the challenges of contemporary Croatian society and contemporary Croatian school] in *Crkva u svijetu* (Split, Croatia), 47, No. 1 (2012): 89.
6. Todorović, *op.cit.*, 187.

CONTENTS

LIST OF TABLES

CHAPTER 1

Introduction

Gorana Ognjenović and Jasna Jozelić

Even though the series of wars in former Yugoslavia during the 1990s had been long over, the segregation amongst members of different ethnic groups has never before appeared greater and more systematic. Societies in a post-conflict transition are vulnerable to political manipulations, which potentially throughout the transition period pull a society back into conflict. Politicization as misuse of freedom of religion is an example of one such manipulation.[1]

The politicization of religion[2] had been proven in this context to be one of the most effective mechanisms (as we pointed out in our two first volumes on politicization of religion), by which nationalists traditionally keep ethnic groups separate from each other and in constant coercion with each other, both within and across the borders of the newborn successor states.

The reason why we, in this third volume on politicization of religion, analyze particular samples of school textbooks in primary and secondary

G. Ognjenović (✉) · J. Jozelić
University of Oslo, Oslo, Norway

© The Author(s) 2018
G. Ognjenović and J. Jozelić (eds.), *Education in Post-Conflict Transition*, Palgrave Studies in Religion, Politics, and Policy,
https://doi.org/10.1007/978-3-319-56605-4_1

1

schools, as one of the primary cornerstones of educational policy in the Southeast, is quite simple: education in a post-conflict transition is precisely where a society chooses to either progress or regress, to either continue to move in the direction of reconciliation or to regress back into the original conflict or apartheid. In the school textbooks of the Southeast, we can evaluate the states' intentions through the educational policy to either build a society according to human rights convention or to build a society built on continuous hate and segregation between the groups.[3]

There are two reasons why school textbooks for religious education in public schools are interesting as a subject for our systematic analyses. On the one hand, religion or more precisely, the politicization of religion (as we have shown in our first two volumes), was a strong factor in encouraging and accommodating ethnic violence in Southeastern Europe since the 1990s, including genocide. However, it is interesting to remark that the religious curriculum in public schools was not immediately considered as problematic or explanatory for quite some time, as certain other so-called national subjects were (i.e. language, geography and history).[4] On the other hand, the Yugoslav successor states ever since have also claimed as part of their transition procedure that education has been used as one of the instruments for introducing reconciliation processes only, between ethnic and religious groups.

The reason why analysing early education is of such great importance is that this system concerns children and young people who grew up after the war, and who have no recollection of what life in former Yugoslavia was like, a community without intolerance towards others in contrast to what they experience today. The absence of this particular memory made new generations vulnerable to the cynical political games by the local elite, who got away so many years after the war, with the original plan of dividing the people as never before. Consequently, they managed to forge the history of the Southeast in cooperation with the national secular successor states who until this very date encourage religious conflict as ethnical conflict for the purpose of achieving their (primitive) political gains of ethnic assimilation or ethnic segregation within their national borders.

How is this possible?

In order to find some answers to this question looking into the primary and secondary school curricula of religious education appeared to be a prerequisite for understanding the origins of this systematic segregation, that is, from where does it spring as well as how it is reproduced within educational practice. Our analyses had to go deeper into a multidisciplinary academic research where answers were to be found in the crossroads between educational politics, social psychology, political science, theology and history, including the history of religion, cultural studies, sociology, linguistics, philosophy, anthropology as well as social anthropology and gender studies.

One research question this study does not ask is 'whether religion is politicized in public school textbooks in the Southeast'. The research questions this study asks and, hopefully, answers are to what degree religion is politicized in various examples of school textbooks used in public schools and for what purpose.

What also makes this particular study unprecedented is that it deals with two of the three Abrahamic religions, which are considered to be the main religions in the Southeast. As we will see, it is also very interesting considering how both Abrahamic religions (Christianity and Islam) have many overlapping views and a similar understanding of certain issues. For example, their mutual relationship (towards each other) as Abrahamic religions, their relationship to other religions as well as their relationship to the world at large.

There are a number of examples in the history of Yugoslavia, which show how religious institutions even during the Tito's period acted as political agents when it came to expanding their populous of followers. One of the reasons why this kind of study was not carried out before could be due to the age of its subjects it belongs to the deep dialectics between the private and public (family life parallel to primary and secondary education): dealing with underage children. This fact has trivialized the depth of seriousness of such an undertaking, since, as Maca Jogan shows[5] it is exactly the institutional protection what makes religious socialization simpler and more effective especially when it comes to one of the primary targets: family as the context wherein people are formed. It is, nevertheless, the easiest within the institution of the family during one's formative years (the primary, secondary and high school) to create the impression that religious formation just like childbearing is one of the life's natural processes. The context of family, in addition, is also a context of the interpretation of women's bodies as a means to family and therefore religious territory. The political approach of religious institutions to gender-related issues, regarding the control of women's means of reproduction seems even more grotesque, so soon after the bloody war and genocidal rape of women that was carried out as a form of demarcation of physical territory.[6]

The positive position towards religious plurality remains something talked about in general rather than something locally referred to or attempted to capitalize on.[7] There are no discussions of the problems or issues that might arise from religious plurality, or no discussion of internal diversity and the dynamics of the various religions. There is no discussion on the local history of religion. Atheism is completely unacceptable, while new religions are not to be understood as part of the positively attitude plurality.

Make no mistake, the relation between State and Religion in the Southeast today is one of equality before the law and that of Church and State are separate. The problem is that at the same time this is a relationship of protection and assistance.[8] In the case of the Catholic Church in Croatia, the contract between Croatian Catholic Church and the Holy See resulted in cooperation in the field of education and culture (1996) which introduced religion into preschool, primary and secondary schools, while the introduction of 'religious culture' as an alternative subject for those who do not wish to attend religion classes is firmly blocked by political sabotage as well as a threat of a systematic social exclusion.

How is it possible that in the secular state where public schools are financed by the state budget, by the money of all employed citizens that such an intolerant discriminatory attitude towards atheists and agnostics has been allowed?

It is easy to forget when confronted with an issue as sensitive as the formation of a young person, that the control over the content of textbooks is more than anything an instrument of an effective control over a means of survival for a religious institution.[9] The question is not whether the textbooks are politicized, but to what degree they are politicized, in the sense that the level of politicization also reflects the institutional ability to adapt to an ever-changing world. Religious institutions are expert at pointing out at every opportunity how disappointing it is that religious socialization is not part of general education. Allowing religion to become such an essential part of general education is according to the religious institutions themselves a subject for the improvement of democratization.

The biggest problem in Bosnia and Herzegovina is people's identification with the nation instead of with the common identity of the citizens.[10] Religion as one of three (religion, language and cultural heritage) demarcations of ethnic identity in groups in Bosnia has played a role of differentiation in ethnic/national policies for the last 30 years. The reason for this kind of nationalist systematic action, infiltrating education with such categories, was that politicians knew that the division between the people would not last long after the war, because people still held memories of life in harmony. The education was systematically used to ensure a permanent division of the new generations. Demographic politics, the creation of ethnically cleansed pure territories, which did not exist before the war at the state level, have significantly aided the process since the (national) group identity of new generations was only strengthened through the separation of other identities. This exaggerated homogeneity in each national group resulted also in romanticizing of one's own nation while in essence one is never treated by the large group as anything but a diaspora and they are always referred to by larger group members (Croatians in Croatia or Serbians in Serbia) as Bosnians, independent of whether they were Catholics, Orthodox, or Muslims. One of the most tragic aspects of this situation is that total absence of any trace of a will to use religion in order to create a social cohesion, or to promote diversity, as wealth and 'unity as diversity' which naturally belong in this context.

It is interesting to note how the visibility of religion in the public places/sphere is viewed by all religious institutions as the key achievement brought about by democracy. At the same time, on the one hand the school textbooks completely fail to discuss or explore the socially intertwined nature of Abrahamic religions in Bosnia and Hercegovina while those who do not believe in God's word are only to be pitied. An additional issue in the Bosnian Islamic tradition has become their battle for the preservation of their own Sufi order as a true Bosnian tradition against Saudi Arabian sects such as the Muslim Brotherhood, which have had a huge success in reaching far into the Bosnian educational system and presenting themselves as the only true Islam. Wahhabi tradition has gained an extensive influence even though it never belonged to the Bosnian cultural and religious landscape.

However in other places, Serbia for example, the governments' decision to introduce religious education into public schools took place outside of the existing legal framework.[11] There was no public discussion and the final decision even by-passed the Ministry of Education. In addition, a merge of institutions was carried out in 2004, where the Serbian Orthodox Church (SOC) merged with state-run University of Belgrade. SOC was after a while also given a chairmanship in the Serbian Radio Broadcasting Council, a media regulatory body, which represented a clear case of the political elite manipulating the SOC for their own ends, as a tool of political legitimacy. The SOC's primary survival strategy, the monopolization of its historical role as a safeguard of national identity is yet to bear fruits.[12] Its constant contribution to national homogenization with its powerful ethno-national imprint has only resulted in a hostile attitude towards Islam, a lack of a multi-perspective approach and an increasing distance from others, to name but a few and has therefore opened an invitation to the state to regulate and sanction its actions.

SOC's relations towards interreligious and gender perspectives on selected textbooks, just as in textbooks in Catholicism and Islam are for the most part missing.[13] SOC's textbooks mirror a patriarchal educational model of the community where students live, and not a religious message about spirituality, which is the main goal of religious education.

Is this, however, because SOC is unable to relate to modern times and the change in the reality of the Southeast?

Not quite. Traditionalism might be the message but methods for sending the message have been drastically modernized.[14] SOC is delivering the message founded on an ontologically based Orthodox catechism: the textbooks are furnished with illustrations adequate to children's age, which are presented as children's stories from everyday life that can explain abstract theological concepts.

At the end, it is important also to mention that some Former Yugoslav successor states have done a better job at resisting to introduce religious education into public schools.[15] Per today there is no religious education in public schools in either Kosovo, Montenegro, or Macedonia.

NOTES

1. Gorana Ognjenović & Jasna Jozelić, The Human Rights State and Freedom of Religion in Southeastern Europe: The Case of Bosnia-Herzegovina, The International Journal of Human Rights, Special Issue, Routledge, March 2017.

2. We defined in our earlier volume (the subject) politicization of religion as instrumentalization of religion for political purposes. See Gorana Ognjenović & Jasna Jozelić (eds.) *Politicization of Religion, The Power of Symbolism, The Case of Former Yugoslavia and its Successor States*, Palgrave studies in Religion, Politics and Policy, 2014; Gorana Ognjenović & Jasna Jozelić (eds.) *Politicization of Religion, the Power of State, Nation, and Faith, The Case of Former Yugoslavia and its Successor States*, Palgrave studies in Religion, Politics and Policy, 2014.

3. Jasna Jozelić, *The Politicization of Education in conflict-affected countries: The legitimization of a divided society*, Chap. 3, this volume.

4. Zrinka Štimac, *Islamic Religious Instruction in the context of EU Integration and Education Reform, see chapter one of this volume*, Chap. 4, this volume.

5. Maca Jogan, *Slovenia: social changes and (adjustable) politicization of Catholic Church*, Chap. 5, this volume.

6. Gorana Ognjenović, *Changing Faces Swapping places, Oh Sister, Where Art Thou?* Chap. 2, this volume.

7. Zrinka Štimac, *From Vrhbosna to Brussels, Catholic Religious Education Between Local and European Perspectives*, Chap. 6, this volume.

8. Ankica Marinković, *Analysis of Catholic religious instruction textbooks in Croatian primary school: how do they teach atheism?* Chap. 7, this volume.

9. Maca Jogan, *Politicization of the religious textbooks in Slovenia*, Chap. 8, this volume.

10. Dženana Husremović, *Religious Education and Large Group Identity*, Chap. 9, this volume.

11. Bojan Aleksov, *Religious Education in Serbia as a Litmus Test for Church-State Relations*, Chap. 10, this volume.

12. Srđan Barišić & Vladimir Jevtić, *Education and Politicization of Religion in Post-Conflict countries, Orthodoxy in school textbooks, Desecularization and Ethnic distance in Serbian textbooks*, Chap. 11, this volume.

13. Svenka Savić, *An analysis of the Religious Education Textbooks in Serbia*, Chap. 12, this volume.

14. Zorica Kuburić, *An analysis of the textbooks for Orthodox religious education in Serbia*, Chap. 13, this volume.

15. Gjylbehare Bella Murati, *Afterword: Religion at school: to teach or not to teach? The case of Kosovo*.

CHAPTER 2

Changing Faces, Swapping Places: Oh Sister Where Art Thou?

Gorana Ognjenović

INTRODUCTION

Michael Foucault once wrote 'There is not one but many silences, and they are an integral part of the strategies that underlie and permeate discourses.'[1]

For anyone even fairly familiar with the history of religion in the Southeast is aware of the fact that two out of three Abrahamic religions, which are in the majority in the area, are hostile toward women. Once democratic changes began during the 1990s, there was a real hope amongst women in the Balkans that there were now a democratic means, such as respect for Human Rights for all citizens, which would take care of respect for their rights. The need for protection was more than obvious once the two Abrahamic religions were on their way back into the public sphere, as the moral rulers of the newborn society.[2] However, did this protection of women's rights ever see daylight?

As we shall see in this contribution, democratic means of various kinds have been used for a number of years in order to change the situation of

G. Ognjenović (✉)
University of Oslo, Oslo, Norway

© The Author(s) 2018
G. Ognjenović and J. Jozelić (eds.), *Education in Post-Conflict Transition*, Palgrave Studies in Religion, Politics, and Policy, https://doi.org/10.1007/978-3-319-56605-4_2

women after the fall of the Former Yugoslavia and the disappearance of its pro-women legislation. Unfortunately, democratic means are most of the time used for the purpose of enforcing religious nationalism and its politically traditional values in its views of women, the family, and women's role within the primary group, which can hardly be seen as reflecting the view on women in today's modern Europe.

My basic argument is that religious education in public schools, as it is organized in the Southeast today, is socially dysfunctional considering to what degree it provokes the segregation and the conflict at least between the religious and secular populations that choose to base their world view on civil rights and secular values. While having a certain understanding of the emotional needs of religious institutions, to compensate for their marginalization during the time of Tito's Yugoslavia does not mean that one's rights to freedom of religion are violated, when I argue that religious education does not belong in public schools. Respecting one's freedom of religion does not specify where exactly religious education has to be carried out. Let us remind ourselves that Catholic religious education during Tito's rule was without any state interference carried out within churches (around the Former Yugoslavia). Interference from the state was only a threat if and when religion was to be used to cause religious or ethnic conflict between groups.

In my search for some recent concrete examples, I looked at the seventh-grade school textbook for religious education in public schools in Croatia. What I looked for in this textbook is how convincing is the argument that religious values are imposed upon the youth of that age, since there has still not been any other possibility to introduce a substitute[3] for the education of values to those pupils who choose to follow civil rather than religious value systems. What makes this particularly interesting for us is that this is the first time during the use of religious education in public schools that pupils meet with an introduction to the Universal Declaration of Human Rights, in the attempt to adjust the educational form to the needs of children growing up in a secular modern world. However, I will not be making an evaluation of the arguments presented in this textbook, as to whether they are logically consequent or not, as we are aware of the fact that ethical arguments are often far from being logically consequent.

Women's Rights in Tito's Yugoslavia

Despite many flaws in Tito's system, its public policy was in many ways and levels pro-women oriented. This pro-women legislation was simply a continuance of the equality of women demonstrated during the Second World War, where women took part in Tito's anti-fascist movement on equal grounds with men. A proof of this equality is a list of the national hero medals awarded to women for their bravery in the Yugoslav nation's battle against the occupying powers and the local quislings.

What Tito's legislative and institutional politics gave women, independent of their national or religious background was, equal pay for equal work, welfare benefits, the possibility of free education, finding work outside the home, having a career, or just earning their daily bread independently of their husbands, while taking care of the family's needs, as they saw fit.

Most importantly, concerning women, Tito's legislation interfered with religious dogma on two important levels. First, the state legislation made women from some religious groups more visible in public spaces by forbidding the use of the burka in public places. Second, the state legislation gave women the possibility to decide over their own bodies by granting adult women the right to abortion.

This, however, does not mean that Abrahamism[4] did not continue within the private sphere. What this means is that the volume of Abrahamism was challenged by the institutional emancipation and empowerment of women in the public sphere and, consequently, pushed Abrahamism out of public places, forcing it into confinement within the four walls of the family where women's dignity used to be defined, prior to Tito's rule.

The Reborn Abrahamism

The perception in Islam and Christianity of women's bodies as possessions is a well-established historical fact, which characterizes the local Abrahamic culture of the Southeast. Society was en-cultured for centuries through religion to reinforce the repressive patriarchal idea of women. Patriarchy denotes the legal, economic, and social system that validates rule by men over women.[5]

The power of conviction that lies in this en-cultured model of patriarchal social control comes nevertheless from the religious images at hand. The Abrahamic religions'[6] cultural construction depicts women and womanhood as inferior to men, because women are not the full image of God. The images of God in the Scripture are mainly male: Lord, King, Father.[7] The examples that Nena Močnik gives in her essay on genocidal rape in Bosnia during the 1990s for how women in Abrahamic religions define the value of women in the scriptures are of value here: in the Qur'an the inheritance of a female child is clearly stated as half of her male siblings (4.11., 4.176). In the New Testament, for St. Paul, women should remain silent (Timothy, 1:2). For Močnik, this form of the symbolic celebration of a man as a ruler of his property is something that, even in war mythology, is nothing but the extreme expression of accepted practices in everyday lives.[8]

However what feminists often fail to recognize is that women and men are equally en-cultured in this model of Abrahamic culture. It is systematic in every aspect of society to the point that it is experienced as normal, and therefore accommodating for en-culturing women and men to believe something that even reflects a clear disadvantage in their own self-realization as individuals. It is important to notice how the primary nurturers of the family, in the domestic set of Abrahamism, are always women/mothers. This means that mothers are the first carriers of values that are taught directly to children in the privacy of their home, which gives them great power in defining the context and values that later on can be only adjusted in the society at large.

According to the newly established religious nationalism, and its extreme core value traditionalism in Abrahamism, women are to be subjugated to men for the primary purpose of reproduction. This is how religious extremism reduced women's wombs to the womb of the new independent nations. Women's wombs have become national territory as an expression of a new form of domestic slavery. This is why in today's society in the Southeast, women's individual ambitions for self-realization are kept strictly focused on the level of realization of women's potential, but only as an instrument of the nation's reproduction. Since sex in Abrahamic culture is only to be practiced for the purpose of reproduction, women are kept away from any possibility of either reaching their full potential as individuals or being treated as equals to men in relationships (or otherwise). Women are socially marginalized through the systematic limitation of their experiences, in order to limit their possibilities of development by traditionally dividing tasks into 'women's' or 'men's' roles. Religious nationalism managed to ensure the enormous increase in the traditional domestication of women's obedience through dependency, by for example, preferably employing men. The climax of the identity building process being that of the Abrahamic core: women's religious affiliation has no say concerning the religious affiliation of the offspring, theirs is automatically determined by the ethnic and religious origin of men. The newly attained homogeneity of the groups helped to accommodate this process so that the occasional offspring of a mixed marriage of any kind preferred to choose only one identity in order not to complicate its relations to the domineering ethnic or religious group, recognizing both parents' origins equally.

In the eyes of religious nationalist institutional psychology, women are breeders of new generations of believers, who represent the survival of the institution itself. This is why they are en-cultured into the status quo of the Abrahamic patriarchal system, and thus trapped as individuals they are essentially instrumental to systems survival which cynically enslaves them.

SEVENTH GRADE TEXTBOOK FOR RELIGIOUS EDUCATION IN PUBLIC SCHOOLS

One of the essential survival strategies of the Catholic Church in modern Europe today has been, nevertheless, its ability to adapt to any new social and political circumstances. Therefore, in this section I shall denote some argumentational mechanisms and techniques to show how well, or maybe not so well, Catholic value rhetoric, within the context of a public, meaning, secular state-run school, functions in the role of an educator.

In our sample textbook for seventh grade religious education in public schools in Croatia, in the section on the 'Ten commandments for living in love and freedom', it is stated that 'consciousness' in a man is God's voice in a human being, an inner expression of God's commandments,[9] only to contradict the same sentence a few pages later by stating how 'conscience is actually something that needs to be taught and learned'.[10] What this example shows is that it appears to contradict essential parts of the doctrine and thus does not seem to pose much of a problem.

In the section on the Declaration of Human Rights,[11] the text begins in a safe manner with a universal statement about how 'All human laws need to be founded on God's commandments, especially on conscience in 10 commandments'. This is then modified by stating that 'If the governmental laws are against the 10 commandments we need to act according to our conscience since "one has to obey the God and not people" (Dj 5, 29). As Christians, we need to co-operate with civil rulers and do everything in our power through different laws and regulations to respect basic Human Rights for the purpose of the promotion of a just society.'

This example shows us how the author of textbooks consciously exhibits a traditional religious truth reference to a modern universal norm, only in so far as the modern norm overlaps the traditionalism in the original universal generalization. This demonstrates a case of a selective reading of the same Universal Declaration, where Article 5 of the Declaration says that 'everyone has the right to freedom of thought, conscience and belief'. It is only under Article 5 that women's rights can be respected in their totality. We can as an example name the two basic women's rights legislations, which Tito in his time imposed: the right to decide over one's own body and the ban on the use of the burka in public places. Women had the right to choose an abortion without the consent of anyone else as long as they were of age. They were no longer forced culturally to cover their faces in public places as a token of belonging to a certain religious culture or ethnic group.

By referring to God's fourth commandment[12] the author of the textbook repeats that if the government acts against Christian beliefs and values, followers of Catholicism are not obliged to respect the state nor obey the state's orders, since 'one must obey God and not Man.' By giving such instructions, the author is challenging the constitution of the state, implying that in such a case, there is a need for 'an institution within the institution' in order to regulate the individual's morally undesirable behavior. Further, by such instruction, the author implies that whenever the two models of rules and regulations do not overlap completely, the state is blamed for being morally weak, rather than the church for misusing its influence on the Catholic faithful.

The author returns to the Universal Declaration of Human Rights later when he refers to the 'right to life'. The right to life is not only a human right, it is also an absolute right (see Declaration on euthanasia).[13] This strong argument, with its reference to the Declaration is in this case strengthened by other statements/examples in the margins on the same page in the textbook.

Example one Abortion and the murder of a child are two horrific crimes (Gaudium et al., 51).[14] This example is supposed to scare young people from committing a crime according to religious truth.

Example two All human beings have the right to life. There is no death sentence in the Republic of Croatia.[15] This example is a warning against doing something that is prohibited by state legislation.

Example three Hitler signed an order in 1939, which resulted in euthanasia for seriously ill patients. A total of 275,000 people were killed because of this decision (Conclusion in the Court in Nurnberg 1945–1946).[16] This example is a warning against taking part in committing a massive crime prohibited by law, associated with one of the worst evils of the twentieth century.

Example four I swear (...) that I shall never even if someone begs me, either give the means which will result in death or give advice to the same effort (Hyppocrates Oath).[17] This example is a warning to stop youngsters from seeking help from health professionals by presenting them as breaching their oath in cases where they hasten death, which does not result from natural causes, such as by carrying out an abortion at a woman's request. Abortion falls under the breach of God's fifth commandment, together with suicide, euthanasia, and war. Women are according to Abrahamic culture supposed to fulfill a pregnancy, independent of circumstances, even where in extreme cases this would mean also undergoing pregnancies and giving birth to children who were the result of genocidal rape, as was the case in Croatia, Bosnia and Kosovo during the 1990s wars.

This kind of selective and politicized reading of Article 5 of the Universal Declaration is only one example of an attempt to bend modern legislation in ways that would legitimize Abrahamic traditionalism, soaked as it is with examples of sacrificing their women for whatever the institution defines as the 'greater purpose'. In this sense, the greater purpose adds up to nothing less than the survival of the cultural institution, which in certain cases such as this, acts as a political agent. The political agent has a history of transforming the wombs of their women followers into the womb of a nation, where no other aspect of their person or their lives as a whole is superseded by their sole biological ability of reproduction. This reminds us to what degree the matter of reproduction within religious nationalism in the Southeast since the 1990s has been a question of women's wombs as a nation's womb and, therefore, a means to an end concerning the nationalist territorialism. Women raped during the conflict of the 1990s did not receive the official status of victims of the Home defense war against Serbian aggression before this last year. This tells us just how hard to change the state institutions are and how well en-cultured they already are in the Abrahamic ways of reasoning when it comes to equalizing women's suffering/victimhood with the sacrifices of men during the 1990s war.

BILDUNG AS A BACKBONE OF DEMOCRACY

In order to evaluate how well an institution is able to accommodate a 'self-realization of its followers in the image of God' since all already are in the 'image of God,'[18] we analyzed the textbooks' description and contextualization of critical thought.

The context within which the institution depicts critical thought was at the beginning of the book.[19] However, the contextualization of this depiction somewhat surprised the reader. The context of the definition of the institutional relation toward critical thought is nonetheless the context of the process entailed in reaching sexual maturity, which marks the end of the bodily changes in puberty, the end of the rapid growth and development of the internal organs, and the beginning of the sexually active age for men and women.[20] Critical thought is thus here connected only to the period of puberty, when the young are either overly critical toward themselves as a result of the physical changes, but also of others due to the growing feeling of self-importance.[21]

According to the author, at times in puberty children are rebellious also toward religion, and that is a normal phase of development toward the full maturity of spirituality, while true pure maturity is reached through the difficulties met as one grows up and synchronizes one's own wishes with the duties and obligations in one's family and community.[22] In this way, a well-known fact of how the physical volume of the human brain grows for many years after puberty has been efficiently excluded from the equation. Instead, puberty is categorically marked by developing the ability to accept limitations caused by one's body and mind, as well as by society, a kind of compromise with reality.

If the ideas listed above were a matter of religious education alone, one would always have an option of not exposing one's children to such a breach in a doctrine of human rights. The fact that young people are being taught such a doctrine in (public) state-run schools makes the matter essential for our analysis of the degree to which women's rights in the newly established democratic independence of a successor state are actually ignored as a legislative fact. Any secular/worldly explanation of life is all about what is taught in public schools should be subject to a broader moral scrutiny if it allows itself to contextualize the concept of critical thought as a subject of adolescent rebellion during puberty, as the religious explanation appears to do so in school textbooks.

By teaching and encouraging critical thought amongst young people, society is simultaneously promoting its own self-realization: developing the individual's ability to achieve self-realization is an indicator of how well society is organized to accommodate the self-realization of the community.[23] An Individual's self-realization overlaps with self-realization of the society. It includes the development of the citizen's courage and ability to think differently and reflect over the whole, which eventually results in a civilized progress for the community. Here, Hegel's Phenomenology of Spirit,[24] read as a *Bildung* novel[25] comes to mind, where there is an exchange between the main character's experiences and his development. Hegel's civil society reflects just one of few phases through which the individual goes on its way to becoming a citizen of the state. Civil society is a form of *second family*,[26] and in this way the family and civil society are two sides of the same process, the process of the individual's self-realization. Without a doubt, in today's modern Europe it is nevertheless the constitutional obligation of the state to defend the individual's right to choose to live by religious dogmas. Today, religious institutions misuse the right to freedom of religion in order to overcome whatever secular grounds there may be for defending the democratic society, for which the people fought and for which their children bled to death only a few years ago. Individual development, where freedom is the final good, creates a society well prepared to meet the challenges that arise when inherent totalitaristic tendencies become more than obvious.[27] Such tendencies when analyzed in relation to the situation of women in the midst of this newly established religious nationalism in the Southeast are reflected in constant attempts at the disempowerment of women, the neutralization of women as social agents in the public sphere at any given opportunity.

CONCLUDING THOUGHTS

Judging by the above described and documented sexism, misogyny, and religious nationalistic politics that rule the Balkans today, including the systematic ignorance of women's rights as prescribed by the constitutions of each successor state, one is forced to conclude that a regression in civilization on this account is a historical fact. It would have been difficult to get women to give their democratic vote to nationalist political parties during the 1990s if they had known what the price for traditional values that came as a reborn Abrahamism or religious nationalism would be paid by the ruined lives of women and the loss of their children's lives as its main currency. This perspective on the result of a democratic vote is a part of the evaluation of political alternatives, whose expiry date never comes, since in reality we are talking about the votes of 50% of the Balkan population.

If the rapid march of the two Abrahamic religions taking over public education is not challenged soon by concrete measures of defense of the state constitution, the defense of all of its citizens who choose not to be religious, the damages caused could bring even more tragic results. The free flow of religious truth that has ruled these societies for thousands of years is going to become the only truth that young people will learn as a part of their educational path: that it was a male God who was the historical and eternal creator of patriarchal structures and 'the way life is.' The religious truth that overlaps with the primary goal of the religious institutions is to improve further democratization by gaining a total control of the general education of the young. If achieved, this goal will ultimately make any reargumentation completely impossible. The questioning of human rights or ultimately, the eligibility of such non-questionable subjection of women was supposedly unable to be decided, recreated, or re-established by humans—who were, after all, only God's creation.

NOTES

1. Michel Foucault, *The History of Sexuality, Volume 1: An Introduction.*
2. Gorana Ognjenović & Jasna Jozelić, The Human Rights State and Freedom of Religion in Southeastern Europe: The Case of Bosnia–Herzegovina, The International Journal of Human Rights, Special Issue, Routledge, March 2017.
3. See in this volume Ankica Marinković, *Analysis of Catholic religious instruction textbooks in Croatian primary schools: how do they teach atheism?*

4. By Abrahamism here is meant, the culture of oppression based on the common view of women across Abrahamic religions. Individuals who are not necessarily religious still follow the same cultural code of behavior based on religious values.

5. Suzan Rakoczy, "Religion and Violence: The Suffering of Women", Religion & Spirituality 61 (2004). p. 33.

6. In my analysis, I focus on two out of three Abrahamic religions.

7. Ibid., p. 10.

8. Nena Močnik, *Religious Symbolism and Mythology in Sexual Violence and Rape during the Balkan Conflict, 1992–1995*, in Politicization of Religion, The Power of Symbolism, The Case of Former Yugoslavia and its Successor States, (eds.) Gorana Ognjenović & Jasna Jozelić, Palgrave studies in Religion, Politics and Policy, 2014.

9. *Ankica Cicvarić, Vesna Galić, Josip Periš, Vilma Rađa, Zajedno u ljubavi, U džbenik za katolički vjeronauk sedmog razreda osnovne škole, KRŠĆANSKA SADAŠNJOST*, ZAGREB, 2009, p. 32.

10. Ibid., p. 33.

11. Ibid., p. 39.

12. Ibid., p. 50.

13. Ibid., p. 51.

14. Ibid., p. 51.

15. Ibid., p. 51.

16. Ibid., p. 52.

17. Ibid., p. 52.

18. Ibid., p. 51.

19. Ibid., p. 6.

20. Ibid., p. 13.

21. Ibid., p. 14–16.

22. Ibid., p. 14.

23. Jay Martin, *The education of John Dewey; A biography 2003*, Columbia University Press, p. 69.

24. Georg W. Hegel, *The Phenomenology of Spirit*, 1977, trans. A.V. Miller, Oxford University Press, paragraph 78.

25. Josiah Royce, *Lectures on Modern Idealism*, 1919, Yale University Press.

26. Robert R. Williams, *Hegel's Ethics of Recognition*, University of California Press 1997, p. 229.

27. Srečo Dragoš, *The Separation between Church and State in Slovenia: A Political Fiasco*, Politicization of Religion, the Power of State, Nation, and Faith, The Case of Former Yugoslavia and its Successor States, Gorana Ognjenović & Jasna Jozelić, Palgrave studies in Religion, Politics and Policy, 2014.

CHAPTER 3

The Politicization of Education in Conflict-Affected Countries: The Legitimization of a Divided Society

Jasna Jozelić

INTRODUCTION

This article will discuss the challenges and identify the possible violations of human rights in regard to religious education as a part of the public education system in the post-conflict society (the case of Bosnia and Herzegovina). Education is understood as a powerful tool in the development of individuals as well as in the development of societies, which can be used/misused for different purposes. In this case specifically, religious education as a part of the public educational system in a post-conflict society (Bosnia and Herzegovina), especially, a multi-ethnic community riven by conflict, may have a negative role in the educational policy for the purpose of nation re-building (identity policy), which may indirectly lead to greater division and segregation between the groups in society and therefore maintain an intention opposite to that which is usual in education.

J. Jozelić (✉)
Norwegian Centre for Human Rights, University of Oslo, Oslo, Norway

© The Author(s) 2018
G. Ognjenović and J. Jozelić (eds.), *Education in Post-Conflict Transition*, Palgrave Studies in Religion, Politics, and Policy, https://doi.org/10.1007/978-3-319-56605-4_3

Therefore, it is natural to ask, was the state obligation to protect, respect, and fulfil the right to education for all their citizens, regardless of their "race, colour, sex, language, religion, political or other opinion, national or social origin, property, birth or other status"[1] realized and, if not, what is the objective of the state?

Education is undoubtedly the most important and significant factor in the development of the individual, of communities and of the society at large. It provides not only the empowerment of the individual, but also increases the progress of society as a whole. As such, education represents an effective tool for human development in a way that affects the development of knowledge, skills and the values each individual and society strive to reach. Essentially, education is considered as a fundamental human right that promotes empowerment and freedom and as such is elementary for the practice of all other human rights, as is stated in the Universal Declaration of Human rights Article 2; "Everyone is entitled to all the rights and freedoms set forth in this Declaration, without distinction of any kind, such as race, colour, sex, language, religion, political or other opinion, national or social origin, property, birth or other status..." and Article 26. "(1) Everyone has the right to education. Education shall be free, at least at the elementary and fundamental stages. Elementary education shall be compulsory. Technical and professional education shall be made generally available and higher education shall be equally accessible to all on the basis of merit. (2) Education shall be directed to the full development of the human personality and to the strengthening of respect for human rights and fundamental freedoms. It shall promote understanding, tolerance and friendship among all nations, racial or religious groups, and shall further the activities of the United Nations for the maintenance of peace...."[2]

Why is education considered so important? Education remains and is considered by many as a powerful tool for several reasons. First, education is a powerful tool for the empowerment of the individual, which enables him/her to meet and cope with challenges in the best possible way. Second, education is considered as an essential tool in the fight against poverty and is an important element in improving the living conditions for many. Finally, education can be/is a powerful tool that may be used/misused for different purposes that may have both positive and negative sides in society. Such an interpretation and understanding of the role of education in individual lives as well as in society is explicitly expressed in the Millennium Development Goals (MDG) where the main emphasis is "on achieving universal, free and compulsory primary education through education for all."[3]

Education is not only about the cognitive development of the one, it also includes the development and reflection of the values system the society depends on. In such a context, it is expected that the state has the guarantee to protect the citizen's right to education prioritize and take measures to protect the realization of individual rights.

EDUCATION IN POST-CONFLICT SOCIETY

In the case of post-conflict societies, as Bosnia and Herzegovina, where the multi-ethnic community has been riven by conflict, the state should be concerned for the protection of children and respond to the negative impacts of conflict on their education. Educational policies and systems in post-conflict societies can play a major role in the re-building of a conflict-wounded society. In this context, it is of essence that education is provided in a way that "does no harm" and has a preventive role in future conflicts. In such an environment, it is of huge importance to remember that learning takes place in both formal and non-formal ways, which makes a non-formal learning environment have greater significance than the traditional formal schooling and thus weakens formal schooling.

Unfortunately, in the case of Bosnia and Herzegovina, where the education system is decentralized and "victimized" by the "children's disease" of the transitional process, education is left open to manipulation as a political objective. A Divided state structure based on ethnic lines, which was created by the Dayton Peace Agreement, has a number of negative effects on the educational system. By placing "constituent nations" as the foundation of the state, the society has established a contradictory system that cannot function without generating conflict, and this directly undermines the state as well as the educational system. It creates a discriminatory and dysfunctional institutional framework where the salience of ethnic differences has been maintained by 'ethnic' political institutions: On the one hand they cripple the efficient functioning of the state through their mutual blockade potential, while on the other hand they continue to "reinforce the very ethnic division that had helped to fuel the conflict."[4]

The war continued in the amended form, which is especially evident in the educational sector. Thus, step-by-step, politics has created three educational programmes in Bosnia and Herzegovina: two that were taken from the neighbouring countries, and the Bosnian programme.

A Unified education policy and system, curriculum, textbooks, common goals in education or common values are almost non-existing.[5]

THE RELIGIOUS EDUCATION

In a multi-ethnic community such Bosnia and Herzegovina, religion has been used and became a major agent in re-building the nation and state. In the environment created after the war Bosnian society at large identified religion as one of the core elements in the re-building of nations a process, that has made it a significant political element in the mobilization of citizens.

Practicing freedom of religious belief plays a new role in society. In reality, Bosnia and Herzegovina today is split along ethnic borderlines and, ideologically, religion has taken the role of a mechanism of ideological dogma necessary in re-building national/identity unity. Providing religion with a new public role as a unifying "power" in the new nation states has resulted in a much closer relationship between religion and politics, which has been expressed in the education system as well as in society at large.

> The newly formed educational systems led to the 'blossoming' of national identities and cultures, which in this part of the Balkans is synonymous with religious faith.[6]

The Constitution of Bosnia and Herzegovina guarantees citizens freedom of religion, which affirms the right of every citizen to religious education. Religion as a subject was introduced in all public schools in the early 90s. The state legislation regulates religious education in private pre-schools, primary schools and universities. The teachers of religion are employees of the schools in which they teach, but receive accreditation from the religious body governing the curriculum.[7]

In The Current Status of Religious Coexistence and Education in Bosnia and Herzegovina from 2009; "Culture of Religions is a secular course, which, drawing on the students' knowledge of their own faith acquired through traditional religious instruction, teaches students about the country's main religious traditions. Deeply rooted in Bosnia and Herzegovina's reality, the course gives students the practical skills to recognize, understand and appreciate the religious diversity reflected in the society in which they live, and to be able to engage in constructive dialogue with people of different fait."[8]

The distinctive contribution that religion could make in education, and could positively transform conflict-affected societies in an attempt to build a common ground for all, has been in the case of Bosnia and Herzegovina sacrificed in the name of nationality.

The main aim behind introducing religious education in the public education system could be seen as an enrichment in the development of a values system, that reflects universal values and as such responds to the negative impacts the conflict had on the society at large.

Did such a role of religious education manage to be maintained?

To begin with, everyone is free to choose the religion they want to study, but often only one of the major religions of the area is offered. Such a practice in a conflict-torn country has divided society even further. One can say that citizens enjoy freedom of religion, but only in areas where their particular ethnic group represents a majority.[9]

> Religious education classes are also frequently a source of conflict between students. Furthermore, intolerance is inculcated through textbooks that favour a particular faith while disparaging others in order to stress the differences between them by comparison.[10]

By reconstructing the religious belief in this way, as an enemy "of others," religion as an institution has become a part of the politicized system that contributes to further division among its own citizens.

THE LEGITIMIZATION OF A DIVIDED SOCIETY

According to the Civil Rights defenders report from 2015 "The education system in Bosnia Herzegovina is characterised by ethnic divisions. In the Republika Srpska, only a Serbian curriculum is taught, discriminating pupils of other ethnic backgrounds. In November 2014, the Supreme Court of the Federation of Bosnia and Herzegovina ruled that ethnically divided schools constituted discrimination and ordered schools to integrate their education facilities. However concrete, efforts to integrate schools have not yet been made. More than 50 schools in the Federation of Bosnia and Herzegovina alone still separate Bosniak and Croat children today."[11]

In such an environment, religious education is mostly perceived as a powerful political tool for ideological development rather than "enrichment" for further development of knowledge, skills or universal values. As the report states, it is the range of forms that education, particularly religious education, has been used in nation building and, in extreme cases, political indoctrination. Many of the textbooks used in religious education transmit such social and cultural values to new generations, and these may convey negative stereotypes and encourage attitudes that explicitly or implicitly generate conflict and thus a further division in society. The statements "we cannot leave together" or "the others" are our enemies, or that children from different "ethnic" groups are purposely kept away from each other, reinforce the attempt to use educational policies as a political tool by the political elite.

Evidence of education being used/misused for ideological or political purposes is transparent, usually by the political involvement in determining the curriculum, textbooks, or education appointments.[12]

In the context of Bosnia and Herzegovina, politics are strongly involved the teaching of history, language, religion, and so on. History education in many cases has become a source for promoting particular versions of history (there are three different versions of history in Bosnia and Herzegovina); in some textbooks, we see attempts of revising historical events, and a lack of a critical way of confronting the past. Such a teaching approach is not new and is often used as a tool to raise sensitive and offensive issues by keeping and continuing the status quo in society.[13]

While the authorities do not restrict academic freedom at institutions of higher education, academic appointments are heavily politicized, with ethnic favouritism playing a significant role. Primary and secondary school curricula are also politicized; some Bosniak returnees in the Republika Srpska have sent their children to temporary alternative schools in protest against curricula they call discriminatory. Depending on their ethnicity, children use textbooks printed in Croatia, Serbia, or Sarajevo. At some schools in the Federation, Bosniak and Croat students are divided into classes on the basis of their ethnicity, meeting in segregated classrooms despite attending school in the same building. In 2014, the Federation's Supreme Court ruled that these divisions are discriminatory, but at the end of 2015 no action had been taken to implement the ruling.[14]

The established theory that the indigenous Bosnian people oversimplify the real state of affairs with the presumption that all Catholics in Bosnia are Croats, all Orthodox are Serbs and all Muslims are the only Bosniaks gives religious education a role that guarantees that same theory.

Such conceptual constructions of identity give support to the process of further division and segregation among students and the society. By manipulating religion and the role of religion in a self-understanding of ethnic and national identities, education takes the role of an agent in re-building these ethnic and national identities in addition to being a political strategy aimed at achieving the legitimatization of segregation in schools and in society in general.

Religious institutions as a part of the educational system become promoters of political ideology and, by doing so, represent the interests of certain groups of citizens as the interest of the whole population. In such a context, religion plays the role of a marker of identity for certain groups, instead of safeguarding the possibility of choosing a common ground for values. Religious education increasingly becomes the source of segregation. Educational institutions become homogenized where students have little or no contact with members of other ethnic groups.[15]

The nationalist elites in control of educational policies together with local politicians have "introduced" a systematic institutional segregation of students. Their project of ethnically dividing the country between the three main ethnic and religious groups is best seen in the education system in the introduction of the "two schools under one roof" system, which is based on the "linguistic differences" between the "ethnic" groups.[16]

Where Is the State?

The state has an obligation to guarantee fundamental civil rights to all citizens, including the right to education as and freedom of religion, but at the same time it underrates the right to choose as well as the right to be protected from having to choose. Through such an educational policy, where indoctrination of the students is extensive, the state breches one's right to education by not acting or by interfering with their agenda of particular politics. Education, considered as a tool for the individual to develop values, skills and knowledge is also essential in building a ground for critical thinking in the individual, and hence, it is of crucial importance that it is protected and independent.

The state must prioritize education and take measures to protect the educational system in such a way that it will serve all, regardless of their ethnicity, nationality or gender. Second, the state has an obligation to protect children from the negative impacts conflict has on their education and encourage education to contribute to the development of common values through textbooks that will build unity rather than division. This highlights the need to bring education back to the schools and away from extensive political interference.

The minimum that all citizens can ask for is that the state be responsible to promote and protect human rights in society, especially through education. In 1993, at the UN conference of Human Rights, clause 33 clearly states: "...that states are duty-bound... to ensure that education is aimed at strengthening the respect of human rights and fundamental freedoms. Education should promote understanding, tolerance, peace and friendly relations between the nations and all racial or religious groups and encourage the development of United Nations activities in pursuance of these objectives."[17]

In the case of Bosnia and Herzegovina, the state has been allocating its responsibility for education as a basic human right to political and religious institutions. Keeping in mind the notion of state responsibility can we then claim that in Bosnia and Hercegovina freedom of religion through religious education is realized, if religious education in public schools, promotes discrimination? Or can we claim that the right to education as knowledge-based training is accessible to everyone and that the state has fulfilled its obligation?

In Bosnia and Herzegovina today, a large part of the educational system is more a source of conflict than a place for knowledge-based training. A part of the curriculum (some textbooks) often promotes a dominant set of values that are more based on identity politics and as such permits the development of ethnicity-based institutions, favouring us the interests of a majority group. By doing so, the school system legitimizes the objective of religious and political institutions rather than protecting and realizing one's right to education. Frequently, the content of the curriculum in textbooks clearly provides segregation among the students based on an intrusive religious-, ethnic-, cultural- and language-divisive education policy. In this context, education takes on a political dimension and schools become a playground for nation building, considered as "national subjects" closely "controlled" by the agents of national politics, Under the parole "We er separate but equal!"

Such an educational system can have a devastating impact on individuals; therefore, the state has an obligation to provide education for all, free from improper external influence and intimidation, which means without the transmission/promotion of particular political ideologies.

> Education shall be free....., It shall promote understanding, tolerance and friendship among all nations, racial or religious groups, and shall further the activities of the United Nations for the maintenance of peace.[18]

Does such an education system violate the right to education?

In the case of Bosnia and Herzegovina, it is clear that the basic principle of non-discrimination is not met. Though indirectly, the state participates in violating the principle by allowing a political approach of interference and discriminatory ethnical-based segregation. This includes the fact that the political ideology strongly influences the educational system, as well as its structural, administrative and, in the end, legislative features. When religious education is used/misused as a political tool, it may have significant implications for non-discrimination and the equal access to education. The Convention against Discrimination in Education[19] clearly provides the legal basis for the state's obligations regarding any form of discrimination in education as well as the right to education. [20]

To conclude, the picture is very clear; division in education through textbooks that are based on biased ethno-national identification, religion, language, ongoing segregation by introduction of "two schools under one roof" system, and lack of a unifying common educational system undoubtedly gives the answer that the state of Bosnia and Herzegovina violates the basic human right to education on several levels.

The state's inadequate actions regarding the educational system violate the right to education. First, the quality of children's education is diminished by intrusive political interference making schools a playground for political objectives. Second, textbooks used in education do not promote understanding, tolerance and friendship among all nations, racial or religious groups. The marginalization of minorities is institutionalized, and discrimination based on religious, ethnic and gender ground is widespread. By not addressing these issues, the state acts in violation of the right to education.

Conclusion

To secure the quality of education in a way that is in accordance with a free, democratic society, especially in a post-conflict setting, is not an easy task. It is difficult to raise society again after the devastation that took place and which had an enormous impact on the individual as well as on society. Therefore, the greatest challenge now is to find a way that will bring society together. Education is one of the basic elements that may make this possible.

The goal is to educate new generations in such a way that democratic principles and human rights become a ground for learning about themselves and others, without prejudice. This includes the necessity to raise critical questions about the content, structure and form of the textbooks used in schools, on education as a whole and on the kind of implications these have on the relation between people, groups and nations subjected to such a politicized education. Many young people in Bosnia and Herzegovina no longer have any contact with others outside their own group.

Despite efforts to present the introduction of religious education in public schools positively, among other elements, religion-based education is more of a barrier than an aid in promoting sustainable coexistence. Polarization, segregation and ethnic extremism make the religion of others, in the context of Bosnia and Herzegovina, stranger, more distant and more threatening. The political division of society has been introduced forcefully in schools and education, in a place that should be protected from such kinds of influences. The lack of interaction between the groups, even in school playgrounds, is because political and religious leaders are more interested in a comprehensive approach in order to promote the interests of their own group, or in furthering other political agendas.

In such an environment the state must prioritize education as a universal minimum and impose a minimum ban on extreme nationalism, and in this case, introduce a unified educational system.

Notes

1. Universal Declaration on Human Rights, http://www.un.org/en/universal-declaration-human-rights/.
2. Universal Declaration on Human Rights, http://www.un.org/en/universal-declaration-human-rights/.

3. The Role of Education in Peacebuilding: Literature Review, May 2011, https://www.unicef.org/infobycountry/files/EEPCT_Peacebuilding_LiteratureReview.pdf.

4. Richard Caplan, "International Governance and War-torn Territories: Rule and reconstruction" (Oxford University Press, 2006).

5. Adila Pašalić Kreso, "The War and Post-War Impact on the Educational System of Bosnia and Herzegovina," International Review of Education, Vol. 54, No. 3/4, Living Together: Education and Intercultural Dialogue (May–July, 2008), pp. 353–374, Springer.

6. Adila Pašalić Kreso, "The War and Post-War Impact on the Educational System of Bosnia and Herzegovina," International Review of Education, Vol. 54, No. 3/4, Living Together: Education and Intercultural Dialogue (May–July, 2008), pp. 356, Springer.

7. https://www.state.gov/documents/organization/238574.pdf.

8. The Current Status of Religious Coexistence and Education in Bosnia and Herzegovina, 2009, by Renata Stuebne, http://www.erisee.org/downloads/2013/2/bh/religion_education_bosnia_herzegovina%202009%20ENG.pdf.

9. Freedom in the World, Report Bosnia and Herzegovina, 2016, https://freedomhouse.org/report/freedom-world/2016/bosnia-and-herzegovina.

10. Adila Pašalić Kreso, "The War and Post-War Impact on the Educational System of Bosnia and Herzegovina," International Review of Education, Vol. 54, No. 3/4, Living Together: Education and Intercultural Dialogue (May–July, 2008), p. 356, Springer.

11. Civil Rights defenders report, 2015, https://www.civilrightsdefenders.org/country-reports/human-rights-in-bosnia-and-herzegovina/.

12. https://www.unicef.org/infobycountry/files/EEPCT_Peacebuilding_LiteratureReview.pdf.

13. Wolfgang Höpken (2003) 'Textbooks and Conflicts. Experiences from the Work of the Georg-Eckert-Institute for International Textbook Research' (Washington, DC, World Bank Symposium).

14. Freedom of the Word, Report Bosnia and Herzegovina, 2016, https://freedomhouse.org/report/freedom-world/2016/bosnia-and-herzegovina.

15. Nejra N. Čengić. Podijeljeno školstvo u BiH ili „volimo se po razlici"! (Divided education in B & H or „love each other based on our differences"!) In. Dvije škole pod jednim krovom – Studija o segregaciji u obrazovanju, pp. 91–137. Center for Human Rights of University of Sarajevo & ACIPS. 2012. Available at: http://www.2skole1krov.info/wp-content/uploads/2013/02/Dvije-s%CC%8Ckole-pod-jednim-krovom.pdf.

16. Tony Judt & Denis Lacorne. Language, nation, and state: identity politics in a multilingual age. Palgrave Macmillan, New York. 2004.
17. http://www.ohchr.org/EN/ProfessionalInterest/Pages/Vienna.aspx.
18. Article 26. The Universal Declaration of Human Rights, http://www.un.org/en/universal-declaration-human-rights/.
19. http://unesdoc.unesco.org/images/0013/001325/132598e.pdf.
20. http://www.unesco.org/new/en/education/themes/leading-the-international-agenda/right-to-education/.

CHAPTER 4

Islamic Religious Instruction in the Context of EU Integration and Education Reform

Zrinka Štimac

INTRODUCTION

The signing of the Dayton Accords in December 1995 brought the war in Bosnia and Herzegovina to an end. The peace agreement stipulated that Bosnia and Herzegovina (henceforth BiH) was to remain a sovereign undivided state within its borders as recognised by the international community; however, it was to be divided into two "entities," the Republika Srpska (Serbian Republic, henceforth RS) and the Bosniak and Croat Federation of Bosnia and Herzegovina henceforth Fedaration , in addition to Brčko District.[1]

The international community created the Office of the High Representative (OHR) for the purpose of implementing the Dayton Accords. The Accords incorporated a new constitution for BiH, which defined the three constituent peoples as Bosniaks, Croats and Serbs,

Z. Štimac (✉)
Georg Eckert Institut, Braunschweig, Germany

© The Author(s) 2018
G. Ognjenović and J. Jozelić (eds.), *Education in Post-Conflict Transition*, Palgrave Studies in Religion, Politics, and Policy,
https://doi.org/10.1007/978-3-319-56605-4_4

whose languages (Bosnian, Serbian and Croatian) and scripts (Latin and Cyrillic) it placed in a state of equality before the law across the whole of BiH.

Further, the constitution of the entirety of Bosnia and Herzegovina provides, at least theoretically, for an equal status throughout the nation's territory of its four "historical churches and faith communities," the Islamic and Jewish communities and the Serbian Orthodox and Roman Catholic churches. In practice, however, the clause stipulating equality has been interpreted in markedly different ways in the two entities. The constitution of the Federation BiH provides equal rights for all people living in its territory (freedom of speech, of thought and of the press, freedom of religion and the freedom to practise one's faith). While the constitution of the Republika Srpska likewise guarantees its citizens these basic rights, it affords the Serbian Orthodox Church a privileged status as the church of the Serbian people.

In relation to questions of education policy, the constitution for the whole of BiH divides powers between the state in its entirety and its constituent entities, assigning to the latter responsibility for the practical development and implementation of education policy and to the former a coordinating role only.[2] In the RS, which is centralised in structure, the education minister, based in the Ministry of Education and Culture in the RS' seat of government Banja Luka, is in charge of education policy. In the Federation, whose name reflects the structure of its governance, responsibilities are assigned in a more complex manner: alongside the federal education ministry in Sarajevo and a regional office run by the Croatian side of the Federation in Mostar, there are an additional ten regional-level education ministries, one for each of the cantons of which the Federation consists. This means that in practice, decision-making on education is a matter for every level of governance, from the federations through the cantons and municipalities down to individual schools. Brčko District represents a further special administrative case. As a consequence of the wartime division of BiH along ethnic lines and the state's ethnically based structure, three separate school systems and three distinct curricula—in three different languages—have emerged in the country since 1995. A study conducted in 2001, by the Federation's Ministry of Education on the cantons' education legislation, came to the conclusion that the education system as it then existed could not be regarded as conducive to the preservation of peace.[3] Douglas Davidson, former head of the OSCE's Mission to BiH, said that as recently as 2006 the country's education system was the most influential factor in the polarisation of its society, with religion playing the decisive role in dividing its population. In Davidson's view, the Bosnian school system represented a continuation of hostilities and thus called urgently for reform.[4]

Education Reform and Education Legislation as Steps Towards EU Integration

In recent years, several steps have been taken towards reforming the education system in BiH; they have included reforms to the legal basis upon which the system rests, the overhauling of curricula in primary and lower secondary education, modernisation of the administration of education in line with European standards and an increase in the flexibility of vocational training. We should regard all these measures as steps towards integration into the EU, emerging as they did either from the commitments entered into by BiH in the context of the Stabilisation and Association Process (SAP) in the year 2000 and with its Stabilisation and Association Agreement with the EU in 2007 or from its obligations, to which it has been subject since 2002, as a member state of the Council of Europe.

The restoration and renovation of school buildings destroyed in the war, which took place from 1996 to 1999 and was funded by UNESCO, UNICEF and the World Bank to a total of US $172 million, represented a precursor to reforms to the education system in BiH.[5] A further significant step in the direction of reform was the first round of textbook revisions in this context, which took place in 1999 and was initiated by UNESCO, the OHR and the country's education ministries. A number of teams of experts were formed and an independent commission was established for the process of revisions to textbooks in what are referred to as the "national" subjects (history, geography and languages). The teams met in Mostar in July 1999, to share their experiences and identify passages in textbooks that needed to be removed or obscured. Religious education textbooks were not included in this process.

In May 2000, BiH's education ministers—in other words, those of the Federation and of the Republika Srpska—signed a general declaration on the fundamental reform of the country's education system and ratified a further declaration on reform of schooling, thereby committing to uphold the following principles: European standards in education, a joint core curriculum, mutual recognition of the Federation's and RS' school-leaving qualifications, and the rejection of segregation through education and of parallel (ethnically based) school systems.[6] Between 2002 and 2004, several international projects and schemes were run with the aim of supporting the process of reform in BiH. In 2002, the OHR relinquished its responsibility for education reform to the OSCE, which, working with local and international experts, published its strategy for "Reforming Education to Give BiH a Better Future". The strategy gave rise to a document issued by the country's education ministers containing five pledges with the primary aim of depoliticising education.[7]

The document served as a basis for the framework legislation on first-stage (primary and lower secondary) education, which came into force at the start of the 2003/2004 academic year.[8] The principal focus of this legislation was the duration of compulsory schooling, which was raised from 8 to 9 years, and the school-leaving qualifications and grades awarded by the two entities, which with the advent of the new law were to be recognised throughout BiH. Further, the legislation enabled the country to take initial steps towards a shared core curriculum in the subjects considered as "national". Article 9 of the framework legislation upholds freedom of religion in its clause stipulating that "schools are to promote and protect religious freedom, tolerance and dialogue in Bosnia and Herzegovina". Further, the legislation emphasised the right of all students to faith-based religious education and conferred responsibility for its curricula and their realisation on the churches and religious communities of the country. This marked a new status of faith-based religious education as an official component of the state education system in BiH. The practical implementation of the legislation in the two entities was accompanied by a number of problems. One was that the law did not make any provisions regarding the introduction of religious education for religious minorities; another was that it remained silent on the potential case of children or their parents rejecting the idea of participation in faith-based religious education classes. The High Representative signed a supplementary law in 2004, which addressed and clarified these issues.

The legislation called for a further round of revisions for language, history, geography and religious education textbooks and for the harmonisation of the various curricula to be found in BiH to the end of creating a shared core curriculum, from which, however, religious education was to be excepted.[9] This second textbook revision was accompanied by the first official classification of religious education as a "national subject" by the OSCE.[10]

Islamic Faith-Based Religious Education and "Culture of Religions"

As early as 1991, the Office of Education, Science, Culture and Sport in the Yugoslav republic of Bosnia and Herzegovina had been making preparations for the introduction of religious education at state schools and had called for the submission of suggestions from all churches and religious communities that wished to be involved. The results of these efforts was published in 1994, during the most recent war under the title "A Plan and Programme for Islamic, Catholic, Serbian Orthodox, Jewish and Adventist Religious Education in State Schools".[11] The programme was approved by the renamed Ministry of Education, Science, Culture and Sport on 15 July 1994, leading to the addition of religious education as an optional subject in the school curriculum.

However, it quickly became apparent after the war that only the Islamic community and the Catholic and Serbian Orthodox churches were in a position, in terms of their organisational structures and numbers of potential students, to offer religious education at state-run schools. The state took over funding of religious education after the religious institutions found themselves unable to continue providing funds for this purpose. Responsibility for the content of religious education curricula remains with the faith communities, subject to approval of the education ministry.

New legislation on religion issued in BiH in 2004 helped improve the legal position of churches and faith communities and hence of religious education in the country. In 1997, through the mediation of the World Conference on Religion and Peace (WCRP), BiH's four "traditional" churches and faith communities had founded the Inter-religious Council of Bosnia and Herzegovina, which in 2003 published a draft of legislation on religious freedom and the legal status of faith communities in the country, which had been produced in cooperation with the WCRP and local lawyers.[12] The parliament of BiH approved the draft legislation on 22 January 2004 (signed into law on 9 March 2004), thus cementing the legal position of faith-based religious education in BiH. The legislation is divided into six sections: general provisions; provisions on freedom to practise one's faith and hold opinions; the legal status of churches and faith communities; the relationship between the state and churches/faith communities; the foundation of new churches and faith communities; and interim and closing stipulations. It enshrined in law the following principles: (1) that of the separation of church and state (article 14); (2) the status of churches and religious communities as legal entities (article 8); (3) the right to religious education at state schools (article 4); and (4) the right of churches and faith communities to publish textbooks and disseminate them in line with the law (article 7).[13]

The international community, led by the OSCE, has expressed emphatic criticism of the model of faith-based single-faith religious education as it is practised in BiH, with particular reference to its tendency to focus on the faith in whose name the teaching is being delivered and the concomitant neglect of, or tendency towards, discrimination against religious minorities. The critics consider that a multifaith society such as that of BiH needs a different approach to teaching about religion in state schools, ideally centring around teaching on the faiths existent in the country from a perspective not affiliated to a particular faith. To this end, the introduction was planned, as a part of the reform referred to above, of a secular subject in school to be called "Culture of Religions". The OHR informed the public on 5 December 2000 about the new subject, to be taught as part of first-stage (primary/lower secondary) education, whose express purpose was to be the dissemination and promotion of non-discriminatory information on BiH's four traditional churches and faith communities.[14] This pilot project, and the reform in general, initiated a debate within BiH society on religious education, which had a direct or indirect impact on all churches and religious organisations in the country. We will explore in the discussion that follows the issue of whether, and to what extent, the process of education reform and the international community's presence in BiH has exerted their influence on the country's Islamic community and the religious education it delivers.

Despite all the criticisms made of religious education, a study conducted by the Open Society Fund Bosnia and Herzegovina, entitled "What are we Teaching our Children?" and published in 2007 indicated that neither parents nor children would like to see the back of religious education in schools.[15]

Islamic Community and Islamic Religious Education at State Schools

The Islamic community in BiH conceives of itself as the religious community of the Muslims living in the country's territory, of those living outside their homeland and of all Muslims who choose to adhere to it. It also encompasses the faith's highest religious bodies, the *mešihat-e* of the Islamic community in the Sandžak region, in Slovenia and Croatia.[16]

The academic literature on the Islamic community in BiH associates it primarily, in both its pre- and post-war incarnations, with the search for national identity. On 28 April 1993, after Yugoslavia had collapsed and BiH had descended into war, a small number of Islamic theologians and intellectuals convened a renewal assembly (*Obnoviteljski Sabor*), which was controversial both within the Islamic community and politically,[17] and declared all internal religious stipulations and determinations issued by the previous Islamic community to be invalid. The assembly ruled that the Muslims in BiH were to refer to themselves henceforth as "Bosniaks" as opposed to "Muslims," in order to set a clear signal marking the transformation of BiH's Islamic community into a political and national grouping with particular territorial claims.[18] Alongside this, the assembly deemed the language of the Bosniaks to be the "Bosnian language".

It was during this period of a search for and attempted assertion of national identity that religious education was introduced in state schools in BiH. We would, however, be failing to take account of the full picture were we to hastily conclude that this means the latter was driven by the ideas behind the former. We need to be aware of the negative influences continuing to live on in the aftermath of the war and the period of communism that preceded it. Further, it was precisely religious education, or rather the visibility of religion in the public sphere of which it was an indicator, which all religious institutions, including the Islamic community, viewed as the key achievement brought about by democracy.

The Intra-Islamic Modernisation of Religious Education

Over the past 15 years, two events took place in the Islamic community in BiH, which exerted a decisive impact on areas of Islamic life in the country including the way in which the religion was taught in schools.

The first of these was the renewal assembly of 1993 referred to above. As a part of this assembly, a discussion was held in Sarajevo on 22 February 1993 on "Faith and Education"; at this event, a number of participants outlined fundamental approaches to Islamic education in BiH.[19] A majority proceeded from the assumption that state education should be based on the Islamic "civilisatory code"; this is primarily a reference to the Islamic religious tradition, which was viewed as having been outlawed under communism[20] and as encompassing physical, intellectual and spiritual components as well as relating to human moral and material life and the holistic effects of human activity on earth.[21] Omer Nakičević takes the view that this holistic approach, or, as he calls it, "the Islamic message of universalism," stands in contradiction to the "usual" separation of education into the religious and the secular.[22] Other participants in the discussion expressed the need for Islamic terminology and Arabic language both within the practice of the religion and in everyday life, including state education.[23] Among the key decisions reached during this event were those concerning the adaptation of textbook content "to the cultural and cognitive reality of Muslims" and the foundation of educational offices and institutes within the highest religious body of the Islamic community, *Rijaset*.[24] A manifesto issued by the Islamic community in BiH defines education in the Islamic sense in clear and concise terms:

> The task of the highest importance for the Islamic community is the development of the Islamic personality via Islamic education, cultural schemes, public media and all other available methods.[25]

The second decisive event of the past 15 years was the publication in 2006 of the Islamic Resolution (*Islamska Rezolucija*), a collection of pieces which once again reiterates the position in which BiH's Islamic community currently sees itself. Among other documents, a *fetwa* included in this collection explicitly determines that "traditional Bosnian Islam" is to be defined as Sunni Islam practised in accordance with Hanaphite theological law and thus that this manner of practising the faith is to be compulsory in mosques, at burials and in other public places of devotion, as well as being prescribed in all religious books.[26] We might from this draw the general inference that the document's intent is not only to initiate internal processes of reform, but also to combat allegations of Wahhabi infiltration into Islam in BiH.

The Resolution views education as an area of great significance to the Islamic community. Grand Mufti Mustafa Cerić considers the institutions and Islamic learned authorities (*Ulama*) to be of central importance both in terms of education and in all other areas of Islamic life.[27] In his view, it is necessary for all educational institutions to continue to centralise under the guidance and leadership of the Islamic community. The further institutionalisation of Islam is regarded as key in view of the fact that it is seen as representing an important part of Islamic tradition in BiH.[28]

Grand Mufti Cerić interprets "modernisation of education" as primarily meaning an increase in the quality of education at all levels.[29] His contribution to the Resolution points out explicitly that the Islamic community of BiH regards education reform as necessary and intends to support it fully; further, the text continues, it is the intention of the state of BiH [sic] to support cooperation with the OSCE on education reform.[30] Despite this, theoretically open-minded attitude towards tendencies of modernisation in education, Grand Mufti Cerić's piece emphasises that teachers of religion should aim principally to promote the "spiritual" unity of Muslims and themselves practise this as an attitude.[31] We can thus observe that "modernisation through education" is evidently conceived of, to refer to and bring together, two distinct elements of education: on the one hand the religious tradition and consolidation of national identity held by BiH's Islamic community, on the other hand access to modern techniques, media and other means of education.[32]

Islamic Religious Education in Practice

Decisions on religious education in BiH are taken exclusively within the *Rijaset* of the Islamic community. Although the *Rijaset* bears the principal responsibility for Islamic religious education, the task of drawing up the curriculum and organising its delivery falls to the religious and public institutions of the Office for Religious Education (*Vjerskoprosvjetna služba*), which also takes care of the preparation, design and publication of religious education textbooks and of all other information relevant to this education via the conventional and electronic media.

Education within the Islamic community takes place at a number of levels. Religious education teachers (*muallims*) are responsible for delivering religious education classes in state schools, while imams cover instruction in religious schools and at theological faculties. Imams, muallims and other teaching figures belong to *Ilmijja*, an association for religious educators, which is based in Sarajevo and was founded in 1912 for the purpose, among others, of training its members.[33] *Ilmijja* publishes the periodical *Novi Muallim*, which is dedicated to exploring issues around education in state and religious schools.

Islamic religious education was officially introduced in state primary schools in the Federation of BiH in 1994. This, as a number of newspaper articles commented at the time,[34] was while the country's most recent war was still in progress; the classes were held primarily in private and religious establishments, with only some of them taking place in schools. At the 476 primary schools, approximately 96% of Muslim schoolchildren attend Islamic religious education,[35] delivered by around 750 teachers.[36] According to the Islamic community's most important medium, the periodical *Glasnik Rijaseta*, the number of students taking part in religious education in state schools is rising continuously,[37] while the numbers enrolled in faith preschools is decreasing, dramatically in places.[38] Islamic religious education is delivered in all the Federation's cantons and in all other lower secondary schools, except in the cantons of Sarajevo and Goražde. Currently, approximately 82% of lower secondary students take part in Islamic religious education classes. The number of lessons taught per week varies between one and two across the various cantons and in BiH's entities.

The introduction of Islamic religious education in lower secondary schools took place years after its commencement in primary schools. The reasons for this are manifold, principally relating to a lack of available staff and the dependence of the processes of its introduction on regional ministers of education. This is the reason why the canton of Sarajevo and the entire RS are as yet without Islamic religious education in lower secondary schools.

Teachers in the subject are trained in 3-year courses at the faculties of Islamic education in Zenica and Bihać and at the Faculty of Islamic Studies in Sarajevo. Graduates of the latter who wish to teach religious education are required to obtain a permit from the *Rijaset*. In general, graduates of the faculties of Islamic education and of the Islamic studies faculty, like those from all other religious institutions in BiH, may only teach in state schools if they pass a state teacher examination. The teachers are paid for a maximum of 20 h a week directly by the state; according to the *Rijaset*, their salary amounted to approximately €270–300 a month. The relevant religious district (*muftijstvo*) is responsible for the delivery of teaching and the rights of the teachers.

Textbooks for the subject are published by the Islamic community and require approval from the federal education ministry. Up to 30% of the books' content may be altered or amended without the book having to go through a repeat approval process. Textbooks can be purchased from state and private bookstores. There are textbooks for each year of primary education, while lower secondary schools have only handbooks. The now compulsory 9-year first stage of education has textbooks for only the first three school years.

Curricula Issued by the Islamic Community

The first curriculum for Islamic religious education in what was then the 8-year initial stage of state education in BiH was published by the *Rijaset* of the country's Islamic community in 1994[39]; the second was agreed upon and approved by the Ministry of Education in 1997, but not published until 1999.[40] This second curriculum for 8-year first-stage education has been amended and gradually adapted for the new 9-year system. This is the third curriculum, which was started to be produced in 2006.

The first two first-stage curricula issued are virtually identical. Of a total of 850 lesson hours of teaching planned in these curricula, 570 are to be held in primary and 280 in lower secondary school,[41] at a rate of two lessons per week and 80 per school year. The two-page explanatory notes to the curriculum, to which no changes were made from the curriculum's first to its second edition, emphasise that the content of lessons is to be kept as simple as possible[42] and advises that the various stories, illustrations and illustrative examples that are available to teachers should be used as often as is practicable. The notes further recommend, without providing further specification, that particular attention should be paid to the teaching methods used, with preference given to dialogic and demonstrative forms of teaching rather than monologic practices, and that modern teaching materials be used. Those delivering Islamic religious education are called upon to draw up their own schedule of lessons on the basis of the curriculum and engage regularly in continuing professional development.[43] The two curricula contain identical learning objectives,[44] with the following expectations from the students:

- become familiar with the key principles of the Koran, i.e. faith in one God, belief in his angels, his revelations, prophets etc.;
- develop the ability to lead their lives in harmony with the religious duties ("five pillars") of Islam, i.e. the profession of faith, prayer rituals, religious discipline [i.e. fasting], material giving, pilgrimage;
- develop a sense of religious duty and responsibility;
- be encouraged to consider and reflect upon their surroundings;
- express their opinion without fear or shame;
- develop an early interest in the Koran, the Sunna and all things Islamic;
- come to understand the core of Islamic teachings;
- become familiar with Sharia laws and learn to apply them[45];
- become familiarised with the Islamic value system;
- develop and shape an attitude of active and conscious love for Allah and for the worldwide Islamic community (*umma*);
- be aware of the development of Islam in "our regions" [*našim prostorima*], of these regions' religious heritage and its cultural monuments;
- attain a conviction/feeling of conscious belonging to the Islamic community of faith;
- develop a determination to preserve and maintain Islam in "our territories" [*našim krajevima*];
- become free, through the knowledge of the truth about their religion, its roots and its progressive role in human history, of the shame forced on Muslims through distortions of Islam's role in these territories [*krajevima*].

All the 14 objectives listed refer to knowledge, capabilities and competencies that proceed from the Islamic faith, or from the five areas or disciplines of Islamic teachings, which are Koranic exegesis, Islamic dogmas Islamic law, the history of Islam and Islamic ethics. This curriculum is therefore a clearly Islamic religious education curriculum. Other religions are not intended to be covered, although they are mentioned in a few cases as follows: In the primary school syllabus from 1994, lesson 41, given in year 5 and covering two lesson periods, is on "Getting to Know the Teachings of Other Denominations," prescribing visits to Orthodox and Catholic churches and a synagogue. This lesson is no longer included in the year-5 syllabus issued in 1999, having been replaced by "The Duties of Muslims Towards Others,"[46] which involves a general

discussion of Muslims' duties towards their parents, children and neighbours. There are no other lessons in the syllabus that explicitly discuss
"others," i.e. non-Muslims.

The Curriculum for the 9-Year First Stage of Education

The new version of the curriculum, for the 9-year first stage of education, shows a notable degree of modernisation in terms of methods and
educational principles compared to the older curricula.[47] The curriculum
lists the subject's significance, its objectives and purposes, the intended
learning outcomes, and educational and methodological guidelines.[48]
The objectives and purposes of the subject are formulated separately
for each of the school years. In year 1, for instance, the objective is to
encourage students to gain a conviction of Allah's importance and significance through their own insights into the matter, based on the revelation of God, the Koran and the teachings of the prophet Mohammed.[49]
In year 2, learners are to be introduced to specific religious content,
mostly Islamic in nature, as well as "the fundamental axioms of intercultural education".[50] Further objectives of the curriculum take this aim as
a basis and seek to expand the ideas gained by the children in year 1 on
a cognitive, emotional and practical level.[51] The curriculum then states
the numerous purposes of Islamic religious education, which have been
reformulated for each school year, yet are identical in terms of content
to the objectives cited above, which were given in the 1994 and 1999
syllabi.

We notice in this reformulated curriculum that the terms used are
now in line with modern principles of religious education. While the
first two versions of the curriculum refer to the "principles of the Koran"
and the development of a "sense of duty and responsibility," now first-
year children are to be given access to "initial knowledge and information on faith, [presented] in an age-appropriate form" and have their
"creative potential and thinking" developed and promoted.[52] The tasks
included in the curriculum have also been overhauled; their purpose is
now to allow first-year learners to "become able to [take part in] the
culture of communication with their peers and adults and [to promote]
mutual cooperation and the acceptance of a relationship of kindness
and humanity towards all living beings".[53] Whereas the older curricula
neglected religious plurality and focused on "Bosnia" (but not "Bosnia
and Herzegovina") as the students' homeland and on Bosnian identity,[54]

the third-year curriculum in the new version has changed the emphasis somewhat: The aim of the lesson on "Leading an Islamic life" (*Islamski se ponašam*) is to encourage children to develop positive feelings of acceptance of others "in an Islamic manner".[55] The 2006 curriculum states and recommends the use of connections to other subjects, with particular emphasis on connections to the subjects of Bosnian language, "My Surroundings," physical education and art. It is thus evident that the curricula, although imperfect, have undergone a noticeable process of modernisation, both in the educational sense and in the terminology used.

ISLAMIC RELIGIOUS EDUCATION TEXTBOOKS IN BiH

The fundamental purpose of Islamic religious education in BiH is to enable students to find and become firm in their own religious point of view. Other religions are nevertheless touched upon implicitly or explicitly in the curriculum, which is a positive development in contrast to the curricula used in the first 8-year structure of first-stage education, in the objectives of which other faiths and religious plurality were not included explicitly.[56]

The other faiths mentioned in Islamic religious education textbooks primarily encompass the monotheistic religions; further groups referred to are atheists and those who adhere to "superstitions". In places, "the West" acts as an "Other," or as a representative of what is different from Islam. Further "other" faiths are what the textbooks refer to as "sects," such as the Ahmadiyya community, the Baha'i faith and Wahhabism.

In order to understand how students in Islamic religious education are taught ideas about different religions and religious phenomena, we need first to differentiate between explicit, implicit and inclusive[57] references to "others" in faith-based religious teaching. We also need to take account of the degree to which a principle operates according to which references to other faiths are explicitly avoided in lessons, a principle that might manifest itself in cases where lesson content or illustrations might point explicitly towards "others" but not actually discuss them. Our close content analysis will revolve around selected examples from textbooks for years 1–8 of schooling. We cannot discuss at length, yet wish to point to the theological and hermeneutical issues connected to the depiction of other faiths from an Islamic perspective.[58]

Different Religions Avoided

The year-1 textbook[59] frequently explicitly avoids references to other faiths in those lessons that would be particularly suitable for such discussion, whether the students might discuss pictures from the textbook or refer to their own friends in this context. Two examples might serve to illustrate this point:

In the lesson on "The Greeting of Peace," children are taught the Bosniak spelling variants *es-selamu alejkum* and *alejkumu-s-selam* and told that *non-Muslims* should be greeted with the words "Good morning" and "Good day" (Religious Education book for year 1, p. 23, henceforth R1: 23).[60] The book does not offer any further information on who the "non-Muslims" are or how students can recognise them.

The lesson "Out in the Street" consists of a picture with questions and information, none of which relate to the things that can be seen in the picture, such as places of worship and a "Club Multikultura". Instead, the most important things about the street scene are listed as being its cleanness, the well-dressed children and pleasant houses to be seen, the attractive displays in the shop windows, well-looked-after plants and flowers, and the children's politeness to older people (R1: 37).[61]

Monotheistic Religions in the Islamic Context

Figures in Islamic religious education who are also relevant to Judaism and Christianity, such as Ibrahim (Abraham), Musa (Moses), Yunus (Jonah) and Isa (Jesus), are first mentioned in year 5, in the lesson "Five Great Gifts from Allah" (R5: 109ff). The names given to these figures are the Islamic ones, and their historical contexts are interpreted from an Islamic perspective. For instance, Ibrahim, Yunus and Musa are shown as praying to Allah, and their names in the faiths from which they originally come are not given. An exception is made in relation to Isa: "*The Christians teach that Isa (Jesus) is the Son of God, that he is a true god* [sic][62] *and truly man, and that he is the foundation and the centre of the Christian faith*" (R5: 111).

The lesson "Faith in Heavenly Revelations" in year 7 contains only one sentence on the four major Abrahamic books of revelation: "The Tevrat [the Torah] was revealed to Musa"; "The Zebur [the Psalms] was revealed to Davud"; "The Indžil [the Gospel] was revealed to Isa"; "The Koran was revealed to Muhammad" (R7: 66). What is discussed here is not expanded upon or placed in the context of other faiths. The questions that accompany the lesson imply that all these holy books of revelation are to be regarded as belonging to Islam; one of them, for instance, asks: "In which way has [knowledge of] the Islamic duties been available to humankind through *history?*" (R7: 66).

The year-8 textbook[63] includes several lessons in which other religions are explicitly referenced from an Islamic perspective. An example is the lesson "Books of Revelation," which names the Torah, the Psalms, the Gospels and the Koran, citing the Islamic forms of their names, Tevrat, Zebur, Indžil and Kur'an, and refers to them as the books revealed to various peoples through the Angel Gabriel, Allah's messenger (R8: 10ff). The lesson covers six pages, around two of which discuss the Koran, while the other four deal with the remaining holy books.

The part of the text discussing the Torah contains only brief asides on the book's religious context, such as "*The original version of the 'Tevrat', revealed by Allah cc, no longer exists today, because the Jews did not preserve it,*" and "*The Jews call the 'Tevrat' Torah, which means 'teachings' or 'knowledge' in Hebrew*" (R8: 11). We can see from such passages that the teaching provides no information, simple or otherwise, on Judaism and does not explore its internal nuances. We might interpret such statements as providing monocausal explanations that transmit a negative attitude towards Judaism, presenting the viewpoint that the Jews, unlike the Muslims later, did not take the word of God sufficiently seriously. It is in our view positive, however, that the textbook clearly gives the book's Jewish name.

The Gospels are initially defined as follows, from an Islamic perspective: "*The Indžil is a set of instructions for those who have remained on the path of the Tevrat.*" The conclusion drawn from this is that Jesus was a Muslim and announced the coming of Mohammed. "*He [Jesus] pointed the world to faith in One God, Allah cc,*" and "*Isa saaw, accordingly, pointed to the same faith as Mohammad saaw and he was a Muslim in the broadest sense of the term, as were all other prophets of Allah.*" (R8: 12) It is not until after this that the book discusses the Gospels as adopted by the "church," without any differentiation of which church is being referred to. It is only in this context that the book uses the term "Gospels"; this is the first time throughout the book that it references— without giving sources—the views of academics who doubt the authenticity of the Biblical narrative. According to the book, these academics claimed that the Gospels "*were written in the second half of the first and the first half fo the second century* [...] *AD, or several decades after the death of Isa or Jesus.*" (R8: 12). The textbook points explicitly to the differences in the ways the Bible and the Koran interpret Jesus' life and teachings, but Christianity is not discussed without being viewed in parallel through the lens of the Koran:

> The Gospels speak of Isa's life and teachings very differently from the Koran. For instance, Christian teaching about the Trinity is that there exists one God – the 'Father', the 'Son of God' (Jesus) and 'the Holy Spirit', - that Jesus was crucified and later rose from the dead. [...] In the Koran, however, it is written that Isa saaw did not consider himself to be the Son of God. About his death, the Koran says that he was neither crucified nor did he die, but this simply appeared to people to be thus. (R8: 12f)

We can see from this that these textbooks consistently refer to other religions from an Islamic perspective, although there a Christian perspective is occasionally presented. However, the books completely fail to discuss or explore the societally intertwined nature of the monotheistic religions in BiH.

"Superstition" and Atheism

The textbooks contain little material on different faiths and worldviews; what there is, however, is extremely interesting to examine. For example, the books' exploration of popular religion begins in year 2, with a lesson entitled "The Witch" (R2: 36), which tells a story about a witch who cannot solve her own problems and follows it up with questions and information on witches, magicians, tarot card readers and others who carry out practices considered forbidden by Islam, including all forms of seeking help from deceased family members at their gravesides. The reference to such practices represents an indirect allusion to Islamic popular religiosity, but does not expand on the discussion. The lesson concludes with the moral that it is not permitted to be "superstitious" and that girls should stop trying to tell their fortunes in coffee grounds (R2: 37).

In the year-6 textbook,[64] atheists are given an explicit mention (R6: 20), with the lesson "The Nature of *kufr*" (Arabic for "unbelief") discussing people who, due to their upbringings, education and/or ignorance, do not believe in any god, adding that the presence of belief in a god is, in the Islamic view of things, the normal human state. The book

deems unbelievers to be those who believe in elements and natural phenomena such as fire and thunder as well as those who "do not believe in
Allah," those who "do not believe in the correct way," and those who
"doubt the word of God" (R6: 20). It describes such people as insecure,
lacking in confidence and pitiable (R6: 19). We are justified in doubting
whether this position can allow the development of fruitful dialogue with
those holding other views.

An example of the interpretation of the productions of other religions
in line with Islamic beliefs and values is the lesson "The Relationship
with Nature and the World Around Us," which is taught in year 8 and
contains a letter written by a Native American chief (R8: 93f). The two-
page letter, which laments from a Native American point of view the
negative ecological and spiritual state of the "modern world" at the time
of writing, is not followed, as one might have expected, by a discussion of Native American ideas of the world, or of environmental issues;
instead, there are questions such as "*Who created our world, and how?*"
and "*What can we find in the Words of the Prophet about the world in
which we live?*" (R8: 95), which relate exclusively to Islam.

INTRA-ISLAMIC CRITICISM OF FAITH-BASED RELIGIOUS EDUCATION

Criticism of faith-based religious education in BiH has been issued by
the OSCE and a number of intellectuals in relation to Islam, several
intellectuals from within the Islamic community have criticised the religious education being given to Muslim children, and it is on this criticism, which has mostly been formulated within interviews or essays,
that we will focus here. The range of points raised extends from general
observations on how the teaching could be improved to emphatic concerns about the *Rijaset*'s manner of proceeding in this context and about
the content taught and the manner of its delivery in state schools.

Figures who have engaged in the first of these forms of criticism
include the Islamic theologians Nedžad Grabus and Dževad Hodžić.
Nedžad Grabus, now the Grand Mufti of Slovenia, has raised concerns
about the image of "others" shown in Islamic textbooks. It is his view
that learning about one's own religion should go hand in hand with
learning about other faiths,[65] faiths whose representation in Islamic religious education is limited to mentions in a few brief sentences.[66] Grabus

recommends that textbooks and educators should discuss the teachings of other religions in more detail and raise cultural issues around these religions in the classroom.[67] Dževad Hodžić, a theologian in the *Rijaset* who is on the editorial staff of the periodical *Novi Muallim,* raises criticisms around the fact that Sufism, despite its status as a part of Bosnian Islamic tradition, is barely represented at Islamic educational institutions in BiH. He is particularly concerned about what is said to be an extensive Wahhabi influence on the content of religious education classes developed at Islamic academies of education.[68] In Hodžić's view, the problem is primarily that the current educational policy of the Islamic community has departed from its own original Islamic teachings and from the Sufi-oriented educational guidelines issued by the first Bosnian supporter and funder of religious education, Gazi Husrev Bey.[69] Hodžić reports that teachings that have left the path of this tradition (Wahabbits) find adherents among Islamic educators more frequently than the *Rijaset* supposes.[70] This claim strikes at the heart of the self-image held by the Islamic community in contemporary BiH: The academies of education, the *Rijaset*'s model institutions, find themselves in ideological conflict with the Islamic Resolution.

Criticism of the content of Islamic religious education in BiH has come from Muslim intellectuals such as Enes Karić and Rešid Hafizović. Karić, minister of education in the Federation during the war, is a professor of Koranic exegesis at the Faculty of Islamic Studies in Sarajevo. His comments in 1998, criticising the unregulated manner in which Islamic religious education had been introduced at schools, launched a debate on Islamic religious education. Karić's view was that Islam was being taught too simplistically and the classes thus taught were doing more harm than good.[71] He also expressed concern about the fact that, in his opinion, state schools were being used for religious, essentially "cultic" purposes, arguing that the school environment was unsuitable for such use, that religious education should not fall into the trap of mirroring the Marxist education of Communist days and that education should not be replaced by religion.[72] Karić considered that the ideological questions around religious education had not yet met with an adequate response.

Rešid Hafizović, professor of Islamic dogmatics at the Faculty of Islamic Studies, has also made repeated negative comments on various aspects of Islamic religious education, including internal processes of content development and decision-making, the role of Grand Mufti Cerić, the design of the curriculum and practical issues such as teacher training. Hafizović takes a critical view of the *Rijaset*'s, having created the subject on its own without consulting the Faculty of Islamic Studies, which was at the time the only academic institution training teachers for religious education. Additionally, Hafizović professes himself unable to identify any consistent concept behind the religious education curriculum and perceives a lack of clarity on its purposes and objectives. He is also concerned about the level at which the textbooks' content is pitched, observing that in his view, their current level makes them counterproductive due to their lack of awareness of the present-day world and the consequently minimal interest they hold for students. Further, he comments, the curriculum ignores the fact that children begin learning Arabic in year 2 of their schooling.[73] His final point of criticism concerns the fact that teachers are not issued with guidelines.[74]

A further critic of both the official interpretive authorities on Islam in BiH and the manner of their argumentation about religious issues is Rusmir Mahmutćehajić, who, after a long active period in the Assembly of the Islamic community, distanced himself from his previous political and religious work. Arguing from the position of an external observer, he has stated that he considers "ignorance" to be the key reason for the rise of "the modern ethno-national ideologies"[75] and that faith-based religious education can have little impact on this ignorance,[76] which he has attempted to resist by founding an NGO, the "Forum Bosnae," dedicated to dialogue and to the mystical side of Islam from the perspective of *philosophia perennis*.[77] Mahmutćehajić's involvement in the discussion around religious education via his co-editorship, with Catholic, Jewish and Serbian Orthodox colleagues, of a handbook for religious education teachers represented an indirect expression of criticism in this context. His essay "On Equality and Difference in Judaism, Christianity and Islam" is primarily a critical discussion of "conventional" religion in BiH, by which he means "official" religion as an institution. In Mahmutćehajić's view, true encounters between people of different faiths can only emerge when—put simply—they approach one another on the level of their shared mystical heritage. [78]

CONCLUSION

The post-communist and post-war period in BiH has presented the Islamic community, as all other churches and religious communities in the country, with the dual challenge of the "external" modernisation being driven by elites in their responsibility for BiH's EU integration, represented primarily by the international community, and the "internal" processes of modernisation unfolding within the Islamic community with its concomitant undergoing of recontextualisation and self-positioning. This modernisation, where it relates to religious education in state schools, revolves, as we have discussed, around acknowledging and adopting the "standards of modern education". Translated into practice in BiH, this primarily means teaching democratic values within the education system. The international community regards the treatment of religious plurality as a yardstick against which adherence to these values can be measured. The Islamic community is attempting to meet these standards, although it finds itself simultaneously confronted with the desire for its religious tradition to take a central place after years of communism and the wish thus to draw the concepts for its religious education from the faith and its tradition.

This dual challenge has given rise to tensions within the Islamic community, which has found a similarly double method of tackling it. These internal tensions have emerged, as we have seen, in the criticisms made from within Islam of Islamic religious education in schools. However, it is precisely these criticisms that have led to the official representatives of Islam in BiH, seeking at all times to promote the impression that there is in fact no internal plurality within the community, neither with regard to approaches to religious education nor on other issues such as the various Islamic legal traditions. This demonstrative internal unity or "continuity" of "Bosnian Islam" is the first strategy used by the community to tackle this challenge, and it is intended to be manifested particularly in public education, which gives rise to discussion in religious education classes around "right" and "wrong" versions of Islam. The key aspect of this attitude is not the religious consequences of following the "right" or "wrong" version, which are detailed in classes, but rather the "national" consequences, as envisaged by the Islamic community's highest interpretive authorities and by the *Rijaset*.

This notwithstanding, there are places within religious education textbooks that attempt to discuss other religions from their faith-specific perspectives. We should emphasise at this juncture that the fact alone that other religions are discussed at all in faith-based Islamic religious education is indicative of a degree of modernisation within Islam in BiH, of an adaptation, albeit reluctant in nature, of the practise of Islamic education to current societal trends and needs, which we might view as the second strategy pursued by the country's Islamic community.

Both the Islamic community's recourse to its tradition through modern educational media and its hesitant acceptance of modern ideas of education bear witness to a fundamental recognition within BiH's Islamic community that the time to modernise has come and to the taking of action to the end of such modernisation. However, further steps will need to be taken if the Islamic community is not to fail to modernise in other aspects of education, a concern raised as early as the beginning of the twentieth century by the Grand Mufti and educational reformer Čaušević.[79]

NOTES

1. For the constitution of BiH as part of the Dayton Accords, see http://www.ccbh.ba/osnovni-akti/ustav/?title=preambula.
2. Cf. the Constitution of the Federation of Bosnia and Herzegovina, Articles III.2a and III.4b.
3. Federalno Ministarstvo obrazovanja, nauke, kulture i sporta: Analiza kantonalnih propisa u oblasti obrazovanja (predoškolsko, osnovno i srednje obrazovanje). Sarajevo, Mai 2001, 4.
4. See www.oscebih.org/public/cro/print_news.asp?id=1560.
5. Terrice Basler: Learning to Change. The Experience of Transforming Education in South East Europe. Budapest, CEU Press 2005, 192.
6. See OHR 10.05.2000, Declaration: Meeting of the Conference of the Ministers of Education of Bosnia and Herzegovina. URL: http://www.ohr.int/print/?content_id=3520.
7. For this document, see OSCE 2002, Dokument: A Message to the People of Bosnia and Herzegovina. Education Reform. URL: http://www.oscebih.org/documents/26-eng.pdf.
8. For the text of the legislation, see „Službeni Glasnik BiH" Nr. 18/03, 425–431.
9. Cf. Astrid Fischer: Integration or Segregation? Reforming the Education Sector. In: Fischer, Martina Peacebuilding and Civil Society in Bosnia and Herzegovina. Ten Years after Dayton. Lit Verlag Berlin 2006, 297–324, here 312.
10. See Note, 8.

11. Ministarstvo obrazovanja, nauke, kulture i sporta, 1994: „Plan i Program vjerskog odgoja i obrazovanja: islamski, katolički, pravoslavni, jevrejski i adventistički" [Lehrplan für die religiöse Erziehung und Bildung: Der islamische, katholische, serbisch-orthodoxe, jüdische und adventistische Religionsunterricht] Republika Bosna i Hercegovina.
12. For the text of the legislation, see „Službeni Glasnik BiH", 09.03.2004.
13. See www.aso.zsi.at/attach/LegposreliginSee.pdf.
14. On the aims and content of the subject, see Christof Ziemer (Hg.) (2001): „Kultur der Religionen" in den Schulen in Bosnien und Herzegowina. Internationale Fachkonsultation zur Einführung eines Faches "Kultur der Religionen" in den Schulen in Bosnien und Herzegowina 18–21. März 2001 in Ilidža (Sarajevo). Dokumentation, ABRAHAM—Vereinigung für Interreligiöse Friedensarbeit & Goethe Institut, Sarajevo.
15. Dženana Trbić; Snježana, Kojić Hasanagić (2007): Obrazovanje u Bosni i Hercegovini. Čemu učimo djecu? Istrazivanje stavova roditelja i učenika o vrijednostima u nastavnim planovima i programima i udžbenicima. Fond otvoreno društvo Bosna i Hercegovina, Sarajevo.
16. Cf., http://islamskazajednica.ba/.
17. The assembly's critics within Islam considered the Islamic community to have installed a politically dependent institution in collusion with Islamic politicians from the SDA party (Party of Democratic Action). Cf. DANI, Nr. 90, 07.12.1998. Esad Hećimović: Hodža u raljama vlasti. https://www.bhdani.ba/portal/arhiva-67-281/90/tekst290.htm.
18. Xavier Bougarel: Islam and Politics in the Post-Communist Balkans. https://halshs.archives-ouvertes.fr/.../Islam_and_Politics_in_the_PostCommunist_Balkans.pdf; see also, Srećko Mato Džaja: Die bosnische Multikulturalität: Multikulturalität als ästhetisches und politisches Problem. In: Valeria Heuberger/Arnold Suppan/Elisabeth Vyslonzil (Hg., 1998): Der Balkan. Friedenszone oder Pulverfaß? Peter Lang Verlag, Frankfurt am Main, 91–97.
19. See Glasnik Rijaseta, Nr. 1–3, 1994, 23f. The speakers were Ferhat Šeta, Omer Nakičević, Lamija Hadžiosmanović, Idris Resić, Rešid Hafizović and Jusuf Žiga.
20. Ferhat Šeta: Ciljevi i zadaci savjetovanja, vjera, odgoj i obrazovanje. In: Glasnik Rijaseta Nr. 1–3 (1994) 25–26. In some instances, however, some contributors to the discussion regarded themselves as in simultaneous relationship with two complementary sets of values and traditions. Šeta commented that "[w]e belong to Europe just as much as we belong to Islam," and proceeds "from the assumption that we will continue to preserve and advance the values of both the one and the other tradition".
21. Omer Nakičević: Koncept islamskog obrazovanja. In: Glasnik Rijaseta 1–3, 1994, 27–31, 28.

22. This text does not state explicitly which kind of education is being referred to here; the context, however, indicates that the reference is likely to be to all non-religious forms of education that were in use in the communist past.
23. See Note 22.
24. See Glasnik Rijaseta, Nr. 1–3, 1994, 23f.
25. Program Islamske zajednice u BiH. Allgemeine Richtlinien, Glasnik Rijaseta 4–6, 1994, 207–215, here 211. Cf. Mustafa Cerić: Mi bošnjaci smo stvarna mjera i europske tolerancije i europskog morala i europske demokracije. In Preporod, 1/627, 1998, 6–8.
26. See Rezolucija islamske zajednice u Bosni i Hercegovini o tumačenju islama i drugi tekstovi, El-kalem, Sarajevo, 2006, 13. For the area affected by this stipulation, see Karčić in „Resolution" 52.
27. See Resolution, 25.
28. See Resolution, 53.
29. See Resolution 2006: 26. This refers both to libraries and adult education colleges for Muslims and to courses for non-Muslims who seek to learn about Islam (and may require English-medium teaching).
30. Cf. Resolution 2006: 28. "Besjeda Reisu-l-uleme dr. Mustafe Cerića" [Speech by Grand Mufti Dr. Mustafa Cerić]. The piece does not clarify the degree to which the head of the Islamic community in BiH regards himself as a spokesperson for the state.
31. See Resolution 2006: 47, section 5.
32. On the—comparable—modernisation process undergone by Islamic education in the era of the Austro-Hungarian monarchy, see Karčić, Fikret: The Bosniaks and the Challenges of Modernity. El-Kalem, Sarajevo, 1999, 92ff. On the role at that time of Grand Mufti Čaušević in relation to education, see Enes Karić: Prilozi za povijest islamskog mišljenja u Bosni i Herzegovini XX stoljeća. Band 1. El-Kalem, Sarajevo, 2004, 227ff.
33. See http://ilmijja.ba/.
34. See, among others, Preporod 15/502, 1.08. 1991, 1, "Islamic Education"; Preporod 5/516, 1.03.1992, 3 "Experimental Religious Education in Sarajevo's Schools"; See also Preporod 9/10, 1 and 10.05.1993, 5: "Education in the Light of Islamic Tradition under the Current Circumstances".
35. This information was given to me by Ibrahim Begović, the member of the Islamic community's *Rijaset* responsible for religious education, in a conversation on 26 April 2007. Cf. Glasnik Rijaseta no. 5–6, 2007, 429.
36. Cf. Glasnik Rijaseta no. 5–6, 2007, 428.
37. For detailed annual statistics in individual districts, see Glasnik Rijaseta no. 4–5, 2006, 485f; Glasnik Rijaseta no. 5–6, 2005, 479f; Glasnik Rijaseta no. 5–6, 2003, 453f; Glasnik Rijaseta no. 5–6, 2002, 556ff.

38. Cf. Glasnik Rijaseta no. 5–6, 2007, 427 and 431.
39. See Rijaset Islamske zajednice u Republici Bosni i Hercegovini (ed.): Program vjeronauke u školi. [Programme for Religious Education in Schools]. Ali Mehmed Abedich, Sarajevo, 1994.
40. Rijaset Islamske zajednice u Bosni i Hercegovini (ed.): Plan i program vjeronauke za osnovnu i srednju školu. [Plan and Programme for Religious Education in Primary and Lower Secondary Schools] Sarajevo, 1999.
41. See Programme, 1994: 6f. Cf. Plan and Programme 1999: 6f.
42. See Programme, 1994: 6f. Cf. Plan and Programme 1999: 6f.
43. See Programme, 1994: 7f. Cf. Plan and Programme 1999: 7f.
44. Cf. Programme, 1994: 5f. Cf. Plan and Programme 1999: 5f.
45. Cf. Zlatiborka Popov/Mette Ofstad: Religious Education in Bosnia and Herzegowina. In. Zorica Kuburić,/Christian Moe: Religion and Pluralism in Education. Comparative Approaches in the Western Balkans. CEIR Novi Sad, 2006, 73–106. The translation of this objective of Islamic religious education is not included here.
46. See Programme, 1994: 37. Cf. Plan and Programme 1999: 28.
47. Each curriculum can be obtained separately. For the curriculum for the first grade approved by Rijaset in year 2006 (Curriculum 2006) see: http://www.vjeroucitelji.ba/skola/npp-udzbenici/osnovna-skola/item/vjeronauka-za-1-razred-osnovne-skole. For the curriculum of the ninth year of primary education, approved by the *Rijaset* in the year 2011 see: http://www.vjeroucitelji.ba/skola/npp-udzbenici/osnovna-skola/item/vjeronauka-za-9-razred-osnovne-skole.
48. Curriculum 2006: 1.
49. Curriculum 2006: 2.
50. Curriculum 2006: 6.
51. Curriculum 2006: 5f.
52. Curriculum 2006: 2.
53. Ibid.
54. See curriculum 1999: 14, specifically the lesson on "Islam in Bosnia"; curriculum 1999: 15, specifically the lesson "Are you proud of your Islamic name?"; curriculum 1999: 36.
55. Curriculum 2006: 23.
56. There is an exception in the year 5 curriculum from 1999, which discusses Muslims' duties towards others; the textbooks, however, indicate clearly that these duties are considered to refer not to adherents of other religions, but to other Muslims.
57. See Klaus hock; Johannes Lähnemann, Wolfram Reiss (eds.): Schulbuchforschung im Dialog. Das Christentum in Schulbüchern islamisch geprägter Länder. Verlag Otto Lembeck, Frankfurt am Main, 2006, 129. An "inclusive" perspective is one which, within the viewpoint of a specific religion, discusses figures from or the holy books of other faiths.

58. On hermeneutical and theological barriers and potential, see Reiss, Wolfram: Schwierigkeiten und Chancen des Gesprächs über Darstellung des Christentums in ägyptischen Schulbüchern. In Hock et al.: Schulbuchforschung im Dialog. Das Christentum in Schulbüchern islamisch geprägter Länder. Verlag Otto Lembeck, Frankfurt am Main. 137–243, here: 198.

59. Hazema Ništović; Dževdeta Ajanović; Edina Vejo: Religious Education for year 1 of primary schooling, issued by Rijaset Islamske zajednice u Bosni i Hercegovini, El-kalem Sarajevo, 2004.

60. Cf. Nedžad Grabus: Iskustvo sa školskim vjeronaukom u BiH i kako vlastiti vjeronaučni priručnici prikazuju "druge" učenicima pluralne sredine. [Experiences with religious education in schools in BiH and how religious education textbooks depict "others" in the context of the pluralistic environment]. In: Vrhbosnensia, Vrhbosanska katolička teologija, no. 1 (2004) Sarajevo, 87–93.

61. For further examples, see Religiouis Education for year 2 of primary schooling, 15 and 61.

62. The term "God" is consistently capitalised in Islamic textbooks when used to refer to the Islamic God, i.e. Allah, and written with a small initial letter where is it used in the context of another faith. This practice evidently represents a narrowing of Islamic teachings in relation to their understanding of Abrahamic religions and is likely to have a negative impact on inter-faith trialogue in BiH.

63. Ševko Sulejmanović; Esma Kapetanović: Religious Education for year 8 of schooling, Rijaset Islamske zajednice BiH, El-kalem, Sarajevo, 2004.

64. See Mensura Ćatović: Religious Education for year 6 of primary schooling. Rijaset Islamske zajednice BiH, El-kalem, Sarajevo, 2004.

65. See Nedžad Grabus: Iskustvo sa školskim vjeronaukom u BiH i kako vlastiti vjeronaučni priručnici prikazuju "druge" učenicima pluralne sredine. [Experiences with religious education in schools in BiH and how religious education textbooks depict "others" in the context of the pluralistic environment]. In: Vrhbosnensia, Vrhbosanska katolička teologija, no. 1 (2004) Sarajevo, 87–93, here: 90.

66. Ibid., 92.

67. Ibid., 93.

68. See Dževad Hodžić: Poste restante. Kuda die Islamska zajednica? [Poste restante: In which direction is the Islamic community moving?], Tugra, Sarajevo, 1999, 88.

69. Ibid., 90.

70. Ibid., 89.

71. Cf. Bosanski Institut, London (1998): Pitanje Opstanka. Zajednički obrazovni sustav za Bosnu i Hercegovinu. Zbornik priloga i diskusija sa seminara odrzanog u travanju 1998, u Samostanu Sv. Ante u Sarajevu. [A Question of Survival: The shared education system in Bosnia and Herzegovina. Edited volume of the proceedings of the seminar in the St. Anto monastery in Sarajevo, April 1998] Promocult, Sarajevo, 7.

72. See Enes Karić: Obredno obrazovanje i vjerske zajednice. Kultura religija u škole. [Ritual Education and Religious Communities: "Culture of Religions" to be introduced in schools]. In: Didaktički putokazi no. 14 (1999) 79–81, here: 79.

73. Cf. The year-2 Arabic language textbook *Arapski jezik. II razred osnovne škole* by Omer Nakičević; Jusuf Ramić; Mesud Hafizović, issued by the ministry of education of the Federation of BiH, Sarajevo 1997.

74. All these criticisms were made in an interview held on 26 June 2007 in Sarajevo.

75. Rusmir Mahmutćehajić: Islam, katoličanstvo i pravoslavlje. O matricama pojmovnih preslikavanja. In Thomas Bremer: Religija, društvo i politika. Kontroverzna tumačenja i približavanja. Wissenschaftliche Arbeitsgruppe für weltkirchliche Aufgaben der deutschen Bischofskonferenz, 2002, 289.

76. On his manner of understanding the term "ignorance," see, inter alia, Malo znanja. O drugome u muslimanskim vidicima [Knowing Little: The Islamic Perspective on the Other] Antibarbarus, Zagreb, 2005.

77. Cf. Zrinka Štimac: Der Islam in Bosnien und Herzegowina. Sophia perennis als ein dialogisches Konzept. In: Jürgen Court; Michael Klöcker (eds.): Wege und Welten der Religionen. Forschungen und Vermittlungen. Festschrift für Udo Tworuschka. Verlag Otto Lambeck, Frankfurt am Main, 2009, 563–574. Cf. Christian Moe: A "Bosnian Paradigm" for Religious Tolerance. The Local as a Sacred Model for Global Society. EASR Konferenz in Bergen, 2003.

78. Mile Babić; Mirko Djordjević; Suzanne Last Stone; Rusmir Mahmutćehajić (eds.): Uputa Nastavnicima. Tolerancija i religijski principi. [A Guide for Teachers: Tolerance and Religious Principles] Forum Bosnae Nr. 23, Sarajevo, 2004, 19.

79. Cf. Enes Karić: Prilozi za povijest islamskog mišljenja u Bosni i Herzegovini XX stoljeća. [Contributions to the History of Islamic Thought in Bosnia and Herzegovina in the 20th Century] vol. 1, El-Kalem, Sarajevo, 2004, 237.

CHAPTER 5

Slovenia: Social Changes and (Adjustable) Politicization of the Catholic Church

Maca Jogan

INTRODUCTION

One of the key fundamental characteristics of the Catholic Church (CC) is its continuous adjustability to the changeable social environment. Upon this historically verified fact is based its stubbornness and permanent vitality. This important Church's capacity has also been conformed by the turbulent changes in Slovene society during the era from the end of the nineteenth century until the present. The permanent main goal of the church's many-sided activity has been the preservation and strengthening of the Christian religious value orientation, in short, God's plan. One of the necessary essential agents for the achievement of this goal is religious socialisation.

Religious value orientation does not exist by itself; it is rather the fruit of continuous self-regeneration or handing down from generation to generation. Socialisation with the goal of maintaining certain religious patterns of behaviour in individuals and their sense of belonging to one uniformly oriented community, can more or less correspond to the socially

M. Jogan (✉)
University of Ljubljana, Ljubljana, Slovenia

© The Author(s) 2018
G. Ognjenović and J. Jozelić (eds.), *Education in Post-Conflict Transition*, Palgrave Studies in Religion, Politics, and Policy,
https://doi.org/10.1007/978-3-319-56605-4_5

recognised fundamental value orientation. The more institutionally protected this orientation, the simpler and more effective religious socialisation; in other words, a structurally prescribed degree of mandatory
conformity with religious behavioural patterns in everyday life and their
seeming obviousness essentially enable the influence of socialisation factors
to be more evenly distributed across its social community, while omnipresence ensures efficient value reproduction.

The pivotal institution managing the complex area of religious education is undoubtedly the Church, regardless of its position in the institutional order as a whole. This is also what the decision-makers within
the Church are aware of and, consequently, it is why the emphasis on
the generational dissemination of religious teachings is one of its key
undertakings when conditions favour the Church's monopoly of people
management, but especially in situations where the Church's dominant
position in public areas has been threatened or even suppressed, simply put, where the activity of the Church is relegated to private realms
only. When such conditions arise, it is in this effort to preserve the religious orientation among members of a certain social community that the
Church in its socialisation pursuits increasingly focuses on the family as
its target institution, one that is always active in the 'building of' people.
It is within families that it is the easiest to create the impression that religious formation—just like childbearing—is just one of natural processes.

The managing of a family—which, in the case of the separation of
the Church from publicly recognised educational agents, must act as the
Church in miniature—follows plans constructed by the holders of power
within the Church (from the highest to the lowest), with catechists
acting as the first disseminators and executors, and parents, especially
mothers, acting as the last, key disseminators. Through religious
interpretation, this process (which actually entails the elements of
coercion or even violence) gains additional validity, since it is presumed
to be a practice elevated above the familiar (universally accessible)
experiential level; throughout, these agents are seen as the assistants of
a supernatural being, God. This kind of ranking individuals into a chain
that recreates the sanctity of life acts as an internal incentive, therefore
appearing natural. This very label can also serve as a defence against
other, 'unnatural' explanations of one's (human) identity and role,
offered by other socialisation factors (e.g. public school[1]) and which,
considering the relevant (the only proper) religious framework, are
labelled as 'improper', and therefore unethical.

Beyond the direct oral (verbal) part of religious socialisation, an important role is also played by various instruments that encourage the active participation of receivers (children) in the formation of the self, according to the principle of the likeness to God, by accepting and internalising holy commandments. During the past few centuries, printed religious textbooks have proven to be effective manuals, while in the twenty-first century they are being joined by digital textbooks.

According to empirical evidence, the religious textbooks used by the CC in Slovenia in the socialist and post-socialist era have never been politics-free. The biblical discourse on the 'truth' of human engagement and draped in the omnipotence and omnipresence of 'God's love' has been interwoven by the covert (latent) or uncovered (manifest) politically clearly oriented explanations. This way the multidirectional politicisation has been realised regarding the social and political system. On the one hand, it was a politicisation through silence on the existing socialist system, and with a (indirectly expressed) recommendation for the believers not to actively participate in the 'atheist' forms of association. The politicisation of religious textbooks in post-socialism has been completely directed to the (one) main goal: an all-out fight against the 'worst totalitarianism'(which signs communism, socialism) by the comprehensive and multilayered active participation of 'proper Christian people' in varied forms of associations in all areas so as to (finally) consolidate the 'new morality'. In both the periods, religious teaching has served particularly as the instrument of gaining and reinforcing the power of the CC.

Considering that the content of these textbooks depends on a wider social environment and the place the Church holds in it, and that the actual activity of the Church is always oriented towards a specific space-time situation, we shall be interested in how some great social changes, different turning points, have reflected in the Church's position and in its many-sided activity. This chapter will represent in a chronological order the great social turning points that took place in the twentieth century and at the beginning of the twenty-first century, when Slovene society experienced changes in terms of the citizenship of its inhabitants, socio-economic order and the status of the Church (or churches).

Pre-first World War Period—the First Re-Catholicisation

For centuries (until the end of the First World War), the Slovene national community lived within the reaches of the Habsburg Monarchy under the domination of Christian religion and the CC), which acted as the undisputable holder of true morality, while its religious education functioned as a guarantee for maintaining the social (class, gender and national) order.[2] Marking the critical period and challenge for this bulwark of order was the start of endeavours for gaining economic, social and political rights for the majority of the population, especially in the second half of the nineteenth century. Although the nineteenth century was also known as the century of true physical dearth, for a long time this had not bothered the Church. The developments only became bothersome when organised rebellions against this general misery had begun. It is no coincidence that only then did the Church firmly intervene in the turn of events and direct all its powers to the condemnation of rebelliousness.[3]

Near the end of the nineteenth century (in what was then Austria–Hungary) the activity of the CC in both spiritual and completely practical social life experienced a terrific revival with one goal: to fight against the 'social evil', which was the label given by the supporters of power structures that maintained ordered to the socio-democratically organised actions of workers. The aim of this 'social disease' which manifested in demonstrations, public mass rallies and written demands, was to shorten the workday from 11 h to 8, raise miserable workers' wages and introduce measures for ensuring social security in the case of illness or old age.[4] This was enough of a motive for the CC in Slovenia too, to 'launch itself into the political fight with a renewed vigour' because 'the chaos' was perceived as a consequence of weakening faith and the influence of 'unchristian science'.

The radical engagement of organised workers, which was fuelled by the actual misery of their situation, was interpreted by Catholic ideologists as a result of non-belief and defection from Christianity. Due to the obvious weakening of influence exerted by the principle of 'work, save money and pray' and by the notion of work as obligation and 'punishment for sin', which the CC in the past had used to justify great social inequalities, the CC's main role now presented as a need to design and strengthen a Christian way of solving the social issue.

The key incentive for this kind of orientation was the recognition of the prevalence of moral destitution,[5] 'defection from faith, a complete religious disregard which dominates both the very public and family life', as the media proclaimed for mass consumption.

The basis for 'unified resistance' was created by Pope Leo XIII (1878–1903) especially with his well-known encyclicals, which comprehensively covered 'social evil' and also clearly set the programme and determined 'correct principles' together with the holders of endeavours for 'peace and harmony'. This is how Pope Leon XIII prompted and substantiated re-catholicisation,[6] which not only attempted to systematically 'colonise the faithless spirit' but also interfere on every level of human activity. This direction was later carried forward by Pope Pius X (1903–1914), who in his encyclical of *Pascendi* (1907) 'threatened that everyone who is marred by the faintest shadow of modernity would be banished from public service and education'.[7]

In order to bring the 'fundamentally anti-Catholic Austria' back to the 'old Catholic Austria',[8] within which the security would also be granted to the Slovene who 'can be generally seen as religious, pious and devout to the Catholic Church ...', it was necessary to 'wake the nation's catholic consciousness'.[9] Religion was postulated by one of the leading theological intellectuals and catholic sociologists, A. Ušeničnik, as the key basis for moral well-being, social integration and the existence of Austria in general[10] because:

There is one thing we know, and that is: without religion, Austria is inconceivable! ... There will be no real freedom or prosperity in Austria if we fail to put morality first, and as there is no unwavering, stable morality without religion, the religion should be put first. ... The more the private and public lives become imbued with the spirit of religion, the spirit of Christianity, the spirit of the Catholic Church, ... the more the discords will resolve, violence shall be tempered, hatred shall decline, the more our peace will return, and with this peace our contentment, happiness, prosperity.

BETWEEN THE WORLD WARS: 1918–1941

After the First World War and the disintegration of Austria–Hungary, most of the Slovene national territory became part of the newly established State of Slovenes, Croats and Serbs, which did not gain international recognition but in which the Slovene national community entered as an independent state formation. The independent operation of the Slovene government met its end when, a good month later, the newly formed multinational country became the Kingdom of Serbs, Croats and Slovenes (1 December 1918), and the budding federalism was suppressed by a centralist system with the Serbian dynasty of Karadjordjevićs at the helm.[11] By the time of the Second World War, political and cultural splits within the Slovene national community, which had already begun in the nineteenth century, only deepened and had throughout the 1930s reflected in the nation's attitude towards Fascism on the one hand, and communism on the other. Due to the increasingly threatening menace of Fascism and Nazism, democratic parties, societies and groups with active membership in the then illegal communist party had joined together in a people's front and fought for peace, democratic freedoms, social justice and national existence. This is how bringing together class and national concerns considerably increased the role of the communist camp, although its attractiveness later faded as the communist refrained from opposing the Hitler–Stalin pact of 1939.[12]

On the anti-communist side, there was the 'Catholic camp' with the CC as the centre of the wide-ranging scope of activities in clubs and societies behind the wheel. The CC as the leading religious institution also maintained its influential position in political decision-making (through the People's Party) and cultural life. In its fight against the 'social evil', i.e. communism, it built on the strategy of a universal CC (most notably expressed in papal encyclicals and letters), which saw in communism a greater threat to the existing order than that represented by Fascism or Nazism.[13] The radical part of the Catholic camp, in particular, strived for a complete catholicisation of social life,[14] which included firm opposition against all efforts for the emancipation of women and the abolishment of great social inequalities.[15] This was the goal that was worked towards, in addition to regular religious rituals, by many printed media as well as mandatory religious education in public schools (catechism was a compulsory subject).

SECOND WORLD WAR IN SLOVENIA: 1941–1945

The CC in Slovenia was most fatally affected by the Second World War (1941–1945), which is why it is first necessary to mention a few peculiarities of the complex social activity of that time. It is essential to note a few key facts, which represent an inseparable and richly documented ingredient of the discussion on the position and role of the CC till the present day. The neutrality of these explanations grows lesser and lesser the greater their distance from verifiable sources becomes, or the more these sources get pushed to the margins or even get erased.

The first indisputable fact is that by occupying the Slovene territory (in April 1941), all of the occupying countries (Germany, Italy, Hungary and partly even the NDH) had the same goal, the extermination of the Slovene national community (ethnocide) which they were also carrying out with extreme brutality. Because of this practice, the occupation of the Slovene nation largely differed from the occupation in other countries (e.g. France, Norway, etc.), where it was mostly a matter of economic subjugation.

The second fact is that the majority of the population did not accept this plan; they raised an organised resistance and joined the national liberation war. A historic role in this fight against the destruction of the national community was played by the Slovene Liberation Front, which put the 'unrelenting armed action' against occupiers first in its programme.[16] After the end of the Second World War, this unique phenomenon of occupied Europe was thus assessed by B. Grafenauer[17]:

> In the whole of Slovene history, the Liberation Front and its successfully realised four-year liberation fighting represent the most distinct watershed. ... The greatest success of the Liberation Front was the fact that, in the interest of the national community, it had overcome party affiliations, brought together the entire Slovene nation despite people's differences in world views and their sociological variation, and led them into their fight for freedom.

In addition, what was extremely important was the fact that the ruling minority (the bourgeois camp) welcomed new rulers and offered to help them, while also actively collaborating with them in the implementation of their occupational goals. This was especially in the Province of Ljubljana, where the collaboration with Italian and later German authorities had been systematically organised, and where the MVAC police units—and the Slovene Home Guard from autumn 1943 onwards—were acting as the military. Their many-sided (criminal and traitorous) activities, where a very important part was played by the leadership of the CC,[18] were justified by their members through their goals of fending off the Liberation Front and/or 'communism'.[19] The programme of the Liberation Front of the

Slovene Nation[20] (Godeša 1997: 21–23; Mally 2011), which represented the organisational and political glue in the all-round resistance against occupying authorities, first came to fruition with the liberation and joining of the Slovene Littoral, then in the post-war period with the development of the socialist social order.

EARLY SOCIALISM AND SECULARISATION: 1945–1990

Despite different denationalising measures, the Slovene national community survived the Second World War, which had proved total for the nation[21] because, in addition to its tremendous death toll (about 96,000 people), immense damage had also been caused to the basic material living conditions (infrastructure had been demolished, villages burnt down).[22] Immediately after the Second World War, there were reprisals against the pro-occupation collaborators who were mostly returned by the English occupying forces from Carinthia to Slovenia or Yugoslavia and included Slovene Home Guard, Croat Ustasa, Serbian Chetniks and others.[23] About 8000 to 12,000 Home Guards were killed (according to different statements), in addition to those who had been sentenced on grounds of other forms of collaboration, in particular terrorist invasions from Austria (e.g. Matthias's Army[24]) or due to their opposing certain revolutionary measures until the start of the 1950s when 'the most brutal forms of repression, including judiciary' started to fade.[25]

Following the victory of the Slovene partisan army with the help of units from other Yugoslav nations, this community continued to develop within the framework of the Federal People's Republic of Yugoslavia (renamed the Socialist Federal Republic of Yugoslavia according to the Constitution of 1963) which had a one-party system with the Communist Party in the leading role.

Post-liberation, the revolutionary measures which in those first few years followed the patterns of the Soviet Union, related to the initial abolishment of the capitalist economic order (expropriation) and gradual introduction of a new socialist order on the foundation of public property[26]; the introduction of self-management (1950, 'factories to workers!') was meant to, at all levels, encourage the generation of conditions that would reduce social, class and gender inequality. The first decade had a lot in common with other socialist countries ('the Eastern Bloc') but, especially during the 1970s and 1980s, the system in Slovenia kept increasingly departing from the ruthless centralist regulation of the everyday life in some other socialist countries that excluded individual initiative and efforts.

It needs to be emphasised that the Slovene model of real-life human relations management was not imposed one-sidedly by the state only, it was masses of people (citizens) that took part in this management by increasing the funds allocated by the state through their voluntary contributions, hereby enabling that a strong institutional foundation was built (e.g. kindergartens, schools, senior homes, medical clinics, cultural and sports centres) to ensure a certain quality of life. The characteristic of the Slovene society is that it came very close to the socio-democratic practice of ensuring social well-being, which was also confirmed by the data on income distribution gathered by the World Bank,[27] and some other indicators (e.g. on decreasing social gender inequality).[28]

Modernisation processes, along with appropriate reforms, took place especially from the 1960s onwards until the political crisis of the 1980s when various movements advocating a faster democratisation of the society emerged and grew stronger.[29] Different civil social groups[30] contributed to the loosening and internal democratisation of the leading power of the League of Communists as the key political organisation that directed the development and managed the system of self-government. The (ruthless) criticism of everything that existed drew its inspiration, in terms of substance, from contrasting types of social order and therefore included either the (democratised) socialist perspective or the 'modern' perspective of 'developed democratic societies', where their main feature (the capitalist system) was never publicly mentioned. The last faction directed the sharpened end of its criticism, which was supposed to be pure, non-ideological and scientific, especially against the 'totalitarianism', 'Stalinism', or 'Marxism', while refraining from also exposing the modern capitalism.[31] Slovene socialist practice was, without residue, classified as totalitarianism too, even though, in comparison to other socialist systems, it manifested as a comparably free and relatively just regime of self-government in practice (Rus and Toš 2005: 24).[32]

The period of 1945 to 1990 was characterised by the separation of church and state, the exclusion of the CC (and all others) from public life (in political, cultural, educational areas), which was something that its leadership never came to terms with, despite having on the surface accepted the new authorities and their order 'for the love of peace' (and hoping for a return of the pre-war situation). The part of the clerical community ('timeservers' and 'collaborators'[33]) that—especially after the Second Vatican Council—passively or actively supported socialist authorities,[34] failed to receive moral honours from their leadership (bishops).

In the first decade after the victory over Nazism, the tense relations between the CC and the state were not only influenced by the Marxist conviction regarding the role of religion and the Church's engagement in supporting a great class inequality, but also by the tremendous burden of its collaboration with the occupiers during the Second World War (in Central Slovenia), which the Church leadership justified as the fight against communism. It is understandable that the revolutionary actions of the state (such as expropriation, banning the active role of nuns and monks in public services,[35] e.g. health services, social work and education, ban on religious education in public schools, the exclusion of the Faculty of Theology from the realm of University, the implementation of mandatory civil marriage before church ceremonies in 1946, the withdrawal of registry services, the dissolution of the Church-led sports and cultural clubs and societies[36]) went against the fundamental focus of the Church, i.e. the struggle to survive in these very Church-unfriendly conditions. This is how the historically verified ambivalent character of the CC had revealed itself once again; it is precisely the secular state efforts for the elimination of great social inequalities that should, under the very definition of the Church (always on the side of the poor), receive the Church's support. And yet, it was the determined rejecting of these measures throughout the early socialist era that presented latent fuel for the anti-revolutionary activity that came to light in its full-blown proportions later, in the independent Slovenia, when the CC entered the public arena (through the main gate). Before this re-entry into public life, the CC intensively focused on the family as its key transmitter of faith, while remaining a fervent defender of the traditional patriarchal family based on the 'holy' matrimony and the submission of the woman/wife to her husband.[37]

Despite these efforts—with the support of authorities, the strengthening of secular institutions and their openness for everyone—secularisation continued to expand, which happened faster in Slovenia than in many places in the West that also saw secularisation, although in a more concealed (latent) form.[38] In Slovenia, the secularisation was more visible (more manifest), and therefore an easier target for the attacks of its political opponents, with the CC at their core. The secularisation trend was characteristic of Slovenia notably in the 1960s and 1970s, coming to a halt in the 1980s due to growing religiousness, especially in the first half of the 1990s; the second half of the 1990s, however, saw the secularisation trend starting to regain strength.[39]

The constitutionally protected separation of church and state never meant the abolishment of the Church as an institution or of its functioning within the limits of legislative provisions, which is claimed by the church's media production. In contrast to the pre-war period, the Church lost access to its appearances in public media, yet instead prolifically developed its own press, with *Družina* newspaper being published already from 7 May 1952, at first monthly, later weekly; *Bogoslovni vestnik*, a magazine for theological issues, has been published from 1965 onwards, and for the broader pastoral use *Ognjišče* appeared, a monthly which in 1989 boasted a circulation of 105,000 copies; *Cerkev v sedanjem svetu*, a pastoral magazine, has been published since 1976; there is also Mohorjeva družba publishing house, and so on.[40]

It is by this extensive Church publishing[41] that the position of the CC in Slovenia differed considerably from that in other socialist countries, and this can also be read in theologically conceived works, because 'it was precisely through the press that the Church carved out some of the paths that churches in other socialist countries could not'.[42] A testimony to the many advantages this communication channel enabled is also the acknowledgement of Bishop Lenič: 'In our place and time, the Slovene Christian ought to make use of what we have, carefully and correctly. We do not have everything, yet we have a lot.'[43] Naturally, the Church press kept a 'safety distance' from actual worldly social developments, which is why in 1976, the articles in the *Cerkev v sedanjem svetu* magazine were of 'a very principled nature, and probably due to political circumstances never even touched on the existing social situation or risked looking back to post-war times'.[44] However, of course even 'a lot' was not 'heaps' if compared to the pre-Second World War period, as 'in comparison to the pre-war religious press, this was only a good third of what Slovene believers had had at their disposal before the advent of the communist single-mindedness'.[45]

POST-SOCIALISM, RESTORATION AND RE-CATHOLICISATION: 1991–2015

Behind the very convincing goals of parting from the shared Socialist Federal Republic of Yugoslavia (because of an increase in conflicts between its nations that only grew stronger in the second half of the 1980s) and national independence, lay the goal—lesser known to the wider public—of changing the entire social system. This goal was explicitly defended by the coalition of the Democratic Opposition of Slovenia (Demos), founded in 1989, which through its programme argued for market economy and the kind of sovereign state, 'independent or in a confederation with other countries, that will not be based on the utopic project of socialism'.[46] This goal was only achievable through the abolishment of both the existing 'totalitarianism' or 'communism' and the governing one-party system with the leading League of Communists; by achieving this goal, Slovene society was supposed to 'normalise' again. Demos perceived socialism as a pathological phenomenon which should (as all diseases) be immediately and completely annihilated.[47]

The critical evaluation of socialism followed the well-known pattern of a 'combined perversion' with double de-historicisation[48]: the current referenced role model societies are purged of negative structural effects, Slovene socialist society is purged of all the positive traits differentiating it from real socialist societies; and for any historical comparison within Slovene society, there is a handy two-part division on its socialist past (with the exclusion of positive gains) versus pre-socialist past (with the exclusion of negative characteristics). The mainstream of critical examination could therefore mainly be limited to the form of government, while the content reflection of the many-sided consequences of market economy resulting from a free labour market (especially the increase in inequality and poverty) remained on the back burner. What stayed under wraps was something that only later, through the assessments of communism breakdown, got invoked by some historians, namely that 'the true winner of 1989 was not democracy, it was capitalism'.[49]

In Slovenia, the basis for the first radical split from socialism was provided by the results of the first multiparty elections in 1990,[50] while the institutional foundation for the introduction of capitalism was created soon after the independent state had been proclaimed (1991). The key for the establishment of the new capitalist economic system lay in the Denationalisation Act (adopted in November 1991, URL 27/91-I),[51] which was followed by the Ownership Transformation of Companies Act (in November 1992). The denationalisation prompted the emergence of a 'completely new class of rich people' in Slovenia, 'which became wealthy by birth (being born in previously expropriated families), not through their own work'; the denationalisation resulted in a sharp rise in income inequalities already in the first decade.[52]

The supplanting of the socialist social system with the capitalist system contributed to the formation of a society 'that is not only less just but also (at least at the level of organisational democracy) less free', as was justifiably speculated by Rus and Toš after that first decade.[53] The development in the second decade, especially with the start of the crisis, further deepened social inequality, while the 'liberalisation' of market economy descended into 'absurd privatisation, more feudal than capitalist in nature'.[54] 'It seems that the Slovene state failed to protect its well-being from the social marginalisation of those she ought to, instead providing protection for those who could have provided for themselves on their own'.[55]

In the name of 'democratisation', the independent country has seen the attempts of abolishing everything that has been seen as 'ideological',[56] or in any way connected to socialism or even 'communism'. In their discussion of social inequalities, Dragoš and Leskošek[57] come to the following conclusion: 'It is suspected that those things that were characteristic of socialism are not compatible with Europe'. This is why, for the purpose of discursive opposition against socialism, the notion of Europeanisation comes in very handy, and in view of the past national affiliation (to the 'Balkans') it is supposed to convey an additional, higher civilisational meaning. Despite surface insistence that the evaluations of the socialist past and the advocacy of 'European' present and future remain non-ideological, it can be, based on many indicators, possible to conclude that there is a different ideological direction which, on the face of it, recognises the values of civilisation (which remain the same from the French Revolution onwards: freedom, equality, solidarity), while at the same time at a deeper level, due to its embeddedness in the neo-liberalist practice of capitalism, it dismantles social foundations for their actualisation within the majority of population.

Without delving into a detailed discussion (although necessary) of the transformation experienced by the society in different areas and at different levels, let us only call attention to the main aspect of their legitimisation (justification). Leaning on a reductionist and de-historicised approach, the public discourse has been drawing from the ideology of anti-socialism or (in accordance with its prevailing basic approach) anti-communism. The apologising of the new social order as practised by right-wing political parties and mostly carried out in the name of 'real democracy' has been intensifying from the time the nation gained its independence, and has all the while been based on the conjecture that communism is a criminal system,[58] which must be thoroughly demolished, also by reinstating 'true morality' in public life. Reintroduction of 'true morality in public life' now, for the third decade, means the re-catholicisation of a society that is too secularised, especially this post-socialist one.

Based on its own assessment, it is the CC that is the main proponent of this moral renewal[59] (Jogan 2008; Smrke 2008), and it is also the biggest denationalisation beneficiary.[60] It is this institution that has rich experience in the fight against 'social evil', specifically communism, going on for decades, and it is this re-catholicisation role that invigorates the CC, so it remains as 'old but forever young'. While in 'old democracies' the justification of re-catholicisation follows the more 'morally pure' lines or is less involved with political developments, in 'new democracies', post-socialist societies, it is abundantly laden with political past.

For it is in these societies that the 'social evil' which prompted the first re-catholicisation gained its institutional dimension, became the ruling order. The common label for this order is 'communism' or 'totalitarianism', which has been used indiscriminately for all societies that have not followed the linear path of the evolution of democracy as a social system (in the West), down the lane of capitalism as their economic system. Given the persistent and long-standing denunciation of communism, it is understandable that the CC tends to inextricably link the abolishment of this order with its condemnation and with suggesting the pattern of 'true morals' and true order as the alternative, contrary to the 'totalitarian'. By focusing on one type of totalitarianism (the communist one) and disregarding its own (active) role in the formation and operation of another kind of totalitarianism,[61] the salvation and liberation role of the CC can shine in all its glory.

Modern re-catholicisation in Slovenia has been justified and implemented partly within the framework of the general pattern used for the eradication of 'communist evil' in post-socialist societies, and partly through taking into consideration those peculiarities that are Slovene in character. At the level of reasoning, both patterns of action include two—mutually interlinked—traits: reductionism and the de-historicisation of the subject matter.

The general incentive has been provided by the accentuation of the need for democratisation of all types of (post-)socialist societies. Even so, there was only one type that has kept cropping up in public discourse, 'communism', labelled for the everyday use as 'the times of lead' or 'totalitarianism'. The specifics that were—despite certain elements of totalitarian rule—produced and developed by Slovenia at the time of socialist self-government have been completely overlooked. Simply, the key empirical foundation for the general use of 'communism' has been 'real' socialism, while socialist self-government (the soft version of socialism) has been practically erased from theorising.[62]

The emphasis on democratisation as the way for overcoming the totalitarianism of (real)socialist social systems could remain—without acknowledging the multiple differentiation of the actual developed societies and the differences in development strategies among them— within the (safe) domain of the formal model of democracy. This is how the desired model of social order (democracy) has been used in public communication (discourse) with one-sided contents, and the same goes for the market economy model: with no admitted negative social effects (which are an inherent part of the very social structure) and often also without modifications that are typical of these two elements in the present-day existence of people. Democracy per se could, for instance, operate without being 'contaminated' with the model of addressing gender discrimination, and the model of market economy without the inclusion of any protective mechanisms that would ensure the social well-being of the majority of society members (due to 'class compromise' in the second half of the twentieth century).

The creation of 'neutral' and 'apolitical' explanation follows the optionality principle: only certain parts are taken out of social reality as a whole, those that conform with the underlying 'vision'—which is by definition 'pure'—unencumbered with political interests, regardless of where this purity feeds from, whether the system as such, the Holy Ghost or 'social organism'. However, the use of such knowledge, which is considered inherently 'pure', 'apolitical', 'non-ideological'— or precisely because of these attributes—is determined following the (holistic) principle of integrity: it applies to all social life. This is how 'pure' knowledge can act against 'dirty' politics. Those, however, who start from the wholeness of the situation, are labelled as 'ideologically' biased in advance.

This is the framework in which discussions have taken place in Slovenia in the past decades. In clarifying the transition from totalitarianism (communism) into democracy, the idealised model of democracy (in general) has gone hand in hand with a one-sided explanation of the pre-existing social situation. While the target model of the social order has been able to operate without its content label (of capitalism), the pre-existing situation could not escape its highlighted content label and has been laden with negative traits that are part of (every) totalitarianism. This is how the general label of socialism and/or communism has been used as a derogatory term, often without any consideration of the actual historical context. Since the target democratic system has been understood as 'natural' and all the earlier regulative actions in the name of socialist transformation as an aberration in general development, the ('relentless') criticism of socialism was assigned a high degree of justifiedness and at the same time appeal and validity, as it heralded the return of the 'true natural' order.

It has been particularly important that, after the elimination of Church-hostile communism, 'true morality' is established, for which—according to its own continual claims—only the CC has the necessary qualifications, as ascertained by A. Stres:

> We are past being interested in those large and all-encompassing social projects that are meant to build 'Heaven on Earth' right now. However, the crucial question of what is right and what is not remains. That is also how the ethics and morality once again return to our public life and politics.[63]

The absence of morality is therefore presumed to be an important feature of the existence of Slovene society in the second half of the twentieth century; under this definition, even the functioning of individuals is supposedly immoral. The return of the morality to the public means the reinstatement of Catholic moral principles as:

> The social teachings of the Catholic Church principally lie in its moral teachings: their starting-points are moral stands, while liberalism and Marxism do not acknowledge morality as an independent and socially applicable thought.[64]

The emphasised function of the moral teachings of the CC is distinctly practical, as these teachings as 'moral inspiration, motivation, and value orientation, ... should reveal to us which actual goals out of the possible must be selected and realised in social life' (Stres 1991: 12). Since other interpretations of social cohesion and interaction fail to attain the appropriate level as far as acknowledging morality is concerned, it can therefore be justifiably concluded that actions are morally positive (or in simplified terms, 'moral') when (and only when) they are in accordance with Catholic definitions.[65] The exclusivity of Catholic 'moral inspiration' is the common thread of modern re-catholicisation efforts.

These efforts are being additionally substantiated with the consolidation of the impression that the Slovene CC was a grave victim of 'communism'. If for now, we disregard the role the CC played during the World War II and only focus on the post-war era, the findings of empirical research paint a largely different picture. The claim that the post-Second World War period until the early 1990s was not an era of a prevailing disregard of the religious members of society is also corroborated by the findings of various studies from the 1990s. This is how, on the basis of an international study on religion and attitude towards the church (1997), theologian V. Potočnik[66] rejects 'the premise of the general persecution of believers' in the communist era and finds that only 11% of all respondents claimed to be disregarded due to their religious beliefs during that time.

Despite these facts, what is emphasised over and over again is not only that the Church in Slovenia was a victim of 'the period of crime and disloyalty' but that this also marked the faithful with 'humiliating imprints which must be erased from all thinking and acting'.[67] This kind of discourse, however, is present not only at the populist level but has become a normal, unquestionable ingredient of theological (scientific) discussions.[68]

NEW EVANGELISATION (RE-CATHOLICISATION) IN THE TWENTY-FIRST CENTURY

Exactly how this re-catholicisation or 'new evangelisation' should progress in the twenty-first century, 'on the threshold of the third millennium', is determined within the core programme document of future CC activities in Slovenia, *Izberi življenje* ('Choose Life'), which was, following four years of preparations, adopted by Slovene bishops at their plenary assembly on 17 and 18 January 2001 (the Congregation of Bishops in Rome confirmed it as on 5 December 2001) and solemnly given to Slovene Catholics on nineteenth May 2002. The precisely determined tasks in the Final Document convey the content and ways of 'new evangelisation'. This adventure,[69] however, is not limited to the inner domain of the Church, it is also not directed at the celestial realm; it is unmistakably earthly and concerns all the members of society, not only Slovene society but that of all secularised European environments. As highlighted later (2012),[70] it is European secularisation that is supposed to help the faithful community recognise its 'fundamental priority: the confirmation and deepening of personal faith' as the key ingredient of new evangelisation 'through which the CC responds to the modern challenges of secularisation'.

Based on the assurance of the metropolitan, Dr. Anton Stres,[71] the Slovene religious community from clerics to the last lay people, will not indifferently observe departures from the faith, but instead perform the tasks it has been assigned by the 'new evangelisation', invigorated and determined.

> We will not respond to the pressures and phenomena of secularisation with lamentation, as if nothing can be done and as if secularisation is the inevitable fate of the Western World. ... Even though many of the contemporaries have abandoned God, God has abandoned no-one. ... He remains loyal, for he cannot forsake eternal love. ... God perseveres in his eternal love to us, and this is also the deepest motive for us to remain firm in our love for Him. Faith is stronger than the secularised world that rejects God and takes no notice of him.

This claim is additionally substantiated with the conviction that it is only in faith where we can 'once again find the lost human dignity, which has been jeopardised over and over again'.[72] This is why faithful communities face a crucial task: the intensification of those 'activities that will reinforce personal faith and life consistent with this faith'. This kind of orientation is not limited to the individual and his or her immediate private surroundings (e.g. family), it is directed towards the entire sphere of shared life. In this wider area—'yard of pagans'—what is also emerging is a need for a spiritual instrument by which Slovene bishops wish to 'offer' to all the Catholics 'the starting points aimed at understanding the present Slovene moment, and to point out the tasks it brings to our faithful Catholic community ...' where 'the force from above' will also help. Slovene bishops encapsulated their role in this as that of a humble medium, in essence that of good scribes communicating the thoughts of God's Spirit (or the Holy Ghost) who 'as the Spirit of Truth leads' the faithful to 'the perfect truth'.

The fact that this 'perfect truth' remains in fact a half-truth, therefore incomplete, is shown by 'the authentic insight' into recent history as written in the core source strategic document *Izberi življenje* (2002). For Slovene Christians, who often 'live out their faith shyly' and are 'uncertain because of lack of the examples of authentic Christian life in everyday life', this document offers in its presentation of the cultural and historical perspective 'a new consideration of historical facts',[73] since presumably the entire history of humanity until now has been distorted due to its Marxist portrayal. Particularly interesting among the novelties is the reinterpretation of the Second World War that reduces the national liberation struggle to a 'communist revolution that reached its culmination at the end of the war with mass executions and thousands of exiles'.[74] In addition to a general assessment stating that Europe's history is 'a story of never-ending violence', for which the Christians 'assume part of responsibility', what is, for the purpose of dialogue with history, explicitly stressed is the 'issue of reconciliation within the "national body" regarding violence and injustices during and following the Second World War' that is of particular importance for Slovenia.[75] Naturally, there is no mention of any (co-)responsibility of the Church for this violence, the only thing highlighted is 'the persecution of the Church in the communist Yugoslavia', which generated a great many 'witnesses for the faith who can be a model of forgiveness and readiness for reconciliation'. There is no trace in the document of any mention of the collaboration of the official Church[76] with the occupying authorities, nothing about the systematic sowing of dissension in the 'national body' prior to and after the Second World War. The opposite: for future 'eschatological-salvation action' it is highlighted that, throughout history to the present day, the Church has been 'a strong element of national integration, cultural ascent, ethic formation and also a unique contribution to the community of nations'.[77]

Among other matters, its 'factual' review of the social and socio-economic aspect of socialist era and transition period mentions that the legal order in socialism was based on 'the revolutionary principle', while its social system 'followed ideological principles'[78] and worked according to 'the principle of seeming solidarity, which was led by seemingly elected political authorities with the aim of ensuring social peace for themselves'. This destructive evaluation is partly mitigated by the admission that the system's social security was ensured 'especially by a high level of employment' but also at the expense of 'women being overemployed to an above-average degree'. Flaws are also acknowledged for the transition period (high unemployment, 'ruthless drive for profit') when 'hereby emerges a society that is not rooted in social justice and solidarity'. At first glance, this advocacy of justice could give the impression of an extremely humane and anti-capitalist orientation of the CC leadership in Slovenia at the beginning of the twenty-first century. In practice, however, its actions differ considerably from this high moral stance, as this very same leadership, when need be, most determinedly and immediately supports proposals for reforms with the goal of the neoliberal bulking up of the 'slender state'.[79]

While eloquently painting their own concern for justice, the highest representatives of the CC shame the holders of these 'delusional ideologies' and as an argument against all demands for greater social equality emphasise (as a general trait) that 'the society has always been stratified', even at the time of 'communism', dismissing practical protests against the loss of social rights as a 'socialist reflex'.[80] According to the judgement of Cardinal F. Rode,[81] the twenty-first century calls for a different kind of practice:

> It is time to breathe freely; time to shake the past and its delusional ideology. For this ideology experienced a defeat that has no equal in history, and there is no force that could bring it back to life. It should therefore vanish from our reflexes and stop encroaching on our freedom and making our life bitter.

The responsibility for achieving this goal lies foremost with the CC whose first concern is to 'preach the Gospel and bring about God's Kingdom on Earth',[82] for which it must be taken into account that 'traditional religiousness cannot be the only criterion and starting point for pastoral work', as Slovene society has been subject to great secularisation, which is said to be 'the fruit of planned post-war atheisation and development currents in modern society'. This is why, in its pastoral work, when dealing with 'some kind of optional believers' (the faithful 'a la carte') who picks her or his religious and moral truths according to his or her own judgement, the CC must expect a phenomenon where some

> have difficulty accepting the very religious truths that lie at the root of Christian faith, such as the virginal conception of Jesus, Resurrection, eternal life, original sin, God's love, Eucharist, the existence of the Evil Spirit and Hell.[83]

Hence the Church must continually instruct in the faith not only the young but also adults; it must make sure that there is always a genuine community among its faithful, where an important role must be assumed by the priest who ought to be 'personally connected with people', for 'the more distanced the Church as the institution is from the real problems of its people, the less they trust it'.[84] What is to be expected from the Church—especially by the young—is primarily its charitable activity. From the multitude of precise instructions for its current activities 'in the yard of pagans', the Church's perspectives on upbringing and education, and some of its starting points for the 'dialogue with history' are described briefly below.

THE YOUNG—THE PRIMARY CONCERN OF THE CATHOLIC CHURCH

Although it has been true for decades that one of the key interests of the CC is directed towards the young, who are 'the first victims of the spiritual and cultural crisis affecting the world',[85] this document further recommends that, apart from family and community, it is the youth that should become the primary pastoral concern of the Church, even though it is at the same time estimated that 'this generation of young Slovenes is even more religious than the generation of their parents'.[86]

If we compare this data (which originates from the Church and has not been brought in by any 'ideological' impurities from the outside) with statements regarding fear and prosecution at the time of communism, we start to doubt the premise that the main evaluations of post-war history on which the entire document is built actually constitute a 'factual' or even 'objective' perspective. This kind of ambivalence, however, is probably a multipurpose tool that, on the one hand, validates the position of the Church as a victim and hence its demands for its special treatment by the 'state' or secular authorities, while on the other, through its relating of its successes on the path travelled ensures credibility or provides an assurance to the young that they are entering well-tested and organisationally strong forms of associating. This kind of associating is not limited to in-church activities or especially spiritual and charitable work, instead, there is this tendency towards comprehensive oversight of youth at the forefront, clearly expressed in a recommendation for building youth centres across parishes, which should be carried out 'in an organised and coordinated fashion in the domains of individual dioceses and with the cooperation of municipalities'.[87] These centres should—in the framework of youth pastorship—ensure a supply of a great variety of opportunities for spiritual, cultural and physical activities of the young.

The propensity of the CC to control the entire social domain is indisputably pronounced in its approach to the catechesis—comprehensive initiation into Christianity. For it does not suffice that the parish catechesis exists, it should also be stepped up with compulsory public education: 'The introduction of religious contents in the national school system would mean a reasonable extension and complementing of current catechesis'.[88]

Demands that overreach or disregard the constitutionally determined separation of church and state in Slovenia are defended in that document by means of invoking the rights and wishes of parents and by limiting the role of secular authorities ('state'), which ought to only regulate the framework of the national school programme, and 'leave' the other 'levers of decision-making to local communities, schools and parents', arguing that the operation of the state, as it falls 'under the rule of subsidiarity, is only complementary and should not have the monopoly over the education system.'[89] The document underlines the principle of 'the plurality of convictions and religious plurality' in schools, while amending the principle of comprehensive education so that it 'takes into account all the dimensions of human personality, including religious', with a clear demand:

> This is why religious upbringing and education should be regarded and treated as an integral part of the upbringing and education of religious children and adolescents, which must be considered, not ignored by the national education programme if the latter aspires to respect the religious freedom of children, youth and their parents.[90]

Within the *Pridite in poglejte* ('Come and See') pastoral plan (2012), religious education has a more precisely determined priority goal, consistent with the perception of the 'solidary' society as 'compassionate and just' and with the focus on charitableness, which is to train individuals so that 'they are able and know how to help themselves'.[91] It is in vain that we look for at least one sentence mentioning the direct or indirect complicity of the Church in creating increasing poverty that calls for charity work. Instead, this institution is classified as one of those that need special sympathy from the state, and the effects of this sympathy are already recognised in the plan:

> Solidarity and justice are shown in relation to church property. ... The aspiration of the Church in Slovenia to be economically independent is its obligation and a reflection of needs. Slovenia today is one of those countries where the calling of the Church can be wholly realised and carried out without material assistance from abroad.[92]

After this admittance, there is probably none in 'the yard of pagans' who would still wonder about the grounds for the process of the extremely efficient and layered Church colonisation of the public sphere in Slovenia in the past decades.[93] This kind of questioning is surely superfluous, as the economic independence of the CC is inextricably linked with the emergence and operation of the autonomous state. Economic power is also important for the consolidation of the Church's spiritual influence, which should assist the solidary Slovenian society in removal of the 'traumatic injury', particularly aggravated by the happenings during and after the Second World War.[94]

New Evangelisation and Reconciliation

In the description of this 'trauma' already, only one spiritual factor appears ('in a plural society, disunity over ideas is admittedly normal, what is controversial is the spirit of exclusion') as the axle around which the fifth strategy has been formed, that of 'Forgiveness and Reconciliation'. This strategy is supposed to restore individuals' inner peace, achieve national reconciliation and develop a general culture of forgiveness. 'The Slovene Church feels especially addressed and obligated to contribute its share' in the elimination of the national rift and injustices that were inflicted in its 'semi-past' history.[95]

Given the self-ascribed standing of the key moral authority and the holder of the true moral in this new order of the Slovene society, it is worth learning about characteristics and means by which the CC is supposedly acting in a conciliatory way. The role of the CC has been defined very concisely: in this 'semi-past' history, the Church was a victim, the victim of an emerging or functioning 'communism'. This is possible because everything has been erased from this role of the CC that places it as an institution in the category of the perpetrators (or at least co-perpetrators) of various injustices at the time of the Second World War. However, in the name of the truth (or the Spirit of Truth) this fact also cannot be disregarded in the discussion of post-war victims (of executions), since it is the approach to them that is key for the special salvational role of the CC now and in the future.

Instead of taking into account the entire cause-effect sequence in breeding injustices, the pastoral plan offers a torso that, in the past decades, became almost completely acclimatised in the Slovene territory. This is how tradition, already determined in the CC's operational strategy for the twenty-first century (by the *Izberi življenje* document, 2002), continues and is reinforced by the Church's mass media: producing shrunken, biased knowledge about the origin of injustices through cutting certain pieces out of historical developments according to the Church's measure and need, in regard to its position of an almost monopolist holder of spirituality in the present. The denial of the true role of the CC's top leadership (in the Province of Ljubljana) at the time when the Slovene national community was sentenced to extermination, is the precondition for its current 'burden as a victim'. Cleared of this, the CC could, especially via its lay faithful, their clubs and societies, enter the 'new evangelisation' in accordance with the 'Christian understanding of reconciliation'. The crux of this understanding is that the reconciliation

> starts with the victim, not the perpetrator, which also holds true in those cases where the victim has suffered torture or injustice by the Catholics. ... We Christians believe that God first turns to the victim, its wounded and humiliated humanity. With his Mercy, he first heals this and then, through it, also extends to the perpetrator.[96]

The key question is therefore who the victims are or what the truth about the 'burdening past' is. The pastoral plan leaves no doubt, since, in the spirit of the primary Christian perception of reconciliation which 'means recognising the truth of the victims, their suffering, death and also martyrdom', it announces:

> We shall strive for the victims of killings perpetrated during and after the war to be respectfully buried, and the memory of them to be properly commemorated; and for the other victims who have lived in the decades long humiliation and fear to, legally and politically, obtain satisfaction as much as possible, especially to be allowed to speak up and be heard. [97]

Despite their assurance that they will avoid the 'traps of ideological disputes and political passions,' it is already their listing of victims that is burdened with a fairly clear 'ideological' contamination, especially when it comes to the practical examples of achieving reconciliation. This is how, for instance, the Blessed Alojzij Grozde[98] is mentioned as the first martyr whose veneration should be revitalised. The CC, however, can only act as the driving force of reconciliation if 'the truth' is correctly explained, and this 'truth' is that Slovene Christians were the victims of , yet they do not foster 'any desire for revenge ... only a longing for the truth and respectable memory of the killed'.[99]

So, in this seemingly very humanely explained orientation of 'new evangelisation' within the 'national body', the reconciliation involves the holders of good—one-sidedly proclaimed victims (religious Christians)—and the holders of evil, the main perpetrators (communists). The Church community (with a wider community probably implied as well) faces the 'challenge of justice and forgiveness'. There is no peace and reconciliation without justice. There is no justice without the truth.'[100] The role of the church is characterised as decidedly dialogical; its prayer and work should be primarily oriented towards the victims regardless of their 'religious or political conviction and regardless of who their torturers or killers were'. Through this kind of—victim-friendly—stance the Church has allegedly contributed to the 'fostering of the culture of forgiveness that has presented, in the above-mentioned processes, most intrinsically as that of the Christ'. The Church is a victim only because of its faith in the Saviour, and it is because of the faith that 'communists' presumably tortured and killed people (the faithful).

Step by step, this is how the image of the Church as the institution gets cleared, so in the end, it can justifiably 'commit to the precedence of the victim'.[101] Through this, the Church gains a superior position, becomes the role model for 'the other-minded', it is the moral authority whose testimony of the truth is irrefutable and the only acceptable for achieving reconciliation. Thus purified the church could then justifiably be a socially recognised driving force of reconciliation.

The detailed pastoral plan (*Pridite in poglejte*) for the road towards reconciliation with its 'new evangelisation' is, at first glance, a refreshing plan focused on the homogenisation of the Slovene social community, as it is imbued with noble words/values such as love, truth, justice, solidarity, which should be used as glue for a renewed establishment of an undivided society. However, a more detailed insight into the meanings and applicable worth of these values for direct activities indicates a status quo: the CC in its mission actually remains the key institution that, directly or indirectly (through political parties and various forms of organisation—e.g. special Catholic scientific, cultural and other[102] clubs and societies) divides people along the axle of faithfulness. This kind of division, at the open and also occasionally hidden levels, has taken place from the late nineteenth century onwards, when a need emerged for 'the revival of truth', and totalitarian Catholicism appeared in response to the start of the struggle for the basic economic, social and political rights of (the majority of subordinated) people.[103]

This consciously and deliberately divisive (schismatic) role of the Church is extremely finely veiled as a concern for the maintenance of traditional customs and habits and for the restoration of true morality. Likewise concealed is the autonomous, essential (also political) activity of the CC, because it only presents itself as a servant obeying the Holy Ghost, and is increasingly leaving its planned and directed mass activities to lay people, while the leadership of the Church remains only as a mediator balancing this 'spontaneous' performance. Quite simply, anyone 'whoever has an ear, should listen to the words of the Spirit' of the CC in Slovenia, so peace will be achieved, and dignity will be guaranteed to every human.

This cleared historical image of the Church is also a basis for demands that seek to 'launch processes and procedures for reconciliation at all levels of societal life', 'immediately adopt a European resolution condemning all totalitarian systems', in the name of 'the human as human' abandon the differentiation between partisan, national liberation fighting and (Home Guard) fighting against 'revolution', prohibit the denouncement of 'one and the other' for five years, and introduce a moratorium on all organised polarising celebrations. When it comes to the cautioning of dangers, the president of the state should take part and convene 'the summit of national security', so that we could achieve 'order and peace in the country, a greater justice, respect and tolerance in diversity'. Put plainly, order and peace would prevail when the truth as related by the Church is accepted in its entirety.

NOTES

1. The term 'public school' here refers to those schools that are entirely funded by the state (or state budget) and for public use.
2. Religious instruction was the main ingredient of education in the 'real Christian school' where catechists represented almost one half of all teachers—e.g. in 1902, 373 (or 49%) of 762 teachers in elementary schools were religious teachers; see Milan Divjak, *Razvoj laične moralne vzgoje in pouka v slovenski šoli s posebnim ozirom na predmet DMV* (Ljubljana: FDV, 1993), p. 774. The cultivation of humbleness and submissiveness in all its aspects in the name of the Fear of God was also supported in a 'capillary' way by different organisations, especially that of St. Mary's Society. From the second half of the nineteenth century onwards, an important educational device gained prominence in the form of the 'Holy Virgin Mary' whose omnipresence was ensured by special St. Mary's Societies, which had proliferated at the beginning of the twentieth century; see Maca Jogan, *Seksizem v vsakdanjem življenju*, pp. 9–12 and 21–29 (Ljubljana: Fakulteta za družbene vede, 2001). The consolidation of faith was also promoted by the printed word, so the Catechism became the most published work.
3. Maca Jogan, "Rekatolizacija slovenske družbe," *Teorija in praksa*, 45 (1–2), 2008, pp. 28–52.
4. Ferdo Gestrin and Vasilij Melik, *Slovenska zgodovina od konca osemnajstega stoletja do 1918*, (Ljubljana: 1966), p. 222.
5. 'Moral poverty', as the greatest social disease of the time, prompted the emergence of explanations on its causes and treatment also outside the frameworks set by religion. A prominent place in the attempts of 'earthly' sociological elucidation can undoubtedly be ascribed to one of the classics of sociological theory, E. Durkheim, who used the notion of *anomie* as the consequence of functional differentiation to explain moral destitution, while employing organic solidarity to explain the inherent specificity (harmony) of the existing modern social structure; see Maca Jogan, *Sociologija reda*, (Maribor: Obzorja, 1978), pp. 33–48. At the theological level, both the theologically and non-theologically

consolidated explanations are practically equal—the goal is an obedient and disciplined (morally positive) individual.

6. Given that this first re-catholicisation was interrupted at the end of the Second World War by the strict separation of church and state, and by the relegation of the Church into the private sphere, the modern-day striving of the Church for the control of private and public life can be seen as the second re-catholicisation in modern history. This tendency became particularly conspicuous after Slovenia had gained independence.

7. Robert Hutchison, *Opus dei: njihovo kraljestvo prihaja*, (Ljubljana: Orbis, 2002), p. 41.

8. Aleš Ušeničnik, "Ali je Avstrija res katoliška?," *Rimski katolik*, 1895, pp. 403,417.

9. Aleš Ušeničnik, "Zakaj Avstrija ni katoliška?," *Rimski katolik*, 1896, pp. 79–84.

10. Aleš Ušeničnik, "Velika laž naše dobe," *Katoliški obzornik*, 1899, pp. 36–47.

11. Dušan Nečak and Božo Repe, *Oris sodobne obče in slovenske zgodovine: učbenik za študente 4. letnika*, (Ljubljana: Faculty of Arts, Department of History, 2003), pp. 36–39.

12. Ibid., pp. 84–86.

13. That is why in the 1930s, prayers during Sunday Mass concluded with the following plea: 'From hunger, pest and communism, save us, o Lord!' Also dedicated to the fight against communism was a segment of mass media (e.g. *Slovenec* newspaper, which was edited by Ivan Ahčin from 1929 to 1942) and several books were published as well, e.g. Ivan Ahčin, *Komunizem največja nevarnost naše dobe*, (Ljubljana: 1939).

14. Dušan Nečak and Božo Repe, *Oris sodobne obče in slovenske zgodovine: učbenik za študente 4. letnika*, (Ljubljana: Faculty of Arts, Department of History, 2003), pp. 85.

15. In the 1930s, nearly all political parties supported the demand for women's voting rights, the only one opposing it was the Slovene People's Party, see Maca Jogan, *Seksizem v vsakdanjem življenju*, (Ljubljana: Fakulteta za družbene vede, 2001), pp. 239.

16. *Izjava, Osvobodilna fronta slovenskega naroda* (a pamphlet published at the 70th foundation anniversary), on the inside of the cover page. Ljubljana: Svobodna misel 201 (compiled by Zveza združenj borcev za vrednote NOB Slovenije, written by Martin Ivanič).

17. Bogo Grafenauer, "Osvobodilna fronta v slovenskem narodnem razvoju," in Bogo Grafenauer (ed.), *Slovensko narodno vprašanje in slovenski zgodovinski položaj* (Ljubljana: Slovenska matica, 1945/1987), pp. 185, 199, 200.

18. The key character was Bishop Rožman who, also participated in the Home Guard oath ceremony by holding the 'Holy Mass', 20 April 1944. After the capitulation of Germany, the leadership of the CC and a great part of anti-communist citizens first emigrated to Austria and later, when their hopes for a fast return and acquisition of power had not been realised, to the USA, Argentina and Canada, where they continued to prepare for the restoration of the former system. See Peter Kvaternik, *Brez časti, svobode in moči: vpliv komunizma na pastoralno delovanje Cerkve v ljubljanski nadškofiji (194–2000)*, (Ljubljana: Družina, 2003), p. 265.

19. Bojan Godeša, "Ustanovitev Slovenske zaveze", in Marjan Drnovšek and Drago Bajt (eds.), *Slovenska kronika XX. stoletja 1941–1995*, 2nd edition (Ljubljana: Nova revija, 1997), p. 35. Marjan Drnovšek, "Begunstvo in slovenska politična emigracija", in Marjan Drnovšek and Drago Bajt (eds.), *Slovenska kronika XX. stoletja 1941–1995*, 2nd edition (Ljubljana: Nova revija, 1997), pp. 98–99. Silvo Grgič, *Zločini okupatorjevih sodelavcev* (Novo mesto: Društvo piscev zgodovine NOB Slovenije, Dolenjska založba, 1995).

20. Bojan Godeša, "Temeljne točke osvobodilne fronte", in Marjan Drnovšek and Drago Bajt (eds.), *Slovenska kronika XX. stoletja 1941–1995*, 2nd edition (Ljubljana: Nova revija, 1997), pp. 21–23. Eva Malli, *Slovenski odpor: Osvobodilna fronta slovenskega naroda od 1941 do 1945* (Ljubljana: Institute of Contemporary History, 2011).

21. Tone Ferenc, "Množično izganjanje Slovencev med drugo svetovno vojno", in Franc Šetinc (ed.) *Izgnanci* (Ljubljana: Društvo izgnancev Slovenije 1993), p. 30. Dušan, Nečak and Božo Repe, *Oris sodobne obče in slovenske zgodovine: učbenik za študente 4. letnika*, (Ljubljana: Faculty of Arts, Department of History, 2003), p. 240.

22. Ivica Žnidaršič, *Nemčija še ni plačala vojne škode*, (Ljubljana, Društvo izgnancev Slovenije 1941–1945, 2015).

23. Božo Repe, "Vračanje domobrancev in obračun z njimi", in Marjan Drnovšek and Drago Bajt (eds.), *Slovenska kronika XX. stoletja 1941–1995*, 2nd edition (Ljubljana: Nova revija, 1997), pp. 99–101. Dušan Nečak and Božo Repe, *Oris sodobne obče in slovenske zgodovine: učbenik za študente 4. letnika*, (Ljubljana: Faculty of Arts, Department of History, 2003), pp. 244–248.

24. Martin Premk, *Matjaževa vojska 1945–1950*, (Ljubljana: Društvo piscev zgodovine NOB Slovenije, 2005).

25. Dušan Nečak and Božo Repe, *Oris sodobne obče in slovenske zgodovine: učbenik za študente 4. letnika*, (Ljubljana: Faculty of Arts, Department of History, 2003), pp. 253.

26. Ibid., pp. 254–283.

27. In the 1960s and 1970s Sweden, the top 10% of the wealthiest households had 21.3% of the total income of national households at their disposal, 22.2% in Norway and 22.5% in Yugoslavia. For the USA, this number was different, 26.6%. See Srečo Dragoš and Vesna Leskošek, 2003: 29.

28. Maca Jogan, "Slovenska (postmoderna) družba in spolna neenakost". *Teorija in praksa* (Ljubljana) 41 (2004, 1-2), pp. 367–374.

29. Žiga Vodovnik, 'Demokratizacija in nova družbena gibanja', *Teorija in praksa*, 51 (2–3), 2014, pp. 415–433.

30. An important role in these efforts from 1971 onwards was played by the theology course on current matters aimed at students and intellectuals (its precursor was a theology course for lay people at the Theological Faculty in Ljubljana, introduced in 1967), which 'for years was the only relatively free forum' with its conciliary renovative surpassing of 'the spiritual drought of one-sided communist thinking' (Kvaternik 2003: 216–218).

31. A. Kirn analysed this approach in detail, and based on reasoning rejected it on the case of one of the key associates (*Nova revija*, which was, from the beginning, a centre of critical discourse) and later authors of the Constitution of the RS, T. Hribar. See Andrej Kirn, "Tine Hribar v vlogi ideološkega razumnika", *Teorija in praksa*, 21 (5-6), 1984, pp. 539–552.

32. Veljko Rus and Niko Toš, *Vrednote Slovencev in Evropejcev*, (Ljubljana: FDV, IDV, 2005).

33. Peter Kvaternik, 2003, abovementioned, pp. 357–358.

34. Thus oriented clergy gathered under the Association of Cyril and Methodius for Catholic Priests founded in 1949.

35. It must be emphasised that nuns could remain in these services but wearing the civilian nurse uniform and working under an individual contract of employment. In essence, it was a process of laicisation of these professions.

36. Considering the extremely great number and diversification of catholic clubs and societies at the end of the nineteenth century and the beginning of the twentieth century, the dissolution of these forms of church consolidation could also be regarded as a reaction to the former situation.

37. For more see Maca Jogan, *Ženska, cerkev in družina*, (Ljubljana: Delavska enotnost, 1986).

38. This type of secularisation is referred to, especially by theological thinkers, as 'the crisis of values', and the modern Westerner is characterised as a human distanced from the faith.

39. This can also be argued based on the comparison of the percentages of those who do not trust the Church or do so only barely in 1991 and 1998: from 52.4%, the percentage increased to 79.9% (in the meantime, the percentage of those who trust the Church completely or considerably decreased from 36.9 to 11.2%), Niko Toš, et al., in Niko Toš, (ed.), *Vrednote v prehodu II. Slovensko javno mnenje 1990–1998*, (Ljubljana: Faculty of Social Sciences, Institute of Social Sciences, Public Opinion and Mass Communication Research Centre, 1999), pp. 181, 183.

40. Peter Kvaternik, above mentioned, 2003, pp. 237, 240, 249–251.

41. Typical of the early 1980s is the following statement: 'Right after the war we felt a shortage of religious print, while today many already complain that there is too much of it. We have a lot of it, it is true, however, compared to the secular press our press is still far behind' (Z. Bahor per Kvaternik 2003: 251/252). This comparison fully reveals the propensity for an unrestricted, all-out public activity, however, this way, the people are able to choose, and not only according to the CC's wishes, since, as (in 1993) I. Štuhec recognised that 'while we were absent from the media, these have changed the image of the Slovenes' (per Kvaternik 2003: 252).

42. Peter Kvaternik, id., 2003, p. 244.

43. Ibid., p. 251.

44. Ibid., p. 251.

45. Ibid., p. 253.

46. Zdenko Čepič, "Ustanovitev Demosa," in Neven Borak et al. (eds. Jasna Fischer et al.), *Slovenska novejša zgodovina: od Programa Zedinjena Slovenija do mednarodnega priznanja republike Slovenije 1848–1992* (Ljubljana: Mladinska knjiga, 2005), p. 1285.

47. Even before Demos won in the elections, a symbolic purification was performed: on 7 March 1990, new constitutional amendments disposed of the 'Socialist' title, and all that remained was the 'Republic of Slovenia'.

48. Maca Jogan, "Postsocializem in androcentrizem", *Družboslovne razprave—Tranzicija in neenakost med spoloma* XVI (34-35), 2000, pp. 9–30.

49. Mark Mazower, *Temna celina: dvajseto stoletje v Evropi*, (Ljubljana: Mladinska knjiga, 2002), pp. 389.

50. On the occasion of the celebration of the 25th anniversary of these elections (7 April 2015 at CD, broadcast on TV SLO I) it was highlighted several times that the election meant 'the return of democracy'. This event is likewise often emphasised elsewhere. For example, on the occasion of a solemn mass in the Bled Island held on

the Assumption Day (15/8/2014), Cardinal F. Rode emphasised his wish 'that our homeland free itself from the consequences of its totalitarian past ... and exist as a place of true democracy'.

51. According to the estimate of Dragoš and Leskošek, the denationalisation in Slovenia is 'the greatest "social" transfer of all times. Slovenia is the only country in the world that introduced a denationalisation to the extent of 100% reimbursement in kind, which includes feudal property', Srečo Dragoš and Vesna Leskošek, *Družbena neenakost in socialni kapital*, (Ljubljana: Mirovni inštitut, 2003), pp. 37.

52. If we only take into consideration the ratio of property income between the poorest and the wealthiest, in 1993, the 10% of the former received 2.2% of the said income, and the 10% of the richest 17.6%; in 1997–99, the corresponding percentages were 0.3% and 62.5%.

53. Veljko Rus and Niko Toš, *Vrednote Slovencev in Evropejcev*, (Ljubljana: FDV, IDV, 2005), p. 24.

54. Franček Drenovec, *Kolaps elite. Iskanje normalnosti in naprednosti v majhni evropski državi*, (Ljubljana: Založba/*cf., 2013), p. 211.

55. Veljko Rus and Niko Toš, *Vrednote Slovencev in Evropejcev*, (Ljubljana: FDV, IDV, 2005), p. 27.

56. Ever since the Independence, the notion of 'ideology' has been used in a distinctly derogatory manner in the public discourse, yet at the same time extremely broadly, to refer to all the various matters that are in some way linked to the positive valuation of socialism.

57. Srečo Dragoš and Vesna Leskošek, *Družbena neenakost in socialni kapital*, (Ljubljana: Mirovni inštitut, 2003), p. 21.

58. The vocabulary of public discourse in which 'communism' is being shamed, is extremely hostile, rich in the lowest of humiliating branding and slander. As an example, it suffices to list a few labels given to 'communists', as communicated to the public at a rally in support of J. Janša on 10 December 2014: 'communist barbarian horde', 'red leeches', 'heirs to the degenerates of the idiot revolution', members of 'red Satanism over the Slovene nation'. Acting as a support in these efforts is also the Resolution of European Parliament about European conscience and totalitarianism (2 April 2009), according to which it is the communism that is the most dangerous of totalitarianisms.

59. Maca Jogan, ″Rekatolizacija slovenske družbe,″. *Teorija in praksa*, 45 (1–2), 2008, pp. 28–52. Marjan Smrke and Mitja Hafner Fink, ″(Ne) religioznost in socialna distanca do izbranih družbenih manjšin v postsocialistični Evropi,″ *Teorija in praksa*, 45 (3-4), 2008, pp. 285-300.

60. Srečo Dragoš, 'The Separation between Church and State in Slovenia: A Political Fiasco', in Gorana Ognjenović and Jasna Jozelić (ed.),

Politicization of Religion, the Power of State, Nation and Face: the Case of Former Yugoslavia and its Successor States, (New York: Palgrave Macmillan, 2014), pp. 171–192, cited p. 184.

61. The supporting role of the CC in Hitler's rise and actions is reported in a well-considered way in John Cornwell's work *Hitler's Pope* (1999, in Slovene translation 2002, Ljubljana: Orbis)—if only one non-Slovene source is cited here that highlights the activities of the leadership of the Church (already completely centralised in the twentieth century). In Slovene catholically inspired public discourse, totalitarianism is connected to atheism which 'in the twentieth century submerged humankind in an ocean of blood', as established by e.g. Drago K. Ocvirk (in *Dnevnik*, 24th March 2006, p. 5) who initially admits that 'God can also be abused but it is impossible for a civilisation to grow on abuse and endure for 2000 years'.

62. For more on this see the case of overcoming societal gender inequality and the discrimination of women in the following article: Maca Jogan, "Slovenska (postmoderna) družba in spolna neenakost," *Teorija in praksa*, 41 (1-2), 2004, pp. 361–376.

63. Anton Stres, *Oseba in družba*, (Celje: Mohorjeva družba, 1991), p. 11.

64. Anton Stres, *Oseba in družba*, (Celje, Mohorjeva družba 1991), p. 12.

65. As shown by SJM (Slovenian Public Opinion Poll) for 1991, only a meagre minority of respondents (21.9%) accept the conviction that God's plan is the source of morality and that the Church is the preeminent arbiter of the questions of morality, which would legitimise the Church's interventions in public life. On the other hand, a majority (61.4%—with nearly equal results between genders) agrees on the position that 'it should be the society that decides what is right and what not', so they acknowledge that moral principles are socially determined (Niko Toš et al., *Podobe o cerkvi in religiji na Slovenskem v 90-tih*, (Ljubljana: FDV, IDV, Public Opinion and Mass Communication Research Centre, 1999), pp. 748. According to data gathered by this study, the majority of the adult members of Slovene society reject the possibility of the strengthening of the Church's role in public life; in 1991, more than four quarters of all adult respondents (76.6%, with no significant gender differences) did not support the view that the Church should take sides in political issues.

66. V. Potočnik, in Niko Toš et al., *Podobe o cerkvi in religiji/na Slovenskem v 90-tih*, (Ljubljana: FDV, IDV, Public Opinion and Mass Communication Research Centre, 1999), p. 85/based on an international study on faith and relationship with the Church (*Aufbruch der Kirchen in Ost/Mitte/Europa*), which was designed within the Pastoral Forum in Vienna, 1997, and carried out in the framework of

SJM (Slovenian Public Opinion Poll) in 1997/2 on a representative sample (N = 1011 individuals, data summary—Toš 1999: 745–779).

67. This was emphasised by Cardinal F. Rode during the mass in St. Peter's Basillica in Rome at the end of the visit of Slovene bishops with Pope Benedict XVI (*Delo*, 28. januar 2008, p. 24).

68. One of the leading theological thinkers sees 'the totalitarian communism' and revolution as the main reasons for the inappropriate modernisation because: 'The revolutionary logic unfortunately unleashed the demon forces in the nation that influenced the moral and cultural image of the nation. ... The demolition of everything religious or connected to Christianity and the Church that was performed by the revolutionaries during the war and afterwards, has marked our consciousness', Janez Juhant, *Za človeka gre*, (Ljubljana: Teološka fakulteta, 2011), p. 166; based on the assessment of Peter Kvaternik, the end of the Second World War or 'revolutionary storm' or the rise of the 'communist totalitarianism', 'one-sided thinking' and 'communist atheist system', instead of liberation brought a new, even greater slavery (*Brez časti, svobode in moči: vpliv komunizma na pastoralno delovanje Cerkve v ljubljanski nadškofiji/1945–2000/*, (Ljubljana: Družina, 2009), p. 13); according to the opinion of Dr. Ivan Štuhec, professor of moral theology, 'those social structures which fell apart in the 1990s were sinful and their defenders were those who ascribed the authority for forming social institutions to themselves. The influence of citizens and their responsibility for the situation were basically nil, as the communist avant-garde developed a theory on class society which it seemingly disestablished, although it actually reinforced it and made it further radicalised', (″Etična utemeljitev in upravičenost slovenske osamosvojitvene vojne,″ *Bogoslovni vestnik* 74 (4), 2014, p. 593–638.).

69. This is how Cardinal F. Rode referred to the programme *Izberi življenje* (Ljubljana: Družina, 2002), p. 8.

70. This is what Archbishop A. Stres wrote in his foreword to *Pridite in poglejte—slovenski pastoralni načrt* (″Come and See—Slovene Pastoral Plan″), the umbrella document published by the Slovenian Bishops' Conference in the autumn of 2012 (and applicable for the time period from 2013 to 2018).

71. Ibid., p. 8.

72. Ibid., p. 8 (and all of the quotes in this paragraph).

73. *Izberi življenje* (Ljubljana: Družina, 2002), p. 23.

74. Ibid., pp. 25, 26.

75. Ibid., pp. 52, 53.

76. This is the orientation that the leadership of the Catholic Church in the Province of Ljubljana adopted, while the majority of clergy in

Slovenian Styria and Littoral regions had not joined this collaboration, which is why they were among the first who felt the consequences of occupiers' brutal ethnocidal procedures (e.g. the expulsion of priests from the Diocese of Lavant/the Styrian area under German occupation/—in 1941 alone, there were 284 diocesan and 81 religious priests exiled to Croatia/Rybar 1993: 122/). The end of the 20th and the beginning of the twenty-first centuries have witnessed efforts for establishing the image of the CC as the main guardian of Slovene identity and Slovene nation (also at the time of gaining independence in 1991—e.g. the speech of the then auxiliary bishop in Maribor, Dr. A. Stres 17/6/2001 at Brezje). At the same time it presents itself as the supreme (irreproachable) moral arbiter and moral condemner of the entire national community—especially in connection to killings after 9/5/1945. This is conveyed through public castigations every time there is an exhumation of the 'innocent victims' of post-war killings, like e.g. through the claim of F. Kramberger, the Archbishop of Maribor stating (in his sermon at Ptujska Gora 15/8/2007) that it is due to these killings that our tiny Slovene nation carries the greatest moral stain in Europe.

77. *Izberi življenje*, p. 27. The actual attitude towards Slovene emigration is in contradiction to its herein expressed integrative stance towards emigration, as it declares itself solely as the protector of the 'disdained' Slovenes across the world, hereby acknowledging only those emigrants who had to leave the home country (in May 1945) because of communism. However, a much greater number of economic and political emigrants—Littoral Slovenes (around 30,000)—who had been forced to leave their home country before that, at the time of Fascist occupation, and who mostly emigrated to Argentina, completely slipped the CC's memory. (Ibid., p. 175).

78. Ibid., p. 28.

79. An example of the CC's determined advocacy for a neo-liberalist regulation of the entire society can be seen in its attitude towards a reform document of the Slovenian Government (of 25th October 2005), *Predlog konceptov ekonomskih in socialnih reform za povečanje konkurenčne sposobnosti slovenskega gospodarstva* ('Proposal for economic and social reforms towards increasing the competitive ability of Slovene economy'), which (especially with its uniform tax rate) would lead to a deterioration of the living standard among the majority of (working) the population. A mere few days after the Slovenian Government (with J. Janša as its prime minister) published this proposal, the Commission of Justice and Peace of the Slovenian Bishops' Conference publicly supported the foreseen efforts as 'being of vital importance for the

increase of economic performance and efficiency', and at the same time expressed its expectation that 'these reformation efforts would not be to the detriment of the safeguarding and protection of family and education for spiritual and general moral values'.

80. These are the estimates that theologian Ivan Štuhec, member of the Commission for Justice and Peace, expressed in the support of the reforms despite very real warnings cautioning that a uniform tax rate would contribute to a greater social stratification.

81. In a sermon in Rome, (Delo, 28. January 2008, p. 24).

82. *Izberi življenje*, p. 30.

83. Ibid., p. 31.

84. Ibid., p. 32.

85. Ibid., p. 128.

86. Ibid., p.130. This situation is most certainly not random, but instead a result of a systematically organised endeavour of the CC during the last five decades. This is indisputably attested by the listings of important events connected to the pastoral oversight of young people in general, and particularly university students, e.g. the formation of religious education youth groups and student groups, the organising of spiritual exercises in the 1960s, the establishment of Medškofijski odbor za študente ('Inter-Diocesan Board for Students') in 1971, etc. An important role in this has been played by the Catholic press targeted at different youth groups.

87. Ibid., p. 133.

88. Ibid., p. 136. After the adoption of the Final Document, every available moment has been seized by the Church leaders during their public appearances to point out the necessity for religious education in school, since this is the only way for the school 'as needed by the modern human' to become 'more complete, thorough and general', as stated on 29 December 2007 by Cardinal F. Rode on the occasion of the blessing of *Vinum Cardinalium* in Slovenska Bistrica (TV Slovenia, Channel 1, Dnevnik at 7 p.m.). In addition, his sermon at the end of the visit of Slovene bishops in Rome emphasised that 'zealotry' and 'the violations of parents' rights' were 'rampant in Slovene schools' (Delo, 28. January 2008, p. 24). These efforts extend way beyond the mere symbolic level, which became evident in 2007 during discussions on the proposal of the Organisation and Financing of Education Act. In certain environments it can sometimes already be observed that a priest expresses threats against the teaching staff (and shames it during religious classes) if an occasion arises where a certain activity organised for the benefit of pupils in state schools (e.g. for reading badge) coincides with the time when children are expected in religious classes.

89. Ibid., p.148.
90. Ibid., p. 149.
91. *Pridite in poglejte*, p. 33.
92. *Pridite in poglejte*, p. 33.
93. This process has been accomplished by the CC through raising crucifixes on hilltops, establishing small chapels within barracks and hospitals, through the blessings of new wards in some hospitals, new schools, road sections, etc.
94. *Pridite in poglejte*, p. 19.
95. Ibid., p. 34.
96. *Pridite in poglejte*, p. 35.
97. *Pridite in poglejte*, p. 35.
98. *Pridite in poglejte*, p. 54. This was a theology student who had been actively engaged in outing the Liberation Front members. However, among those 'martyrs', it completely fails to mention the Slovene victims of Fascism and/or Nazism before or during the Second World War, such as Alojz Bratuž, a Littoral Region music professor at the theological seminary and the supervisor of church choirs in Gorizia who died (in 1937) in excruciating pain after he had been forced to drink machine oil in prison. Also unmentioned went the first victim of Nazi violence in Carinthia, Vinko Poljanec, a nationally conscious regional deputy of Carinthian Slovenes and active priest in Škocjan, Carinthia, who died (on 25 August 1938) after he had been poisoned with glass powder in Nazi imprisonment. A list of such individual victims could go on and on, even if group mass victims (e.g. the victims of concentration camps or killings perpetrated by the Home Guard and White Guard) are put aside completely.
99. *Pridite in poglejte*, p. 35.
100. *Pridite in poglejte*, p. 36.
101. *Pridite in poglejte*, p. 36.
102. E.g. the increasingly organised Association of Catholic Teachers of Slovenia.
103. Despite the obvious signs of the restoration of the CC's previous monopolistic position, all under the attractive title of 'new evangelisation', theological intellectuals repudiate this conclusion. 'New evangelisation is no programme seeking the restoration of the former Europe; instead, it provides help and encouragement for discovering one's own Christian roots and achieving a deeper civilisation that will be more Christian and therefore more human. This "new evangelisation" subsists on the non-exhaustive treasure of the Revelation which was given to us in Jesus Chris. ... It has been consciously named "new evangelisation" as the Holy Ghost perpetually creates the newness

of God's word, continually waking people in soul and spirit.' This definition, offered by Catholic theologian Karl Lehmann from Mainz, is quoted by a Slovene theologian Jože Krašovec, 'Vrnitev k virom teologije', *Bogoslovni vestnik*, 63 (1), 2003, pp. 139–140.

CHAPTER 6

From *Vrhbosna* to Brussels: Catholic Religious Education Between Local and Global Perspectives

Zrinka Štimac

INTRODUCTION[1]

The political transformations after the youngest war (1992–1995) brought about changes in the structures of the Roman Catholic Bishops' Conference of the former state of the Socialist Federal Republic of Yugoslavia, with separate Bishops' Conferences in the individual successor

The international stakeholders in Bosnia and Herzegovina use the phrase 'From Dayton to Brussels'to indicate the path from the post-war crisis to the EU integration. See Petritsch, Wolfgang (2002): BiH From Dayton to Europe. Svjetlost, Sarajevo. See also Aybet, Gülnur; Bieber, Florian (2011): From Dayton to Brussels: The Impact of EU and NATO Conditionality on State Building in Bosnia & Hercegovina. In: Europe-Asia Studies, Volume 63, Issue 10, 2011, Special Issue: Unconditional Conditionality? The Impact of EU Conditionality in the Western.

Z. Štimac (✉)
Georg Eckert Institute, Brunswick, Germany

© The Author(s) 2018   99
G. Ognjenović and J. Jozelić (eds.), *Education in Post-Conflict Transition*, Palgrave Studies in Religion, Politics, and Policy,
https://doi.org/10.1007/978-3-319-56605-4_6

states of the Republic of Slovenia and the Republic of Croatia. The Roman Catholic Church in Bosnia and Herzegovina (hereafter BiH) was part of the Croatian Bishops' Conference until 1993; it was not until the decree issued on 8 December 1993 by the Congregation for the Evangelisation of Peoples that a separate Bishops' Conference of BiH came into being.[2] It gave rise to and became a space for a number of councils and commissions, such as a Catechistic Council; the Educational Council of the Bishops' Conference, which oversees the Catholic 'Schools for Europe' in the country; BiH's first Catholic press agency; and a Council for ecumenical issues and dialogue among faiths and cultures.[3] The Catechistic Council of the BiH Bishops' Conference is responsible for religious education in schools, and each diocese has a Catechistic Office, with the archdiocese of Vrhbosna having a Metropolitan Catechistic Office.[4]

The bishops of BiH are under the authority of the Holy See in issues of dogmas and discipline and have freedom in political and social matters. Nevertheless the Congregation for the Doctrine of the Faith issues doctrinal notes on the latter, one of which was the Doctrinal Note on some questions regarding the Participation of Catholics in Political Life issued in 2002, on which the Bishops' Conference of BiH based its statements on the political situation in their country. The regular province of the Church, re-established in 1881, comprises the archdiocese of Vrhbosna with its seat in Sarajevo and the suffragan dioceses of Banja Luka, Mostar-Duvno and Trebinje-Mrkan, the last of which has been under the administration of Mostar-Duvno since 1890. Further, there are two Franciscan provinces, each with their own higher education institutions: the Province of Bosna Srebrena (Bosna Argentina), based in Sarajevo, and the Province of Herzegovina, based in Mostar. The official printed organ of the archdiocese of Vrhbosna is the *Vrhbosna* magazine, issued jointly by all diocesan bishops in BiH.

Diocesan priests and Franciscan monks take equal roles in pastoral welfare, catechistic and educational activities; additionally the Dominican, Trappist and Jesuit orders each head one parish in the country.[5] A specific feature of ecclesiastical law in BiH consists in the fact that diocesan clerics and Franciscan monks have been equal in terms of their priestly office since the early Middle Ages[6]; it is for this reason that the country's Catholic parishes are managed in the way described above.

As early as 1991, Roman Catholic religious education in BiH was planned as a regular subject in school together with Islamic and Serbian

Orthodox religious education, through the efforts of the education minister Nihad Hasić in the former Socialist Republic of BiH.[7] The first lessons in the subject were taught during the country's most recent war, and the first curricula and textbooks to be used in BiH were produced in the Croatian Bishops' Conference. Initial issues with textbooks and curricula were resolved quickly after the war due to the effective functioning of the structures within the Roman Catholic Church, despite the conflict and the Communist era that had preceded it.

Later versions of curricula and textbooks were produced in cooperation with the Croatian Bishops' Conference but published in BiH. The catechistic council of the BiH Bishops' Conference is responsible for religious education in schools, and each diocese has a catechistic office, with the arch-diocese of Vrhbosna having a metropolitan catechistic office. The Catechistic Council considers religious education in schools and church-based catechesis to be of equal importance; we will, however, be exclusively discussing the former in this essay. Teachers of Catholic religious education are graduates in theology and trained catechists.

Teachers of Catholic religious education are graduates in theology and trained catechists. Training takes place at the Faculty of Catholic Theology of Vrhbosna (*Vrhbosanska katolička teologija*), at the Faculty of Franciscan Theology (*Franjevačka teologija*), and at the Theological Institute in Mostar (*Teološki Institut Mostar*).

Catholic Religious Education: Background Documents and Curricula

The idea behind faith-based religious education in schools, in this context specifically Catholic religious education, is based on a number of documents issued by the Vatican and other theological sources. The document *Gravissimum educationis*, issued in 1965, opened the way to a new perspective on religious education, church-based catechesis and higher education in a Catholic context. A point specific to BiH is that the document considers schools to be places particularly representative of the pluralism that characterises the country's society as it is now (GE 24).[8] The document *Gaudium et spes* regards human beings as the origin, centre and ultimate aim of economic and cultural activity due to the basis of human dignity in humanity being made in the image of God (GS 12). The same document condemns different pernicious teachings

(GS 19–21); concluding, it considers dialogue to be the only way to overcome internal differences among Christians (GS 92). The Council Declaration *Nostra aetate* discusses different religions, including a brief description of and commentary on Hinduism and Buddhism, whose teachings and precepts, according to the declaration, contain a ray of the truth that enlightens all humankind, although they depart in a number of matters from the truth as conceived of and taught by the Catholic Church. The declaration further contains a separate discussion of Islam and calls for enmity and conflict to be put aside and for efforts towards mutual understanding between the Christian and Islamic faiths (NA 3). In relation to Judaism, the document points to Jews' and Christians' shared heritage and reiterates the Church's official condemnation of anti-Semitism, referring to its confession of guilt and expression of repentance for its past anti-Judaism and making optimistic statements about the future (NA 4). All these 'guidelines' on different religions find expression in Catholic religious education textbooks in BiH.

Alongside these Vatican-issued documents, attention is paid to religious education curricula from other countries, including those of the German and Austrian dioceses of Rottenburg-Stuttgart, Munich, Graz-Steckau and Vienna. Further, curricula cite contemporary theologians and religious educators from German-speaking regions, such as Edward Schillebeeckx, Karl Rahner, Alfred Holzbrecher and Hans Küng, who are considered as representative of an engagement with theological issues that are relevant to the current age.[9]

Aims of the Catholic Religious Education Curriculum

In 1998, after the revision of the first post-war Catholic religious education curriculum for primary and middle schools, originally issued in 1994,[10] the Bishops' Conference of BiH published an official 'Programme for Catholic Religious Education for Primary Schools'. This essay will discuss a version of the curriculum revised and agreed upon by the Bishop's Conference of BiH in 2003.[11] This curriculum, stipulating 70 teaching periods per year and 2 per week, is designed for the 8-year basic education ('primary school') prescribed in BiH. Its key objectives are (1) Enabling children to develop into mature personalities and members of the community of faith, at both the individual and societal level, and in relation to all aspects of human life; (2) educating the Christian conscience in young people in relation to the children themselves, to others, to society and to the world in general; (3) encouraging young people to recognise, encounter and accept the Trinitarian God, Father, Son and Holy Spirit; (4) helping young people to come to know others and develop feelings of respect for other people and cultures, faiths and denominations; (5) raising awareness in young people of the role of the family in the development of social and emotional life and enabling them to develop feelings of responsibility within their own families and towards the wider community.[12] These general objectives indicate that, while Catholic religious education in BiH revolves primarily around Catholic doctrine and the practice of the faith, it additionally aims to enable students to engage with social realities in the shape of other faiths and of interactions and inter-relationships between religions and society. This points to the, at least, theoretical possibility of this curriculum having a positive impact within the pluralistic society of BiH.

Content of the Catholic Religious Education Curriculum

The curriculum's content is described both in brief for its individual teaching units and in a more detailed form, with descriptions of the methodology and educational aims. Different religions are discussed in a variety of ways in 81 lessons of a total of 560. The analysis in this essay will engage with some of these units, for a range of different year groups.[13] In years 1 and 2, other religions do not appear explicitly in the curriculum, with teaching focusing, as the curriculum states, on the primary objective of helping children to come to love God and their neighbour. The curriculum considers this important because learners, in passing through the period of their socialisation as members of the church and society, are becoming members of a wider community than their families of origin.[14] From year 4 onward, teaching revolves principally around the Christian churches and attempts to communicate and bring to life the Christian message of peace and the principles of community with others and of ecumenism.[15] A large proportion of the content of the year-5 curriculum focuses on other people and other religions, with descriptions of the religions of classical antiquity, the monotheistic religions, Hinduism and Buddhism and definitions of terms such as 'religion', 'monotheism' and 'polytheism'.[16] Further, young people at this stage of their education are to learn that people have asked different questions on faith in different ways during different periods in history.[17] Year 7 brings explicit discussion of Judaism, various Christian churches and the ecumenical movement with specific reference to the Greek

Catholic, Orthodox, Protestant and Anglican churches.[18] While the curriculum makes no mention of atheism or New Age spirituality, some textbooks refer to these issues.

Textbooks: Presenting Religions as Static Entities

The most recent versions of textbooks for Catholic religious education at BiH's 8-year primary schools contain some passages of text which, in accordance with the subject curriculum, point to engagement with a range of 'others', including members of different faiths, races and nationalities. These textbooks further contain discussion of other worldviews, such as atheism, and of the Catholic view on new religious movements. Approximately 15% of the content of these textbooks is devoted to topics such as these, compared with 10% of timetabled lesson time as stipulated in the curriculum being dedicated to other faiths. An external analysis has reached positive findings on these textbooks.[19] The study confirmed that the primary school books discussed here are of high educational and design quality and can be considered as textbooks that encourage critical thinking among students. These textbooks discuss religious diversity in a positive light as well as giving critical information on negative roles played in history by the religious communities they represent.

Implicit Depictions of Different Religions: Years 1–4

Catholic religious education in the first 2 years of schooling seeks to enable pupils to locate themselves in the religious spectrum and consequently avoids explicit discussion of religious or cultural plurality. There is, however, engagement with differences among people; in year 1 teachers using the textbooks explore with their students the individual differences between the students in the class (R1: 11[20]), discuss God's creation of different people as brothers and sisters (R1: 22) and state that God extends an invitation to all people to be his people (R1: 32).[21] In year 2, in a way similar to that observed in textbooks for Islamic religious education, the books point students to their friends from their own religious background (R2: 8ff).[22] Further, they discuss differences between the rich and poor, the old and young, the sick and healthy, and between people of different races and colours: '*People have different skin colours and ways of praying to God*' (R2: 20). This rather 'ideal', model way of engaging with what is 'other' is to be found throughout these textbooks, as we have observed above; it both shows interest in the 'Other' and indicates to students that religious education is about, among other things, interacting with others and perceiving and respecting their difference from oneself, including differences in faith.

Explicit Depictions of Religious Pluralism: 'Our Friends Believe in God'
A Catholic textbook for year 5, in a chapter entitled 'Religion in people's lives: Traces of God', contains the first explicit discussion in the Catholic religious education course of questions of the meaning of life, theodicy and religious plurality.[23] Questions such as *'Where do human beings come from? Why am I alive? Why do we suffer and die?'* serve to introduce the key point *'Many people look for answers to these questions in faith'* (R5: 19). There follows an outline of the beginnings of the history of religion and of religious plurality. The history of religion is consistently discussed from the perspective of the faithful (*'the first human beings discover God's traces [in the world]'*). We are struck by the fact that atheists are mentioned as part of this plurality (R5: 21). There are, however, no details at this stage on specific worldviews.

The book communicates facts and information about the 'inhabitants of the earth' and their religions via the fictitious friends David, Ana, Chen and Sanela, who all live in the same town (R5: 22). The lessons in this chapter do not have the aim of giving large amounts of information on the religions followed by 'our friends', i.e. Judaism, Christianity, Buddhism and Islam, or about religious ideas held by the ancient Egyptians, Greeks and Romans; instead, they seek to raise students' awareness of different ways of being religious and of the need to promote dialogue, friendship and mutual respect among the global community of humanity (R5: 32). This gives rise to student engagement on a general level with religious plurality, with other faiths being discussed as independent entities. The chapter takes a positive position towards religious diversity throughout; we can regard it as a successful example of support for religious pluralism, despite its rather idealised character and the fact that it does not relate specifically to religious diversity in BiH.

Buddhism and Islam are on the year-5 curriculum.[24] The former, although the book describes it as a religion from the Far East, is depicted as being part of BiH society: *'Some* [Buddhists] *live among us. They revere Buddha. The grandfather of our friend Chen also came* [here] *from Asia and is telling his grandson all about Buddha's teachings'*. Some errors occur in the book's description of Buddhism in the context of the notion of 'religion' outlined above. 'Buddhism' is presented as a historical religion in which meditation represents 'a path to unity with God's will' (R5: 27). Further, the description of Buddhism is limited to just one of its schools, and the textbook refers to the Tripitaka, the Theravada Buddhist text of the 'Three Baskets', as the religion's holy book (R5: 21) and the Buddhist symbol of the 'Wheel of Becoming' as the symbol of 'Buddha's Way' (R5: 27). Although this information gives a less than complete picture, we can assert that this part of the textbook draws a positive picture of Buddhism.

The book presents Islam as a religion with a relationship to the region and the country by illustrating its 27-line introduction with a picture of the Gazi-Husrev Bey mosque in Sarajevo (R5: 28). The terms 'Allah', 'Mohammed', 'Mecca' and 'Medina' are given visual emphasis in the text. This lesson further contains brief pieces of text on the Koran, Mecca, the Kaab'a, mosques, their minarets, Ramadan and the Hijra. 'Allah' is referred to as the name of God in Islam; there is no mention of the 99 names of God that are an integral part of Islamic tradition. On the positive side, we notice that the book depicts Muslims as approachable partners in dialogue, as evinced by the additional material's encouragement of students to talk to other students in order to find out more about Islam (R5: 28). Further, learners are asked to name the aspects that Islam and Christianity have in common.

The chapter neither compares nor interrelates the various religions upon which it touches, instead consistently emphasising the shared precepts of all of the world's major religions (R5: 33), such as the 'Golden Rule', formulated thus from the Christian perspective: '*So in everything, do to others what you would have them do to you*' (Mt 7:12).[25] There is a distinct emphasis on the positive aspects of religious diversity (R5: 32): '*The community of humanity is made up of various different religions, languages and peoples, all with different customs, faces and ways of dressing. We give God different names and worship him in different ways. But this is our wealth and our future*'. There is no discussion here of problems or issues that might arise in connection with religious diversity, and none of the internal diversity and dynamics of the various religions, which makes these appear as monolithic entities.

Judaism is discussed in the textbooks for almost all year groups,[26] always with a mention of the historic interrelationship between it and Christianity.[27] There is a detailed discussion of this subject in the books for years 5, 7[28] and 8.[29] A total of 13 pages of the year-7 textbook describe the history, holy books, rites and rituals of Judaism and the dialogue that has taken place between Jews and Catholics. The characteristics of Judaism appear as static entities, without any information on intra-religious variations. Similarly, there is no attempt to point out the occurrence of Judaism in students' surroundings in BiH or discuss the history of the religion in the locality. Despite this omission, there is a general—and brief—attempt to point to the presence of Judaism in BiH society: '*We can meet adherents of Judaism in our surroundings. Do you know any famous personalities with Jewish backgrounds?*' (R7: 52). Judaism is described as '*the oldest monotheistic religion and* [...] *the source of Christianity and Islam*'. Its holy books and texts are discussed from a Catholic perspective, which contrasts with the more neutral depiction of the religious history (R7: 54).[30] Rites and rituals find mention in the context of specific holy days and feasts such as Hanukkah and Pesach (R7: 57–60).[31] A subsection on 'Dialogue between Judaism and the Catholic Church' discusses relations between Christians and Jews in the context of the Second Vatican Council (1962–1965). The textbook consistently presents a positive view of the future in regard to the Jewish–Christian relationship.

Diversity Within Christianity and Ecumenism

Year 7 includes teachings on the various Christian churches (R7: 122–135), with individual brief lessons on the Serbian Orthodox, Greek Catholic and various Protestant churches, consisting of text, illustrations and summaries.[32] The chapter ends with a lesson on ecumenism (R7: 133–135).

The depictions here of various churches are similar in their initial relative lack of key facts and figures on the history of these churches, such as year of foundation or schism. They provide a few sentences on the church's teachings without going into detail or following up this information in any way. Each of these lessons concludes with the current numbers of adherents and the presence of the religion in the locality; the latter, however, refers primarily to the Republic of Croatia and not to BiH. At the end of the chapter, the ecumenical movement receives a positive description as '*not a political movement, but the fulfilment of Jesus' will and prayer that all Christians should become one*' (R7: 133–135).[33]

Atheism, New Religious Movements and New Age Spirituality

The year-8 textbook discusses worldviews such as atheism and new religious movements (R8: 29–50), although these topics are not included in

the curriculum as such. The authors evidently pursue the aim of familiar-
ising learners with current societal phenomena and providing an academ-
ically founded approach to issues of people's religiosity. However, it is in
this chapter that we notice the largest number of problematic statements.
There are factual errors, one-sided or one-dimensional definitions, invalid comparisons, deliberately negative assessments of other worldviews
and negatively connotated imagery. The one-sided definition of 'religion'
(R8: 32, as the act of turning personally to God)[34] suggests to students
that the belief in a personal God, in the form of a monotheistic religion,
is the highest form of religious adherence and way of life.[35] The lesson
on 'atheism and human indifference' defines atheism as '*the negation of
God or other higher powers which are above human beings and on which they
are dependent*' (R8: 38). The images used to accompany this definition
are Munch's 'The Scream' and 'Anxiety' and Caspar David Friedrich's
'The Wreck of Hope'. The book states that atheism is entirely unacceptable to Christians (R8: 40) and should be combated with knowledge
about religion. Although it also recommends pursuing the path of tolerance and dialogue (R8: 40), we may wonder how such dialogue is to take
place if atheism is to be regarded as entirely unacceptable.

The key illustrations used in the section on new religious movements
(barbed wire, a person depicted as being alone, a dead and felled tree
and a picture of the Archangel Michael triumphant over Lucifer) likewise place these in a negative light. The book claims that 'new religious
movements' emerged in response to changes in people's worlds (R8:
41), to the increasing pace of life, and through the search for truth via
emotion and curiosity alone and through young people's dissatisfac-
tion with their lives (R8: 42). The text reveals that its authors catego-
rise as 'new religious movements or sects' (R8: 43) various religions
and movements of Christian and non-Christian origin. Religions, practices and belief systems counted within this definition include Hinduism,
Buddhism, Transcendental Meditation and pantheism, alongside 'sects
with a Christian character' such as Jehovah's Witnesses, the Mormons,
the Children of God and the Sun Myung Moon Unification Church[36].
The 'New Age movement' is depicted as a religious movement 'without God', involving esoteric and occult practices[37] and aiming for '*all
religions* [to come together] [...] *in an unnatural fashion [to form] a
"super-religion", a new religion* [encompassing] *all of humanity*'. This
attitude is a clear contrast to the positive approach to religious plurality
taken in the year-5 textbook.

RELIGIOUS EDUCATION IN THE CATHOLIC PRESS: PRINCIPAL ARGUMENTS

The following part of the essay will discuss the rationales and approaches to the legitimation of religious education in state schools in the Catholic periodicals *Vrhbosna*, *Katolički tjednik* [Catholic Week], *Crkva na kamenu* [The Church on the rock] and *Svjetlo riječi* [Light of the Word].

During the most recent war and in the early period of transition to a new political system, specifically between 1991 and 1993, these publications reiterate in detail the Bishops' Conference official position on these issues and provide a rationale for it. A separate Bishops' Conference of BiH was at this time yet to be founded; this means that the rationales provided here for religious education related to both BiH and neighbouring Croatia. A key feature of this period was that, despite the war, a future characterised by democracy and religious freedom was a firm hope of those involved in the discourse and, correspondingly, the future shape of religious education appeared as a promise of better things to come. We can also observe that a range of ideas and considerations emerged during this time as to how to incorporate 'religious culture' into state school curricula. The position of the Catholic Church on religious education within the state system found its official formulation in 1992, comprising various aspects of what religious education might look like in the future[38] as well as ideas on the democratic and humanistic values that might be espoused through this teaching.[39] A commonly represented view was that, in a democratic society, the church should take on an active role and become involved in all relevant sectors, such as education, culture and the media. There is support expressed for the notion, arising in the 1990s, of a *'religious culture in schools'*,[40] whose creation would entail the removal of the *'ideological sediment of the old system'* and the valuing of religious and religious/cultural ideas, notions and curricular content. Discussions around this issue were held in 1990 in Croatia,[41] at a meeting of experts from across Yugoslavia, and in BiH in 1991.[42] The arguments advanced in support of religious education were numerous and varied, coming primarily from those engaged in the field. Theological and ecclesiastical arguments were discussed in curricular terms. A set of arguments defined as 'anthropological-educational' claimed that pluralistic and democratic attitudes '[...] *enable each individual to come to know, retain and develop his or her own religious, cultural and national identity in order to enter into dialogue and live together with all people* [...]'.[43] Continuing, this argumentation suggests that religious education in schools provides a site for comprehensive education of young people that aims to enable them to inquire about the meaning of life and develop skills for the critical observation and evaluation of various value systems. Arguing from the perspective of cultural history, this rationale emphasises the significance of religion, which it considers to enable people to locate themselves in their own history and context; parents' rights to make decisions on the religious education of their children are also emphasised and the view offered that the church and the state are responsible for meeting parents' wishes in this regard.

It is during this period, on 19 May 1991, that the papal document *Dialogue and Proclamation* was issued.[44] The author Msgr. Mato Zovkić described the core statement of this document, as relevant to BiH, as follows: '*Regardless of the internal organisation of BiH, we need to educate our faithful in the spirit of religious and national pluralism*'.[45]

The period between 1994 and 1999 saw a number of decisive events explicitly or implicitly related to issues around education, which were picked up by the Catholic press. The first of these was the foundation of the Bishops' Conference of BiH by the Holy See, which, alongside the end of the war in 1994, prompted the Catholic Church to look back at the path it had travelled and make a pronouncement on its official attitude to religious education. In a letter, the auxiliary bishop of BiH, Pero Sudar, mentions a number of points of significance to Catholic religious education in BiH.[46] They include a change in the political system in the country; the fact that BiH was in the process of acquiring a number of different religious education courses delivered by various churches and religious communities, the need to define the status of religious education in schools; and the need to firm up curricula and arrangements for teacher training.[47] The members of the Bishops' Conference subsequently wrote an open letter to the signatories of the Dayton Accords, which contained a number of calls for action issued during the war as well as pointing out various paradoxical aspects of the accords which, in the view of the church, would only result in new difficulties. The content of this letter is implicitly relevant to education because of the questions formulated within it that touch upon the country's socio-political situation. The bishops express particular concern about the division into three of the country's school system, reinforced in consequence of its division into its constituent entities and resettlement of parts of the population as 'agreed' between the political parties and in accordance with the Dayton

Accords.[48] Other issues of concern in this context include that of three armies within one state, the 'ethnic cleansing' that had taken place during the way, and concern around the principle of 'might is right' and of which authority was to guarantee the implementation of the Dayton Accords, the return of wartime refugees to their original homes, and respect for human rights. The church, as the letter states, considers it to be evident that the Accords give rise to new unrest and insecurities.[49] The archbishop of BiH, Vinko Puljić, considered assistance from Europe as key to BiH's future, in contrast to his view of the Dayton Accords, which he regarded as an 'American' solution. Further, he saw Sarajevo and BiH as a test case for democracy and pluralism in the country itself and in Europe as a whole,[50] and took the view that Europe and BiH were closely connected in issues of democracy and religious plurality in particular.

Another factor of influence at this time was the foundation in 1994 of the Catholic 'School Centres' or 'Schools for Europe', which we will discuss in more detail below. It is important to point out here that these schools emerge from a situation of crisis and war.[51] As Pero Sudar has commented, the Bishops' Conference of BiH was at this time not prepared to accept the negative impact of divisions between people in BiH, nor the expulsion or exodus of its Catholic population. It was for this reason that the first 'School Centre' was founded in Sarajevo, open to students of all faiths and ethnicities.[52]

The period subsequent to 2000, and to 2003 at the latest, has been primarily characterised for the Bishops' Conference of BiH by discussions around education reform, the new school subject of 'Culture of Religions', and the issues around the general 'anti-democratic' situation in the country. The year 2000 saw the Church's third proclamation of its position on religious education. In contrast to previous proclamations, this statement, the first made subsequently to the OHR's announcement of the introduction of the secular school subject 'Culture of Religions', makes use of legal arguments. It states that religious education at state schools constitutes a fundamental right[53] and that, due to the fact that this right was being called into question by international stakeholders in BiH, i.e. the OHR and the OSCE, the church needed to find legitimate legal avenues to protect it. Continuing, the proclamation asserts that it was in conformity with, and respected, the right of parents to have their children educated in religious matters at state schools; that it was modelling its approach on the experience of established democracies with the practice of faith-based religious education; and that this approach was in line with the relevant standards from international law.[54] Another new component of the church's argument in this proclamation related to subjects intended to provide an alternative to religious education without replacing it; the Bishops' Conference stated in this context that it did not accept religious education syllabi based on models, such as 'Culture of Religions' or 'History of Religions'. Its idea of the position and role of faith-based religious education, according to the proclamation, was aligned with German-speaking regions' experience of religious education in schools and centred around teaching influenced by ecumenical ideas and by the principle of dialogue.[55] In the view of the Bishops' Conference of BiH, the only way of successfully resolving the issues around religious education is to organise parallel delivery of various faith-based classes. This notion reflects the Church's idea of religious plurality, which Cardinal Vinko Puljić expressed a year after the proclamation in terms of unity in diversity.[56]

'Our Differences Are Our Wealth': A Catholic View on Education Reform

The Bishops' Conference of BiH has been a keen observer, commentator and critic of reforms to education in BiH, and has commented on both local and international stakeholders and on the content of reforms. The Church's criticism of reform efforts is related to political and identity issues.[57] The year 2003 appears to have represented a significant turning point: while from 1991 onwards the Catholic Church consistently made positive statements on impending social change and very rarely claimed to be speaking 'on behalf of the people', it has regularly made such assertions since 2003; its increasingly negative view of local policymakers and international stakeholders and its disapproval of the school subject 'Culture of Religions' appear to go hand in hand with its perception of an increasingly unfavourable position for Croats in BiH. One of the reasons for this change in tone was the attempt by BiH's federal education ministry, which does not exert central authority, to declare only one curriculum, the Bosniak, as valid in the 'two schools under one roof'[58] on the territory of the Federation of Bosnia and Herzegovina.[59] At the end of 2003, the Bishops' Conference of BiH made a public contribution to criticism of education reform in the shape of a 'Proclamation on the Cultural and Religious Identity of the Croatian Catholic Population of

BiH'.[60] In the same year, the Vatican Congregation for the Doctrine of the Faith had issued a document on Catholics in politics; it is this document that the Bishops' Conference of BiH took as a basis for its statements in this issue.[61] We will now go into more detail on the key points of criticism expressed by the Church in this context.

The auxiliary bishop Pero Sudar, the founder and head of the Catholic School Centres, is of the view that, while reforms to education in BiH are urgently necessary, the central problem in the education system is a lack of awareness of diversity and the importance of upholding and preserving it.[62] He fears that it is the belief of the representatives of the international community who are involved in BiH that the tragic war in that country was caused by the differences among its people and that this means that the education system must deny and obscure these differences. Sudar interprets a number of factors in the education reform, such as the shared core curriculum and the denial of teaching in the various languages of BiH, as indicators of this attitude, and considers both the separation of children into ethnically based groups ('Serb', 'Croat', 'Bosniak') within one and the same school for teaching in the 'national' subjects and the current situation with some institutions being 'two schools under one roof' to be inadequate solutions to the issues.[63] Sudar supports both textbook revision and a multi-perspective approach to the depiction of the various religions in all the so-called national subjects, but has asserted that BiH has as yet failed to guarantee respect for fundamental human rights[64] and that therefore diversity in education is not yet attainable. In Sudar's view, the ideas for reform promoted by the international community, such as equality for all languages in all BiH's schools, have little connection to the realities of a society divided in this way, and the country's education system has become a guinea pig for experiments.[65]

In the view of Archbishop Vinko Puljić, the Croats have since 1991, and subsequently to the Dayton Accords, consistently been committed to preserving BiH's statehood, yet had suffered exclusively negative consequences from the Accords and the country's division into entities and cantons,[66] having found themselves, contrary to the 'promise' given at Dayton, unable to return to the regions from which they had been driven during the war due to a severe lack of employment and fears for their personal safety in non-Croat-dominated areas. Conceding that these issues faced all ethnic groups in BiH, the Archbishop expressed the view that the preservation of BiH as a state was a priority, yet that,

should it remain divided—i.e. into two entities and a district—all its constituent peoples should have access to the same rights.[67]

The Catholic Church has come to regard itself as the guardian of the
national, cultural and religious identity of BiH's Croat population, and
to consider this identity as a component of fundamental human rights
and of democracy, respect for which demands that the Croats be permitted to own and make use of their language, media and institutions and
have their own religious education in schools.[68]

The comments on education reform and the treatment of faith-based
religious education made by the Catechistic Council of the BiH Bishops'
Conference have been exclusively critical in tone. Its regular meeting
on 23 February 2005 issued a statement asserting that language, culture, education, religious rights and education from pre-school to university level were to be categorised as fundamental human rights and as
part of the vital national interests of all constituent peoples of BiH.[69]
Continuing, the council stated that the Church was aware of its task
of preserving these elements of its people's identity, and that the background to this position was the observation made by the bishops in BiH
that the Croats were being discursively turned by stealth from a constituent people into a national minority,[70] a development that could be
regarded as a direct consequence of the implementation of the Dayton
Accords and that indicated that BiH had thus far failed to see an active
emergence of any of the principles that govern the modern state in its
political and societal life.[71]

Criticism of the New School Subject 'Culture of Religions'

A part of the education reform in BiH was the devising and introduction
of a new school subject entitled 'Culture of Religions'. After a number
of consultations held between international stakeholders and local religious communities and churches, the Catholic Church, along with other
churches and communities, rejected the idea of the subject and its implementation. Pavo Jurišić, a professor at the Catholic Theology in Sarajevo,
has criticised the approach to the subject's introduction taken by the
OHR, which stipulated prior to the official announcement on the subject that representatives of BiH's religious institutions were obliged to
contribute to its development: '*Heads of religious communities and members of the Inter-religious Council will each nominate a representative who
will propose to the OHR the content for the subject "Culture of Religions"*

[pertaining to the religion he or she represents].[72] Jurišić has observed that at no stage had this been discussed or agreed with any official representatives of religious institutions. He expressed equal surprise over the speed of the subject's introduction, just 4 months after the OHR's announcement (in the 2000/2001 academic year). Had BiH's religious institutions cooperated, this would have entailed the task of drawing up a curriculum for a new school subject within a period of 4 months. A further problem he identified was that, if 'Culture of Religions' was to be compulsory for all learners and faith-based religious education optional, the latter would be in a weakened position, with parents potentially seeking to avoid overburdening their children by sending them only to 'Culture of Religions'.[73]

The OHR's assertion that the new subject was to give 'objective, non-discriminatory information'[74] on BiH's four major religions attracted criticism particularly from Ante Pavlović, a professor of Catholic theology responsible for Catholic religious education in the Bishops' Conference[75]: '*What does "objective information" mean* [in this context] *and what information does it refer to? Are schools there to simply give information, or do they shape* [pupils'] *attitudes and encourage* [them to adopt] *particular values?* [...] *Who is it giving this objective information* [...]*? Who would write textbooks* [for this subject], *and to what criteria would they adhere? So many questions and no satisfactory answer in sight* [...]'.[76]

Catholic authorities in BiH have also criticised the new subject's content and underlying ideological basis, fearing that this supposedly neutral subject would constitute a one-sided, syncretistic and potentially manipulative approach to religious education.[77] This impression contains elements of the experience of the Church with the previous political system, which claimed to oppose the 'missionary imperialism of religion' in the name of religious pluralism.[78] Further, the Church feels that the subject's content and structure have not been outlined with sufficient clarity[79] and that its limitation to discussion of the four largest religions in BiH amounts to precisely the discrimination that the subject seeks to prevent. Other concerns held by the Church include the matter of which information is emphasised and how, and the lack of an educational intent behind the information transmitted, which it regards as an insufficient approach in the context of an education institution such as a school.[80] In another, more extreme viewpoint, the subject is regarded as completely unfeasible because its proponents would essentially place all religions on an indiscriminately equivalent footing and teach without differentiation or categorisation about their traditions, teachings, rites and customs.[81]

INNER CATHOLIC CRITICISM OF RELIGIOUS EDUCATION

Some representatives of the order of Franciscans in the Franciscan province of Bosna Srebrena (Bosna Argentina) hold views on religious education that do not conform to the Bishops' Conference the of BiH official position. Ivan Šarčević OFM, former editor of the Franciscan periodical *Svjetlo riječi*, has drawn from his analysis of the general discourse on religion in the education system the conclusion that there are two extreme opposing positions on religious education in state schools. One is dogmatically secular and militantly atheistic, and the other dogmatically religious and tending to regard discourses around schools as secular institutions and encouraging children to learn about other religions and worldviews as an attempt to cast the faith represented by the holder of this position in a relative light.[82] Šarčević is in favour of religious education at state schools and considers that there is no real alternative to it; however, he also supports school subjects in which a range of religions are discussed and taught.[83] Luka Markešić OFM, who was involved in drawing up the inaugural curriculum for 'Culture of Religions' of 2001 and in some similar curricula produced subsequently to this, holds the view that 'Culture of Religions' is a model of education that may be able to promote and deepen dialogue and mutual respect among religions.[84] His fellow Franciscan Ivo Marković made a practical attempt to promote developments in this direction, when in 1996 he founded the inter-faith choir 'Pontanima'.

While *Svjetlo riječi* frequently reports on the practical issues faced by the education system in general, there is little, if any, evidence in the Franciscan press of a connection between religion and the nation within the context of education. The situation created in BiH by the Dayton Accords, which affects Croats as it does other sections of the population, does find criticism in these media. Mijo Džolan OFM, the former head of the Franciscan province of Bosna Srebrena, has provided a dispassionate analysis in which he identifies a fundamental political issue, that of the fact that, while the Serbs and Bosniaks are perceived and treated as political subjects by the international community, the Croats are not, being without their own entity and not commanding a majority in the Federation's parliament. This means, he continues, that the international community has inevitably found itself acting indirectly against Croat interests.[85] His analysis, as many others appearing in *Svjetlo riječi*, ends, despite its assertion that the Croats in BiH are in a difficult position, with a warning to Croats against falling into the trap of perceiving themselves as fundamentally threatened; indeed, Džolan calls upon them to invest as many resources of all kinds as possible in upholding the shared state of BiH.[86]

Marko Oršolić OFM is a Franciscan monk whose inter-religious and inter-cultural work focusing on dialogue, and whose activities in the International Multireligious Intercultural Centre Zajedno[87] have won him both multiple national and international awards and public criticism. He supports the idea of a secular school subject on religion, such as 'Culture of Religions' or history of religions, which he considers urgently necessary, and is in favour of it being delivered separately from faith-based religious education.[88] He is critical of the 'German' model of school-based religious education, in which each religious institution delivers its own teaching, as being unsuitable for BiH.

The most vigorous criticism of church policies from the Franciscan perspective has been formulated by Drago Bojić OFM, who denounces the organisational discrepancies between the cantons of the Federation in relation to the status of religious education and the 'religious privatisation' of schools, which he regards as a societal problem.[89] Further, he considers religious education curricula to be severely lacking in appropriate educational criteria and all religious education textbooks in BiH to suffer from ideological taint. A serious problem in his view is the abuse of religious freedom by religious institutions to create employment for their theologians at the cost of the state and to promote their own ideologies; with this in view, he has called for the abolition of faith-based religious education. Bojić regards the behaviour of representatives of religious institutions with regard to religious education as indicative of the continued and ongoing influence of the legacy of Communist ideology in BiH; in a manner similar to those who upheld that ideology, he considers, today's faith representatives claim to be in possession of the only valid truth and seek to propagate it via schools.[90] His views, while not shared by all Franciscans in BiH, can stand in exemplary fashion for a critical attitude towards religious education that is exclusive to this order in BiH and that is also indicative of the current breadth of opinion within BiH's Catholic Church.

'SCHOOLS FOR EUROPE': CATHOLIC SCHOOL CENTRES AS A EUROPEAN APPROACH TO EDUCATION

This section of the essay will discuss the 'Schools for Europe' and their connection to the educational policy activities pursued by the Bishops' Conference of BiH. A total of seven 'school centres' run by the Bishops' Conference of BiH have been in existence in BiH since 1994[91]; they are primary (years 1–8) and academic secondary schools (years 9–12). The first curriculum for these schools was agreed upon in 1996 and encompasses the same subjects as state schools.[92] It is worth noting in this context that the Catholic School Centres provide—at one period per week—50% less religious education than state schools in BiH, at both the primary and secondary levels. Further, they teach subjects conceived as alternatives to religious education, such as 'Morals, Ethics and Spirituality', unlike schools in most of BiH's cantons and entities. We might consider particularly interesting the presence at both the primary and secondary schools of the subject 'History of Religions', whose aim is to teach 'basic knowledge about the world religions from their origins to the present'.[93] The schools are funded by the Bishops' Conference of BiH, foreign Roman Catholic organisations such as the German church charity Renovabis, and the Italian Bishops' Conference (BKI). The establishment of these schools came after the last war, at a time when BiH had no functional state or school system and when, in the view of the Catholic Church, the country's education system was dominated by inadequate curricula and educational experiments. Another reason for both the schools' foundation and their continued existence is that their presence in regions where Catholics now live acts as a motivating factor for these populations to remain living there. The Bishops' Conference of BiH regards these schools as *'schools based on humanist values with a Catholic approach to* [these] *values'* and with as high a degree as possible of respect for learners of all religions.[94] Students from non-Catholic backgrounds and different ethnic groups can receive language teaching in their own language and religious education for their own faith. The schools intend this approach to represent a contribution to the normalisation and democratisation of the situation in BiH.[95] Aware of the pluralistic nature of BiH society, the Church, by its own account, seeks to represent parents who wish their children to receive an education in line with their own moral and religious values.[96] Although the school centres have been recognised as educational institutions by local education ministries and feature a '*multi-ethnic composition of learners*'[97] their buildings have been subject to several bomb attacks.[98]

A further self-declared aim of the school centres is the provision of a European-oriented education, which leads to an emphasis in their curricula on three particular subject groups: classical languages (Latin and Ancient Greek), living European languages (English from year 1 and German and French from year 5) and computer and information studies. The process of democratisation, in the schools' view, also encompasses acceptance of diversity and of minorities as a key to peaceful coexistence among the population of BiH. The name 'Schools for Europe' is intended to indicate that those who learn there are to do so in a European spirit and experience Europe as their extended home.[99]

CONCLUSION

To conclude, we will make some observations on the strategies and steps undertaken by the Catholic Church in BiH to meet the challenges posed by modernising education in the post-conflict and post-Communist setting. The starting point for the strategies with which it has come up is the plethora of aspects and experiences of the current situation which it is seeking to change and/or combat, including the division of the country's education system into effectively three subsystems; the expulsion from their original home areas to which parts of the population were subjected during the war; a perceived lack of respect and appreciation for religious diversity and identities in BiH society, particularly on the part of international stakeholders; and what the church has regarded as an anti-democratic approach to education reform and to the introduction of secular school subjects dealing with religion. Pavo Jurišić has commented that the Catholic Church's position on these matters has been strongly influenced by the experience of the war and even more so by the experience of the ideology of 'brotherhood and unity', which regarded religion as 'fraud [perpetrated] by popes and imams' and excluded it from the public sphere.[100] In his view, this atheistic twentieth-century ideology was matched in its hatred for religion only by the relativistic liberalism of the nineteenth, which he regards as now making a comeback in BiH; he considers both to be authoritarian in nature and to desire to dispense with God.

In this way, the Church has located the cause of all BiH's societal problems as residing in political systems and political thought. The

Bishops' Conference has sought to combat, alter or ameliorate these factors using a number of approaches. First, the Church has engaged with education both within state schools and in catechesis outside them, producing new curricula and textbooks. The curriculum for school-based Catholic religious education is conceived around the catholic denomination, an ecumenical approach and the value of dialogue, as well as engaging, with some shortcomings, with the social reality of BiH as it currently is. It continues to be the only religious education curriculum in BiH to specifically and explicitly raise the issue of religious plurality, and its textbooks evince a comparatively thorough exploration of this plurality and of other religions, looking at both religions practised in the region and Asian religions as well as discussing intra-Christian diversity and new religious movements. There is an issue, as discussed above, with the local examples the textbooks present, which frequently fail to depict BiH as the country to which they are making reference, even where the content is related to Catholicism. Their depiction of atheism is problematic; while we might understand that a Catholic approach would not regard it in a positive light, the one-sided and heavily critical portrayal of atheism in these materials could well be viewed as reminiscent, of all things, of the attitude towards religion taken in the Communist era. Additionally, the textbooks depict other religions as distant, static entities without any internal diversity. This said, these depictions are the only ones in the BiH religious education landscape that engage thoroughly with religious plurality, and the only ones with any traces of critical reflection on the faith from whose perspective they are composed.

A second feature of the Catholic Church's approach to religious education is its close analysis of all relevant documents and events from education reform and policy and its involvement in this manner in societal discourses around these issues. The rationales it provides for its position are drawn from religious lines of argument, but also from social-cultural, education policy and legal concerns. The Church has exercised criticism of education policy decisions, structures (such as the arrangement of the state after Dayton and its impact on education) and procedures, as well as of the ways in which international stakeholders have interacted with local decision-makers and particularly representatives of Churches and religious communities. The arguments put forward by Church authorities have shown changes that are closely linked to the activities of the international community in BiH. A particular flashpoint has arisen around the introduction of 'Culture of Religions', which the Church has felt to have been the imposition of a dubious concept conducted undemocratically. In this context, the Church has consistently pointed to the European and particularly the German context when discussing ways of dealing with religious plurality.

We can identify three basic lines of argument within the Bishops' conference in BiH in relation to these issues. Proponents of a moderate approach regard religious education as, ideally, acting in support of religious pluralism as it is conceived of and expressed in BiH. The 'hardliners' tend instead to supply rationales linked to conceptions of nation and point to the paradoxical situation of the Croats as a constituent people of BiH that has in effect become a minority. A third position, primarily advanced by Franciscans, seeks to critique the Church from within and to encourage it to rethink the religious education it has delivered thus far in local contexts.

Alongside these activities and approaches, the Catholic Church has been actively involved in shaping the educational landscape of BiH through its foundation of School Centres funded by Catholic organisations, yet open to, and attended by, young people across all national groups in BiH. The intent of these schools is to provide an organisational and content-based (classical and modern languages, faith-based religious education for students of all religions, and 'History of Religions') demonstration of the capacity of the Catholic Church in BiH to provide all young people with broad educational horizons. The qualifications offered by these schools are now in line with the requirements of the European labour market. The prospects thus opened up to young people represent the Catholic Church's attempt to both meet European educational standards and demonstrate that innovation in education is possible despite the difficulties posed by the post-war setting and the challenges of modernisation. The ultimate political and cultural objective of the Bishops' Conference of BiH is linked to a desire to see BiH within the EU.

We can perceive in all this a dual strategy on the part of the Catholic Church. First, it is evident that the Church's expression of the societal position of the Croat population, the group with which it is primarily identified, as a constituent people of BiH is essentially framed in terms of a Croatian nation, principally for lack of alternative political options. This represents a clear contradiction to the universalist attitude at the heart of Catholicism and appears problematic to the political stakeholders driving the as yet incomplete process of BiH's development as a state. On the other hand, we observe a marked willingness and potential on the part of the Church to support and benefit BiH society, characterised as it is by the plurality of religions, and to contribute positively to shaping it going forward, working with other churches and religious communities in the process. Such attitudes represent a key factor in protecting, preserving and promoting religious plurality as it is understood and expressed in local contexts.

Notes

1. For the general socio-political and educational setting, the influence of the international stakeholders and their documents see the article about the Islamic RE.
2. See Vrhbosna 1–4, 1995, 49. On the status of BiH's Bishops' Conference, see Vrhbosna 1, 2004, 15ff.
3. See Vrhbosna 1–4, 1995, 66f.
4. Ibid., 30.
5. See Katolička tiskovna agencija Biskupske konferencije BiH [Catholic Press Agency, hereafter KTA] „Katolička Crkva u Bosni i Hercegovini", Sarajevo 2002. Until the most recent war, BiH was home to ten Greek Catholic congregations of Ukrainians, with a total of 5000 adherents.
6. See Snježana Vasilj, Srećko M. Džaja, Marko Karamatić, Tomo Vukšić (1997): Katoličanstvo u Bosni i Hercegovini. Napredak, Sarajevo. In all other matters, the Franciscans are subject to the authority of the bishop responsible for them.
7. See Republic of Bosnia and Herzegovina, Ministry of Education, Science, Culture and Sport, Educational Institute (ed.) (1994): Plan i program vjerskog odgoja i obrazovanja. Zenica, 35–76.
8. See 'Gravissimum educatonis'. URL: http://www.vatican.va/archive/hist_councils/ii_vatican_council/documents/vat-ii_decl_19651028_gravissimum-educationis_ge.html (07.07.2015).
9. See Biskupska Konferencija Bosne i Hercegovine (2003): Plan i program katoličkoga vjeronauka u osnovnoj školi. Zagreb-Sarajevo, 257ff.
10. See Republic of Bosnia and Herzegovina, Ministry of Education, Science, Culture and Sport, Educational Institute (ed.) (1994): Plan i program vjerskog odgoja i obrazovanja. Zenica, 35–76.
11. Biskupska Konferencija Bosne i Hercegovine (2003): Plan i program katoličkoga vjeronauka u osnovnoj školi. Zagreb-Sarajevo, second edition, V.
12. Ibid., 53ff.
13. Ibid., 35–50.

14. Ibid., 58.
15. Ibid., 150f.
16. Ibid., 155.
17. Ibid., 157f.
18. Ibid., 214.
19. Dženana Husremović, Steve Powell, Ajla Šišić i Aida Dolić: Obrazovanje u Bosni i Hercegovini. Čemu učimo djecu? Analiza sadržaja udžbenika nacionalne grupe predmeta. Fond otvoreno društvo Bosna i Hercegovina, Sarajevo, 173f.
20. The abbreviations denote the year group for which the textbook is written (e.g. R1 = textbook for year 1) and the page number on which the content referred to is to be found.
21. Josip Jakšić; Karolina Manda Mićanović (2005): Let's grow to love God and people, religious education textbook for year 1 of primary education; Bishops' Conference of Bosnia and Herzegovina. Glas Koncila Zagreb, Sarajevo.
22. Josip Jakšić; Karolina Manda Mićanović (2005): Let's grow in gratitude, religious education textbook for year 2 of primary education; Bishops' Conference of Bosnia and Herzegovina. Glas Koncila Zagreb, Sarajevo.
23. Chapter II, covering 19 pages (374 lines), with 44 illustrations. See Ružica Razum et al. (2003): I am the Way; religious education textbook for year 5 of primary education; Bishop' Conference of Bosnia and Herzegovina. Kršćanska sadašnjost Zagreb-Sarajevo.
24. Each religion discussed in this chapter is described in approximately 40 lines, referencing selected aspects of its history, facts and episodes from the life of its founder, its places of prayer and its visual imagery. Key terms are given visual emphasis and additional information is provided as supplementary to the lesson.
25. New International Version.
26. For further textbooks, see Ivica Pažin et al. (2004): At the table of love and reconciliation: Religious education textbook for year 3 of primary education, issued by the Bishops' Conference of Bosnia and Herzegovina. Kršćanska sadašnjost, Zagreb-Sarajevo; Razum, Ružica et al. (2003): Invited to Freedom: Religious education textbook for year 6 of primary education. Kršćanska sadašnjost, Zagreb-Sarajevo.
27. See R3: 35ff, R4: 65ff, R4: 71, R5: 53ff, R5: 68–86 and R6: 20–49.
28. Josip Periš et al. (2003): Together in Love: Religious education textbook for year 7 of primary education, issued by the Bishops' Conference of Bosnia and Herzegovina. Kršćanska sadašnjost, Zagreb, Sarajevo.
29. Josip Periš et al. (2005): Into Life with Christ: Religious education textbook for year 8 of primary education. Bishops' Conference of Bosnia and Herzegovina, Kršćanska sadašnjost Zagreb-Sarajevo.

30. The discussion takes up 76 lines (three pages) and uses three illustrations (a Torah scroll, a rabbi and a Star of David).

31. The discussion takes up 105 lines (56 of which are concerned with additional explanations on the temple and the synagogue)/four pages and features four illustrations.

32. This chapter contains explicit discussion of the various Christian churches, which the previous chapter, Chap. 5, on, The church, a new prophetic community, (R7: 89–120) lists in a general historical overview from a Catholic perspective. Page 108 discusses the Catharists and the Waldensians, 110ff. the crisis of the Church, Martin Luther and the Reformation, and 115ff. the Enlightenment.

33. Other textbooks also discuss the ecumenical movement: see R4: 98; R4: 105 on ecumenism and dialogue; R5: 33 for general information about the movement R4: 94 for interreligious meetings.

34. '*People naturally turn to God* [...] *because he* [God] *himself implanted this need in human beings. In spite of this, the development of religiosity is also dependent on society, which may negate God*'.

35. '*History enables us to retrace the development of religion from its lowest forms (worship of natural forces) to the worship of God within monotheistic religions*'.

36. The text refers to this movement only as the 'Moon sect'.

37. '*Esotericism and occultism are terms denoting something "hidden*". [In these practices,] *people attempt via knowledge and* via *particular techniques to penetrate the secret forces of nature, those which evade scientific discovery. People believe that these* [forces] *could provide answers to important questions around eternal youth and immortality*'. (R8: 48)

38. Anto Pavlović: Ponovno uvodjenje vjeronauka u javne škole. In: Vrhbosna, 2, 1992, 97–100, 97.

39. Ibid. '*We are approaching democratic change which promises respect for fundamental human rights and freedoms.* [...] *This democratic society will no doubt be influenced by the creation of a new mentality which will go hand in hand with a shift in values, with political pluralism and with pluralism of ideas and points of view*'.

40. Ibid.

41. For Croatia, see Milan Šimunović: Interdisciplinarni i interkonfesionalni znanstveni simpozij: *Religiozna kultura u školi i društvenim medijima.* Organised by „Školska knjiga", Zagreb, 18.do 21. September 1990, Paper: *Religiozna/vjerska kultura kao specifičan odgoj i obrazovanje u vjerskoj/crkvenoj zajednici.* Ders.: Vjeronauk u Crkvi nije sporan. In: *Kateheza,* XII, 1990, 4, 49. For BiH see Round Table on the Introduction of Religious Instruction (religious education) in primary

and middle schools, Fojnica 14–15 November 1991, organised by the association of middle schools and middle school centres in BiH.

42. Anto Pavlović, Ponovno uvodjenje vjeronauka u javne škole. In: Vrhbosna, 2, 1992, 99.

43. Ibid., 99.

44. Pontifical Council for Inter-religious Dialogue, Congregation for the Evangelisation of Peoples: Dialogue and Proclamation, Reflection and Orientations on Interreligious Dialogue and the Proclamation of the Gospel of Jesus Christ. 19.05.1991; published in Bulletin of the Holy See Press Office 102, issued by Secretariat of German Bishops' Conference. Bonn, 1991.

45. Mato Zovkić: Pastoralni ekumenizam. In: Vrhbosna, 2, 1992, 101. On the Catholic view of dialogue between Christianity and Islam, see also Vrhbosna 1 (1996) 23ff und Vrhbosna, 3, 1997, 215ff.

46. The Catechistic Council of the Bishops' Conference of Bosnia and Herzegovina: Statovi Katoličke Crkve u BiH o vjerskom odgoju i obrazovanju katoličke djece i mladeži u predškolskim ustanovama te osnovnim i srednjim školama na području Bosne i Hercegovine. In: Vrhbosna, 1, 1998, 53ff.

47. These points are listed at ibid., 53–55.

48. On the impact of these factors on the foundation of Catholic school centres, see Pero Sudar: Crkva u BiH – izmedju Evandjelja i politike. In Vrhbosna, 3, 1998, 563.

49. „Otvoreno pismo potpisnicima i svjedocima daytonskog sporazuma". In: Vrhbosna, 1–4, 1995, 63.

50. Vinko Puljić, Pravedan mir u BiH samo uz asistenciju Europe". In: Vrhbosna, 1, 1999, 39.

51. Pero Sudar: Crkva u BiH – izmedju Evandjelja i politike. In Vrhbosna, 3, 1998, 557–565, here 562.

52. Ibid., 563.

53. The Catechistic Council of the Bishops' Conference of Bosnia and Herzegovina: Polazišta, stavovi i odluke Katoličke Crkve u BiH o vjerskom odgoju i obrazovanju. In: Vrhbosna, 3, 2000, 255–257, here 255.

54. Ibid.

55. Ibid., 255.

56. Vinko Puljić: Dijalog kao stil života. Poruka Vijeća za Dijalog Biskupske konferencije BiH svećenstvu i vjernicima. In: Vrhbosna, 1, 2001, 22.

57. Cf. Ante Pavlović: Naše školstvo na ispitu. In: Crkva na kamenu, März 2002, 6. On criticism of the treatment of religious education as a so-called 'national' subject, see Jukić: Vjeronauk nije nacionalni predmet. In: Katolički tjednik, 3, 2002, 30.

58. See Brane Vrbić: Imaju li Hrvati u BiH pravo na svoj nacionalni identitet? In: Katolički tjednik 37, 2003, 7–9, hier 8. Cf. the assertion made by the former federal vice-minister of education to the effect that this had only been possible because just one of the 60 employees of the federal ministry was a Croat. Ibid., 7.

59. Among the criticisms advanced by the Catholic Church has been that reforms to education in BiH pursue aims that unambiguously work against the Croats' cultural and religious identity and the Croatian language and therefore against education and curricula delivered in this language. The inference the Church has drawn from this perception is that these reforms run counter to the diversity which is a fact of life in BiH. Further, the Church has asserted that the international community denies that unity in diversity is possible in BiH. See Priopćenje Biskupske konferencije BiH o kulturnom i vjerskom identitetu hrvatskog katoličkog naroda u BiH. In: Vrhbosna 3, 2003, 264.

60. Priopćenje Biskupske konferencije BiH o kulturnom i vjerskom identitetu hrvatskog katoličkog naroda u BiH. In: Katolički tjednik 38, 2003, 5–6.

61. Priopćenje sa zasjedanja BK BiH. In: Vrhbosna, 1, 2003, 25. The document can be found at Congregation for the Doctrine of the Faith, Doctrinal Note on some Questions regarding the Participation of Catholics in Political Life, http://www.europainstitut.at/upload/publikationen/publikation_43.pdf (18.08.2009).

62. Pero Sudar: Ispod krovova razdora – pod krovovima razuma. Temeljni nedostatak školskog sustava. In: Katolički tjednik 39, 2005, 12–13.

63. See Priopćenje Biskupske konferencije BiH. In: Vrhbosna 3, 2003, 263.

64. Sudar: See Note 62.

65. Izjava Pere Sudara za Katoličkit jednik povodom reforme školstva u BiH. [Statement by auxiliary bishop Pero Sudar on education reform in BiH] In: Vrhbosna, 3, 2003, 262.

66. Nacionalno i političko razočarenje Hrvata u poslijedaytonskoj Bosni i Hercegovini. Izlaganje kardinala Vinka Puljića pred Odborom za međunarodne odnose Kongresa Sjedinjenih američkih država 25. srpnja 2001. In: Vrhbosna 3–4, 2003, 265–266.

67. Ibid., 266.

68. See Katoličkit jednik 38, 2003, 6. Joint statement issued by Cardinal Vinko Puljić, the bishops Franjo Komarica and Ratko Perić, and auxiliary bishop Pero Sudar. Cf. Priopćenje Biskupske konferencije BiH. In: Vrhbosna 3, 2003, 264.

69. Održana redovita sjednica Katehetskog vijeća BK BiH. In: Vrhbosna 1, 2005, 22.

70. Izjava katoličkih biskupa Bosne i Hercegovine. In: Vrhbosna, 1, 2005, 125.
71. Priopćenje za javnost komisije Justitia et Pax BK BiH. In: Vrhbosna, 1, 2006, 23.
72. Pavo Jurišić: Predmet „Kultura religija" s aspekta Katoličke Crkve. In: Vrhbosna, 1, 2001, 101–105.
73. Ante Pavlović: Kultura religija – kukavičje jaje u školi. In: Crkva na kamenu, März 2001, 7.
74. See OHR announcement of 01.12.2000: School Subject ,Culture of Religions'. URL: http://www.ohr.int/ohr-dept/presso/pressr/default.asp?content_id=4129 (11.07.2009) 'It [Culture of Religions] is meant to provide objective, non-discriminatory information to all pupils on the four major religions practised in BiH and their respective traditions.'
75. Jurišić, see above, 101.
76. Ante Pavlović: Kultura religija – kukavičje jaje u školi. In Crkva na kamenu, March 2001, 6.
77. Cf. Ante Pavlović: Vjerski odgoj u reformi obrazovanja. In: Crkva na kamenu, November 2003, 6.
78. Jurišić, 104.
79. Ibid., 105.
80. Ibid., 105.
81. Ante Pavlović: Kultura religija – kukavičje jaje u školi. In Crkva na kamenu, March 2001, 6.
82. Ivan Šarčević: Vjeronauk u školi. Presentation given at symposium on religious education in BiH's education system organised by the WCRP and the Friedrich Naumann Foundation and held in Sarajevo, 8–9.02.2001. Unpublished manuscript.
83. Ibid.
84. Luka Markešić: Vjeronauk u obrazovnom sustavu BiH. Presentation given at symposium on religious education in BiH's education system organised by the WCRP and the Friedrich Naumann Foundation and held in Sarajevo, 8–9.02.2001. Unpublished manuscript.
85. Mijo Džolan: BiH, Dayton, Hrvati, fratri...In: Svjetlo riječi, December 2005, 7–9.
86. Ibid., S. 9.
87. See Gerhard Voss: Für einen interreligiösen und interkulturellen Dialog in Sarajevo. In: Una sancta 4, 49. Jg., 1994, 343–357. (Sonderdruck) Cf. Marko Oršolić: Multireligiöser Dialog in Bosnien und Herzegowina. Archiv IMIC-Zajedno, Sarajevo.
88. Marko Oršolić (2003): Zlodusima unatoč. Novinski intervjui 1988–2002. IMIC/adamić, Sarajevo-Rijeka, 275.

89. See Drago Bojić: Bosanska vjeronaučna trakavica. In: Kalendar sv. Ante (2007) 107–114, here 111. Bojić regards the schools as having effectively turned into churches and mosques.

90. Ibid., 114.

91. KTA, Nr. 34, 28.08.2005, 18.

92. For curricula, see Miljenko Brkić (ed.) (2006): Sustav katoličkih „Škola za Europu". Nastavni plan i program za osnovnu školu. Sarajevo. See also Pavo Jurišić (2006): Katolički školski centar. Nastavni plan i program za gimnaziju. Nakladnik Sustava KŠC, Sarajevo.

93. Ibid., 207.

94. KTA, Nr. 3, 8.12.2002, 11.

95. KTA, Nr. 34, 28.08.2005, 21.

96. Ibid., 119.

97. Pero Sudar: Crkva u BiH – izmedju Evandjelja i politike. In Vrhbosna, 3, 1998, 557–565, here 563.

98. See, *inter alia*, Vrhbosna, 3, 1997, 212f.

99. KTA, Nr. 3, 8.12.2002, 10.

100. Pavo Jurišić: Predmet „Kultura religija" s aspekta Katoličke Crkve. In: Vrhbosna, 1, 2001, 101–105, p. 103.

CHAPTER 7

Analysis of Catholic Religious Instruction Textbooks in Croatian Primary Schools: How Do They Teach Atheism?

Ankica Marinović

INTRODUCTION: CROATIAN SOCIAL AND RELIGIOUS CONTEXT

The change in the position of religion and religious communities in Croatia after the 1990s has been followed by a considerable increase in declared religiosity. The high level of declared Catholics together with the high level of religious identification, and religious belief, practice points to a highly visible trend towards the desecularization and revitalization of religiosity after the fall of communism. Such a trend places Croatia among the countries with the highest level of religiosity in Europe, behind Poland, Romanian Transylvania, Malta, Portugal, Italy, and Ireland.[1]

Unlike the stable trend of a general decrease in church religiosity and the influence of the Church within society in the countries of Western Europe,[2] socioreligious researches point that the opposite process is taking place in Croatia. Unlike the disappearance of a general religious

A. Marinović (✉)
Institute for Social Research, Zagreb, Croatia

© The Author(s) 2018
G. Ognjenović and J. Jozelić (eds.), *Education in Post-Conflict Transition*, Palgrave Studies in Religion, Politics, and Policy, https://doi.org/10.1007/978-3-319-56605-4_7

frame organizationally expressed as a universal church, the opposite process in Croatia is directed towards the strengthening of such a frame
(whose role assumes the Catholic Church). This is a case of the process
of revitalization and deprivatization of religion through a regathering
around the Church institutions.[3] As owners of significant "symbolical
and cultural capital", religion and religious institutions declare themselves as owners of universal knowledge and values, as owners of generally
accepted human morality and common sense and as a factor of original
national being.[4] As Vrcan stressed, they build Berger's protecting sacred
canopy. These changes, in addition to reaffirmation of the significance of
religion and Tradition within culture and reaffirmation of the presence of
religion in social life, also affect the role of religion and religious institutions in global society, state, political society and even civil society.[5] These
social circumstances made a politicization of religion possible.

According to the 2011 Census, 93% of the Croatian population belongs to some religion and 5% of them are without confession.
However, the majority (86.28%) declared as themselves Catholics. There
are small categories of Orthodox (4.44%) and Muslims (1.47%), while
adherence to other different religious communities was slightly over
1%. Less than 5% (4.57%) declared themselves as non-religious, atheists,
agnostics and skeptics.

The results of socioreligious research in Croatia showed a significant increase of religiosity in all dimensions researched so far.[6] Research
showed that the prevailing type of religiosity in Croatia is a traditional,
church-oriented, collectivistic one (the similar findings were those of
research in the 70s and 80s), firmly associated with the nation and the
family. It is a type of religiosity mediated by family socialization, with the
usual elements: the sequence of the sacraments from baptizing to the last
rites, attending religious instruction, religious education within the family and at least occasional church attendance.[7]

The same results show that the Catholic Church became present as an
active protagonist in almost all aspects of social life in Croatia: political,
social, economic, educational and cultural ones.[8]

From 1945 to 1991, Croatia was a part of the socialist Yugoslavia
that had a specific stance towards religion and religiosity. "As with many
other social spheres, religions (covering here both the religious communities and religious people) lived in a double reality: the one that guaranteed the religious freedom and autonomy of religious communities
and another that favored the non-religious worldview".[9] Ideological

"struggle" against religion and Church had been fought in different areas of social life. On the institutional level, religion and Church were invisible—for instance, in the educational system and in the mass media.

However, religion and Church did not disappear from people's personal and family lives. They were, as two authors wrote, widely spread in traditional forms across all segments of society, being constituent of traditional rural as well as "modern" urban ambient (although lesser in the latter).[10] Croatia was, together with Slovenia, the most religious Republic of former Yugoslavia. Sociologists recognized this widely spread traditional religiosity as a potential for revitalization of religion in different social circumstances.

Table 7.1 presents changes in religious self-identification in a 25 year period.

RELIGIOUS SELF-IDENTIFICATION IN CROATIA 1984–2009 (%)[11]

The data from the table, among other changes, show a change in the category of non-religious respondents through a period of 25 years. During the 1980s, in relation to the 1960s and 1970s, the number of irreligious respondents increased and the religious and irreligious respondents got closer. The data showed that non-religious respondents, concerning sociodemographic features, were more men than women, respondents of all ages (excluding the oldest), mostly the youngest, more educated, students, clerks, executives, soldiers, and the richer ones, living in towns.[12]

The biggest changes are visible through the period of transition and the period of war: the significant increase of religious and decrease of non-religious respondents. One author says that the increased religiosity could be "the return to the forgotten God, for some – a manifestation on the level of group behavior or form of conformist behavior, for some – an intimate and deep experience/revival of new spirituality, for

Table 7.1 Changes in religious identification 1984–2009

Religious identification	1984	1989	1996	2004	2009
Convinced believers	10	14	36	40	30
Religious	25	27	38	38	47
Uncertain/indifferent	24	22	13	14	12
Irreligious	41	37	12	9	11
Total	100	100	100	100	100

some – a finally free and complete declaration of existing affiliation and for some – a discovery of something never thought and known about".[13]

CHURCH AND STATE IN CROATIA: ELEMENTS OF LEGAL FRAMEWORK

In this chapter we will present some provisions from the legal documents relevant for this topic: the *Constitution of the Republic of Croatia*, the agreements between the Government of the Republic of Croatia and the Holy See, especially the *Agreement on Cooperation in the field of education and culture* and the *Religious Communities Act*.

The Constitution of the Republic of Croatia guarantees that all citizens enjoy rights and freedoms regardless of race, colour, gender, language, religion, political or other convictions, national or social origin, property, birth, education, social status or other characteristics—equality for all persons before the law (*Article 14*), freedom of thought and expression (*Article 38*), freedom of conscience and religion, freedom to demonstrate religious and other convictions (*Article 40*). *The Constitution* postulates general principles addressing the relation between the Church and the State: equality before the law, separation of Church and State (*Article 41*). For our theme Article 41 is especially relevant.

All religious communities shall be equal before the law and shall be separated from the State. Religious communities shall be free, in conformity with the law, to perform religious services publicly to open schools, educational and other institutions, social and charitable institutions and to manage them, and shall in their activity enjoy the protection and assistance of the State.[14]

As some sociologists of religion noticed, "the main constitutional idea was the model of separation of the Church and State but at the same time the idea of cooperation: protection and assistance. How this support (protection and assistance) should be implemented has remained one of the contested issues in the years that followed".[15] It is often difficult to determinate the border between cooperation and possible misuse. That point is relevant for our topic.

The diplomatic relationships between the Republic of Croatia and the Holy See were established in 1992. The regulation of the position of the Catholic Church was completed by signing four agreements of mutual interest between the Republic of Croatia and the Holy See in the period from 1996 to 1998: an "*Agreement on Legal Issues,* an *Agreement on Spiritual*

Care in the Military and Police Forces, an *Agreement on Cooperation in the Fields of Education and Culture* and an *Agreement on Economic Issues*". By signing the agreements with the dominant Catholic Church the Government recognized "its special historical and cultural role and social position". From the very beginning, some aspects of these agreements provoked scholars to public disputes.[16] Different social actors consider that some agreements' provisions put in question the fundamental constitutional postulate on the separation of the Church and the State and some constitutional rights and freedoms of Croatian citizens—those who are not Catholics as well as those who are not religious.[17]

With the international agreement on *Cooperation in the field of education and culture,* signed between the Republic of Croatia and the Holy See in 1996, the Croatian state assumed the legal responsibility to implement Catholic instruction in primary and secondary schools and pre-school institutions, as an optional subject. *The Agreement* defines as follows:

- The program of Catholic religious instruction will be arranged by special contracts between the Government of Croatia and the Croatian Conference of Bishops;
- Religious instruction can be taught by the person to whom diocesan bishop issues a document about canonic mandate (*mission canonica*);
- The possibility to organize additional religious activities in the school is also guaranteed[18];
- The programmes, the content of textbooks and didactic materials will be made by the Croatian Bishops' Conference, submitted to the responsible authorities (the Ministry) to be included into curriculum;
- All expenses of publishing textbooks covers the Republic of Croatia as it does for all other school textbooks;
- Both the Church and the State authorities are in charge of monitoring the quality of religious instruction and its accordance with the Church and State laws[19];
- The right of choice is guaranteed for all parents and students and excludes any possibility of discrimination in school activities;
- The possibility to withdraw from the religious instruction is declared—written withdrawal should be submitted to the school principal at the beginning of the school year.

The following three items have been highlighted in *the Agreement*:

1. "irreplaceable historical and present role of the Catholic Church in Croatia in cultural and moral education of the nation and its role in the field of education and culture";
2. the fact that "the majority of Croatian citizens belong to the Catholic Church";
3. that "the educational system in public pre-schools and schools including higher education institutions will take into account Christian ethics values".[20]

The Religious Communities Act was finally approved in 2002. The *Act* was reached 6 years after the agreements with the Holy See were signed. That fact provoked a doubt that the *Act* has been adjusted to previously signed agreements and highlighted doubt about the privileged position of the Catholic Church in Croatia.[21] Among other issues, the *Act* regulates the position of religious instruction in the public school system in general.

Article 13 of the *Act* defines religious instruction in pre-school, primary schools and secondary schools. *The Article* states that:

• On the request of parents (or foster parents) the programme in pre-school institutions includes religious instruction;
• On the request of parents (or foster parents) of students younger than 15 years and upon declaration of both—parents and students older than 15 years, the confessional religious instruction is established as an optional subject in accordance with the curriculum of primary and secondary schools;
• Only persons who fulfill legal conditions can perform confessional religious instruction;
• Religious communities suggest and the Ministry of Education confirms the programs for religious instruction in pre-school institutions, primary schools, and secondary schools, together with textbooks and didactic materials;
• Religious instruction in pre-school institutions, primary schools and secondary schools is separated from religious instruction in religious communities.

Religious Instruction in Educational System in Croatia

Croatia in the European Context

Europe is characterized by four dominant types of religious instructions in public schools: strictly confessional, loose confessional, non-confessional[22] and a variant without religious instruction.

1. The first type represents teaching religious contents in the traditional, confessional manner (as catechism). Austria, partly Germany and Croatia (and most of transitional countries) are examples of such a trend. The curricula explicitly relate educational contents to the catechetic, pastoral and evangelization ones;

2. The second type represents looser confessional religious education. It is more of a confessional-cultural than a doctrinal and normative approach to the phenomenon of religion. Such an approach is characteristic of many Northern and Western European countries. The main goal is primary education—to help in building the student's worldview and improvement of his/her general education.

3. The third type, non-confessional religious education, characterizes, for example, Slovenia. The subject *Religions and ethics* stresses the educational level of presenting religious contents, with emphasis on the transfer of tradition (emphasizing Christianity as the predominant religion in both Slovenia and Europe) and advocating human rights.

4. The fourth variant—without religious education is presented in France and the Netherlands.

Different European approaches to teaching religious contents, Grace Davie vividly puts, is the European "comprehensive spectrum of religious education – from the almost undiluted confessional message to the conscious preparation of children for living in a world where a wide range of religious ideas makes a significant part of cultural exchange".[23]

In the post-communist era, most of the transitional countries, including Croatia, opted for confessional religious instruction with elements of traditional catechism in public schools (which represented a continuation of the kind of religious education that existed before 1945). Their aim was to indicate the affiliation to Christian Europe where, in the meantime, opposite trends had become a reality. In most of the Western European countries, in accordance with social and religious changes, confessional religious instruction in public schools lost elements of catechism and acquired elements of loose confessional approach to the phenomenon of religion.[24]

Introduction of Religious Instruction in Public Schools: Key Documents

According to the decision of the Ministry of Education and Culture of the Republic of Croatia, confessional religious instruction was introduced in public schools as an elective subject in 1991/1992. The Ministry came to a decision on introducing confessional religious instruction without consultation with experts, professors and teachers and public opinion. The Catholic Church was given a mandate to define the way of teaching, textbooks, as well as to provide a necessary number of instructors and to train them.

Based on Article 2, the Agreement on cooperation in the field of education and culture an additional Contract between the Government of the Republic of Croatia with the Croatian Bishops' Conference about Catholic catechism in public schools and public preschool institutions was signed in 1999.[25] That contract regulates Catholic religious instruction in public primary and secondary schools as an optional subject equal to other subjects, the number of students needed in order to organize the class (7 students), the obligation of the Church and school authorities to inform parents and students about the goals and content of the subject, the number of hours per week (2), the competency for creating curriculum (Croatian Bishops' Conference) and who confirms it (Minister of Science, Education, and Sports), the responsibilities for teacher training and the level of education needed for the teachers. The Croatian Bishops' Conference is obliged to submit to the ministry a list of institutions in which teacher training is undertaken. The National Catechetic Institute is responsible for Catholic religious instruction in schools. The diocesan bishop and a counselor in diocesan offices for catechesis together take care of religious instruction in pre-school institutions and in primary and secondary schools.[26] The production of curriculum and textbooks followed the promptness of reaching political and legal decisions regarding introducing of religious instruction.

The *Program of Catholic Instruction in Primary school* was made in 1999. The Catholic religious instruction, according to the *Program*, emphasizes the holistic education of man, bearing in mind the religious dimension and the promotion of personal, social, universal, and religious values. The confessional characteristic of religious instruction is based on the universal educational and cultural meaning of religious facts for the person, culture, and the society. The principles on which religious instruction is based are the following: faith in God and man, ecumenical openness, open dialogue and correlation in catechetic education (cross-curricular teaching in accordance with the principles of holistic education) and an intercultural approach.[27] The *Program* highlights, as an important aspect, the correlation between religious instruction and other subjects ("in accordance with the principles of full education of students").[28]

The purpose of the Catholic religious instruction in primary school is, according to the *Program*, to provide a systematic and harmonious theological-ecclesiastic and anthropological-pedagogic connection of God's revelation and church tradition with the experiences of students. Its aim is to familiarize students with the Catholic religion through systematic, holistic, ecumenical and open dialogue at different levels: the informative-cognitive, experiential, and active levels, in order to reach the maturity of the Christian faith and achieve holistic human and religious education of students. This compulsory-elective subject does not have any alternative in primary school.

The aforementioned items from the *Program* and some research findings show that the Catholic instruction in Croatian schools appears as a strict catechesis (growth and development in faith) with a pastoral aim (connection with ecclesiastical practices and celebration) and an evangelization aim (testifying to faith in one's personal and social life).[29]

Public Discussions and Controversies on the Introduction of Religious Instruction in Public Schools

According to Marinović Bobinac, Marinović Jerolimov, 2006, the 'first public discussions on introduction of the religious instruction have started by midst of 1990. Political authorities have speeded up this process which the dialogue between the representatives of religious communities and scholar public could not follow. The opinion that the politics made this decision and that the discussions organized in a hurry were a mere alibi and have been held only because of the need for, as the newspaper *Slobodna Dalmacija* stated, "quasi-scientific verification of the political decision" is prevailing in the public'.[30] The discussions concentrated on two possible approaches to teaching religion in public school: confessional and non-confessional. The basic tone has been given by the theologians of the Catholic Church favouring the confessional approach. Two streams have been crystallized among the participants of the discussion: the majority and more "conservative" one which advocated religious instruction, mostly consisted of Catholic theologians and another minority and more "liberal" one (that, besides some Catholic theologians, consisted of the members of the minority religious communities and secular experts) that was pointing at the danger of possible politicization of the religion and advocated non-confessional subject that most of them called "religious culture".[31]

The main arguments for introducing Catholic religious instruction were as follows[32]:

1. Catholic religious tradition is deeply rooted in the Croatian cultural heritage[33];
2. In the past religious contents have been suppressed or distorted for ideological reasons;
3. It enables getting acquainted with and developing one's own cultural-religious identity and respecting somebody else's.

The arguments against introducing religious instruction in public schools were as follows[34]:

1. Religion cannot be the frame or philosophy of life in a public school and the separation of State and Church should be respected in a consistent manner;
2. The deficit of spirituality and knowledge about religions should be compensated with non-confessional instruction taking into account a multiconfessional character of society, as spirituality should not be reduced to the confessional model;
3. There is a danger of proselytism—since confessional religious instruction, such as carried out in Churches, can become the subject of confessional and other worldview misunderstanding[35];
4. Religious instruction as upbringing in belief and for belief belongs to family and religious communities;
5. The place for doctrinarian contents is within religious communities.

After introducing confessional religious instruction, the subject that was created by a sort of summarizing of parish religious instruction and confessional religious culture, the debates on introducing a confessional neutral subject (*religious culture*) more or less stopped. Only sporadic some isolated expressions of support in its favour could be heard and some initiatives emerged. One of the initiatives is briefly presented.

Protagora—Association for the protection of rights of irreligious persons and the promotion of irreligious concept of the world was the most persistent. After a sequence of demands to resolve such a discriminative situation—to introduce alternative subject, they proposed to the Ministry[36] a peaceful solution of the dispute[37] (2012), under the following conditions:

- The Ministry should admit the fact of discrimination of the students (concerning faith, worldview or other convictions), who do not want to attend religious instruction and do not have the possibility to choose an alternative subject;
- The Ministry should add the alternative subject to the Curriculum as soon as possible;
- The Ministry should determine the deadline for introducing of the alternative subject.

After failure of that initiative, *Protagora* sued the Ministry of Science, Education and Sport (2013) in the *County Court* in Zagreb, because the Curriculum for primary schools did not provide the subject alternative to religious instruction, for students who did not want to attend religious instruction because of worldview or other convictions. The *County Court* decided that there was no discrimination and the *Supreme Court* acknowledged the *County Court* sentence.[38] *Protagora* continued with a procedure on the *Constitutional Court* (2014) as highest legal instance in Croatia.[39] The procedure is still not finished.

Till date, a similar subject has not been introduced in public schools. The concept of non-confessional subject (*religious culture*) was strongly criticized by the Catholic Church, even by the cardinal Bozanić who wrote about an intention "that through some *religious culture* syncretistic religious message will be introduced, some kind of neutral religion as a part of the new world order.[40]

THEORETICAL AND METHODOLOGICAL STARTING POINTS

The main goal of this paper has been to find the position of atheism/ irreligiosity in Catholic textbooks for primary schools (from first to eighth grade) and to analyse public responses on a potentially discriminative contents. The above analysed social context, legal acts, process of the introducing of religious instruction in Croatian schools, public discussion and controversies have been used as a starting point in this paper. In addition to the analysis of Catholic religious instruction textbooks for primary schools, letters, documents and reports of different public actors and related contents on some web pages and portals have been analysed.

Some aspects of the thesis of Srđan Vrcan that confessional belonging and religious self-identification in Croatia became an almost general phenomenon and an indicator of social authenticity in the state, political society, civil society and the public, while confessional, and religious non-belonging become an indicator of social abnormality, will be considered in this paper.[41]

RESEARCH RESULTS

According to the data of the Ministry of Science, Higher Education and Technology for the school year 2014/2015, 91.61% of children in Croatian primary schools attend Catholic religious instruction. As already noted, there is no alternative subject for the students of primary schools who do not attend religious instruction, which causes certain problems for students, parents and schools.[42] According to the last Census conducted in 2011, 5% of the citizens declared themselves as nonreligious, atheists, agnostics and sceptics. It could be supposed that most of the students of primary schools who do not attend religious instruction are children of nonreligious parents.

Textbook Analysis

Religious instruction textbooks (the same as *Program*) are firmly based on doctrinal teaching of the Catholic Church and its normative theology. Textbooks communicated moral values originating from Catholic ethical teaching—from the Catholic truth and the Catholic origin of morality. The review of programmes and textbooks showed that they emphasize the formative nature of the Christian (Catholic) values in education—helping to form the Christian (Catholic) identity.[43] According to the formulations in the analysed textbooks, on Catholic (Christian) religion, it is not presented as one of the existing worldviews in the world (Croatia), but as the only genuine religion. This is visible from the number of statements in all the textbooks.

A general tolerant attitude towards all people, regardless of race, nation and religion is present in all the analysed textbooks. Such an attitude is documented by the quotation from the UN Declaration on human rights: "Everybody has a right to freedom of thinking, consciousness, and faith...", by the corresponding quotations of non-Christian religious books, and religious persons which "support Christians in a struggle against evil" (Confucius, Buddha, Bhagavadgita, Kur'an...), and by the words of famous writers and philosophers (M. Selimović, G. Flaubert, R. Tagore, T. Ujević, A. Huxley, B. Pascal...).

"Building of just and better world is not a task of some individuals only, but the inhabitants of all world countries, members of all races and religions, religious people and atheists, people of all professions. Nobody is excluded. *Christians have to contribute on special and dependable way.* They are invited to do that by Jesus Christ".[44]

Unlike such a generally open and tolerant attitude towards "all people of good will" (including even atheists) and the context of "ecumenical openness"[45] that is present, to some extent, towards other world religions,[46] the books authors extract atheism and the new religious movements[47] as completely unacceptable.

Teaching atheism, authors of the eighth class textbook highlight headlines: *Every human seeks God. Religiosity exists in each human. All human by the nature is turned to God.* Atheism is neutrally defined in general, as "an absence of belief in God". But religious indifference is stated as the only origin of atheism. Non-religious person "is born and raised in religious desert".[48] Atheism is not considered as an authentic worldview, among other worldviews, with authentic values. Besides theoretical (philosophical) atheism there is also practical atheism. As a worldview, it is influenced by science and technology (if they are uncritically accepted), success and fame, humanism without God and customary religiosity. "As a way of life, atheism was introduced by the new ideologies and worldviews, glorifying the man and his power".[49] Atheism is presented as a worldview "that intends to push out from the person any religiosity and any connection with God". All people, according to the textbooks, are basically religious, but religious upbringing is necessary in order to recognize God.

Atheism is situated in the context of extremely negatively connotated notions, as spiritism, blasphemy, simony, curse, damn, perjury and sacrilege are. The textbook authors stated: "The biggest sins against the first Gods commandment ("You shall have no other gods before Me") are: superstition, idolatry, horoscopes and astrology, augury and magic, blasphemy and simony, atheism and indifferentism".[50]

Atheism is absolutely unacceptable from the Catholic point of view. According to the textbook authors, atheism as a secular worldview has no credibility and integrity. It is completely wrong. Clear evangelization recommendation for students is present as follows: "Christian should know to recognize contemporary forms of atheism... The best way to prevent atheism is knowledge about faith and testimony of the faith".[51]

Authors highlight the importance of evangelization in cases of atheism and during contacts with atheists: 'If Christianity as the "civilisation of love would be offered", if persons, media, and society would be engaged for the truth about the men, and the God', the number of atheists in the world would be gradually decreased.[52]

To corroborate the state of emptiness and hopelessness of people "caught" by atheism and similar ideologies, the authors use quotes from *Munch's Scream, Munch's Fear* and *Friedrich's Wreck of Hope* along the text. They put, as well, quotations of some planetary eminent persons, for example, Goethe ("Who does not know to take from the three thousand years deep origin, lives from today till tomorrow".[53]

The authors chose one of Pope John Paul II's quotes, which is completely opposite to the spirit of the relationship towards atheism (and especially the atheists) of the Second Vatican Council, proclaiming tolerance and dialogue with non-believers and the spirit of the Pope Frances towards atheists. The Pope John Paul II said: "Atheism is upbringing without God. Some people claim that atheism is an expression of prosperity. From the experiences of the newest events we know that it is not possible to raise noble people without God or against God. On the contrary, without God were raised people like those who created Ošviencim".[54]

The authors even did not mention the distinction made by the Second Vatican Council between atheism as ideology and the atheist as a person who should be taken with respect and empathy. As a ground of relation to atheism, the authors take some general conclusions towards atheism presented by the Council's Constitution *Gaudium et spes* (1965), but they do not take into account conclusions of the main document explicitly devoted to the phenomenon of atheism—*Dialogue with non-believers*. A fundamental presumption of the relationship towards non-believers is the dignity of the human being. A fundamental presumption of its realization is the acceptance of the pluralism: acceptance of the person thinking different as equal, as the person's dignity and freedom to think responsively, in accordance with his consciousness and also, the acceptance of the fundamental equality of his thoughts nevertheless and because of his difference.[55]

The recent attitudes of Pope Frances towards atheism follow the continuity with the spirit of the Council document *Dialogue with nonbelievers*. Unlike the chosen quote of The Pope John Paul II, Pope Frances highlights the continuity with the II Vatican Council, advocating the Church's openness towards the world—to all people. "The Church is not custom", says the Pope, "it must not be a barrier to anyone, irregular people do not exist".[56] He also said: "Lord redeemed all the people, not only Catholics but as well those who do not believe".[57]

Between the hundreds of possible choices from the rich inheritance of Church social doctrine during and after the Second Vatican Council about atheists (in addition to the mentioned *Dialogue with non-believers* and pope Frances' statements), between hundreds of possible choices from the rich inheritance of pope John Paul II, textbook authors chose only such a terrible sentence.

Social Reactions on the Textbooks Treatment of Atheism

The lesson on atheism provoked a lot of controversies and polemics in public: parents, scholars, media, civil associations and even the Ombudsman for children reacted. Reactions especially intensified after an open letter to the Ombudsman for children (sent as well to the Ministry of science, education and sport and to a few more addresses). The letter was sent by a mother atheist, protesting against discrimination of atheist children in public schools.

This is a part of her letter to the Ombudsman for children:

"I am addressing you, as a Mum of an atheist girl, the only one in the class who does not attend religious instruction. The school does not know what to do with her during religious instruction class and she stays in class. Fortunately, she skipped a lesson on atheism (because of illness), but she was mentioned as an atheist during the class... The teacher did not use the lesson from the textbook... but, those who will teach from it, will teach that my daughter could not be noble..., that she could be the possible creator of something like Auschwitz... that students, as devoted Catholics, have an assignment to suppress her worldview as soon as they meet her (similar situation already happened...) This is not only complaint, this is my attempt to explain that such awful situations are taking place in our public schools. I know, individuals cannot do a lot, but institutions could do. All the best, Mum".[58]

The question was set in public: how is it possible that in a secular state where public schools are financed by the budget, by the money of all employed citizens—and of the atheists and agnostics, such intolerant, discriminatory speech has been tolerated?

The already mentioned Association for the protection of rights of irreligious persons and the promotion of irreligious concept of the world —*Protagora*[59] also sent a letter to the Minister of science, education and sport and to the Ombudsman for children. All complaints related to the textbook for Catholic religious instructions for the eighth grade of primary school "With Christ in life" and discrimination of atheists.[60] They requested the Ministry to acquaint with the content of the textbook and to react promptly, in accordance with its authorities.

The Ombudsman for children[61] reacted immediately. Controversial lectures in which persons of atheistic worldview are presented extremely negatively she considered as unacceptable. She wrote: "Provoked by this (mum atheist—op.a.) and some other parents' complaints, we recommend to the Ministry of Science, Education and Sport to inspect the textbook's content on the basis of its legal authority and take measures to decline contents opposite to principles of the democratic order relating to protection of human and minority rights, fundamental rights and freedoms of man and citizen... Besides, the *Convention on the rights of the Child* guarantees rights to every child, without discrimination of child, parents or foster parents".[62] The Ombudsman for children asked for an explanation from the Ministry concerning the textbook of the eighth grade, particularly concerning contents relating to atheism. She said that the Ministry, which approves and pays the publishing of these textbooks has to check their content.

At the beginning of the school year 2015/2016, the Ombudsman for children sent to the Ministry 20 recommendations on the protection of the rights and interests of children in educational institutions concerning the most frequent complaints about the breaking rights of children in the educational process. Two of them directly relate to religious education. The first recommendation reminds all educational institutions of the obligation to respect provisions on the implementation of religious education and religious upbringing and the *Law on prevention of discrimination*. It relates to the praxis of organizing of religious contents inside schools. She highlights: "The engagement of students, including those who are followers of some other religions or who are not religious, to attend religious events in school, points to discrimination of children on the base of religion and/or conviction and violation of the *Convention on children rights*".[63] The second recommendation relates again to removing of discriminating contents from the religious instructions textbooks. She claims that some textbook contents detract and discriminate non-religious children. That is why she sends recommendations to the Ministry of Science, Education and Sport and as well to the Croatian Bishops' Conference. At the end, she highlights the importance to carry out the supervision of the textbook contents and to turn away discriminatory contents.[64] She reminds also 'that the UN *Committee on the rights of the child* recommended recently to the Republic of Croatia to foster intercultural and interreligious dialogue within local community and schools to prevent discrimination of any group of children. She warned: "Attitudes on atheism from the religious instructions textbooks are not in accordance with the recommended dialogue".[65]

Despite the Ombudsman for children pointing out that there is a significant increase in complaints on the issue of discriminatory treating of atheism and atheists in the religious instruction textbooks from year to year, the Ministry of Science, Education and Sport in its answer[66] interpreted the problem as a misunderstanding, referring to the content of religious instruction *Program* only, highlighting the general goal from the *Program*: "to accept an attitude of tolerance towards nonbelievers", not mentioning textbooks at all. The Ministry highlights that they, while reaching the *Program*, took into account the promotion of tolerance towards all groups of students in the educational system. The Ministry informed that its administration responsible for the textbooks together with the Croatian Catechetic Office, will examine disputable allegations and arrange for possible changes in the textbook "With Christ in life" to eliminate all misunderstandings and possible manipulations indicating promotion of intolerance to anybody.[67] But till today, the same religious instruction textbooks with controversial contents are in use.

CONCLUSION

There were a lot of indicators of politicization of religion in Croatian society from the 1990s, especially in the periods under the governments of the conservative Croatian Democratic Community (HDZ).

The strong link between the Church and State, the privileged position of the Catholic Church and its strong influence within the society were maintained. The influence of the Church in political and social life is additionally strengthened by the agreements signed between The Holy See and The Republic of Croatia. One of illustrative example for that claim is the *Agreement on the issues in the field of education and culture. The Agreement's* provision that "the educational system in public pre-schools and schools including higher education institutions will take into account Christian ethics values"—implies not only a school subject called religious instruction, but the educational system in general. That provision favours Christian ethic values in relation to ethical values of other religious and irreligious worldviews and opens the path to possible and real discrimination, especially among the most sensible category of the population: primary and secondary school students. That is clearly visible from the analysed textbooks and the reactions from the actors of civil and political society.

Textbooks analysis indicates that religious instruction textbooks are not tolerant and dialogical in the case of atheism and irreligious people at all. Atheism is absolutely unacceptable from the Catholic point of view. Textbooks do not develop a spirit of tolerance towards atheism and atheists postulated by the Second Vatican Council, but offer to students a confusing image of the world, in which, non-believers (living with their parents among believers) become "people with mistake" and "an object of urgent correcting". Textbooks' instruction to the students is quite clear: not acceptance of difference but correction of atheists and prevention of atheism, by evangelization. The textbooks transform the Second Vatican Council dialogue principle "to know to better understand" in "to know to prevent and convert".

Periods of ruling of left coalition (with the Social Democratic Party (SDP) at the head) in the last mandate (2010–2015) was characterized by contemporary tensions between some ministers and Catholic bishops concerning worldview issues, mostly in the field of education, and by the general distrust of the Church towards the Government. The Government was very cautious towards the Church and showed such an attitude during the whole mandate. Basically, the left coalition preferred compromise to confrontation, preferring "closing eyes" to solving the problem. It is clearly visible, for example, from the subject of this paper: the position of atheism in religious instruction textbooks. The Minister who was involved in that case and most of the Government members are atheists or agnostics, but they do nothing to check and solve this case of discrimination.

The thesis of Srđan Vrcan that confessional belonging and religious self-identification in Croatia became indicators of social authenticity while confessional and religious non-belonging became indicators of social abnormality, has not been the characteristic social climate in Croatia in general, at least not in the past 5 years (2010–2015). However, it is acknowledged by the example of the treatment of atheism in public schools and the unsuccessful actions of different actors of political and civil society.

NOTES

1. Gordan Črpić, Siniša Zrinščak „Između identiteta i i svakodnevnog života", in Josip Baloban (ed.) *U potrazi za identitetom* (Zagreb: Golden marketing—Tehnička knjiga, 2005), pp. 45–84; Gordan Črpić, Siniša Zrinščak, „Religija, društvo, politika: komparativna perspektiva, in Josip Baloban, Krunoslav Nikodem, Siniša Zrinščak (eds.): *Vrednote u Hrvatskoj i u Europi* (Zagreb: Kršćanska sadašnjost, Katolički bogoslovni fakultet, 2014), pp. 13–42; Dinka Marinović Jerolimov, „Religijske promjene u tranzicijskim uvjetima u Hrvatskoj: promjene u dimenzijama religijske identifikacije i prakse" *Sociologija sela*, 1–2 (2000), pp. 43–80; Dinka Marinović Jerolimov „Tradicionalna religioznost u Hrvatskoj 2004: između kolektivnoga i individualnoga" *Sociologija sela*. 2 (2005), pp. 303–339.
2. Peter Berger, *The Desecularization of the World. Resurgent Religion and World Politics* (Washington D.C.: Ethic and Public Policy Center; Grand Rapids, Michigen: William B. Erdmans Publishing Company, 1999); Grace Davie, *Religija u suvremenoj Europi: Mutacija sjećanja* (Zagreb: Golden marketing—Tehnička knjiga, 2005); Danielle Hervieu-Leger, *Religion as a Chain of Memory* (New Brunswick, New Jersey: Rutgers University Press, 2000).
3. Srđan Vrcan, *Vjera u vrtlozima tranzicije* (Split: Glas Dalmacije. Revija Dalmatinske akcije, 2001); Ankica Marinović Bobinac, „Images of the Religious Other in Religious Instruction Textbooks in Croatia", in Christian Moe and Zorica Kuburić (eds.) *Images of the Religious Others* (Novi Sad: CEIR i Kotor Network, 2008), pp. 201–217.
4. Srđan Vrcan, Vjera u vrtlozima tranzicije.
5. Ibid.
6. Ivan Cifrić, „Percepcija nekih odnosa crkve i države i uloga crkve i religije u društvu", *Sociologija sela*, 1–2(2000), pp. 227–269; Gordan Črpić,

Siniša Zrinščak, „Između identiteta i i svakodnevnog života"; Gordan Črpić, Siniša Zrinščak „Religija, društvo, politika: komparativna perspektiva; Dinka Marinović Jerolimov, „Religijske promjene u tranzicijskim uvjetima u Hrvatskoj: promjene u dimenzijama religijske identifikacije i prakse"; Dinka Marinović Jerolimov „Tradicionalna religioznost u Hrvatskoj 2004: između kolektivnoga i individualnoga".

7. Ankica Marinović Bobinac, Dinka Marinović Jerolimov, "Religious Education in Croatia", in Zorica Kuburić and Christian Moe (eds.) *Religion and Pluralism in Education. Comparative Approaches in the Western Balkans* (Novi Sad: CEIR & Kotor Network, 2006), pp. 39–71.

8. Ivan Cifrić, Cifrić, „Percepcija nekih odnosa crkve i države i uloga crkve i religije u društvu"; Ivan Cifrić, „Svećenici, Crkva i društvo: moguće promjene. Javna uloga svećenika i odnosi između vjerskih zajednica" *Sociologija sela*. 2(2005), pp. 439–470; Gordan Črpić, Siniša Zrinščak „Religija, društvo, politika: komparativna perspektiva; Goran Goldberger, „Revitalizacija religije u sjeni nasljeđa liberalne zakonske regulative: stavovi prema pobačaju" *Sociologija sela*, 2(2005), pp. 409–438; Ankica Marinović Bobinac; Goran Goldberger, „Glas koncila – poslanje ili tek ime: analiza sadržaja komentara u razdoblju društvena tranzicije" *Sociologija i prostor*, 3–4(2007), pp. 269–300; Ankica Marinović Bobinac, Dinka Marinović Jerolimov, "Religious Education in Croatia"; Ankica Marinović, Ivan Markešić, „Vjerske zajednice u Hrvatskoj pred europskim izazovima", in Vlado Puljiz, Slaven Ravlić and Velimir Visković (eds.) *Hrvatska u EU: Kako dalje?*, (Zagreb: Centar za demokraciju i pravo Miko Tripalo, 2012), pp. 349–372; Srđan Vrcan, *Vjera u vrtlozima tranzicije*.

9. Siniša Zrinščak, Dinka Marinović Jerolimov, Ankica Marinović, Branko Ančić, „Church and State in Croatia: Legal framework, religious instruction, and social expectations", in Sabrina Ramet (ed.) *Religion and Politics in Central and South-Eastern Europe: Challenges Since 1989*, (New York, Basinstoke: Palgrave Macmillan, 2014), pp. 131–154.

10. Ankica Marinović Bobinac, Dinka Marinović Jerolimov, „Catholic Religious Education in Public Schools in Croatia: Attitudes towards Other Religions in Primary School Textbooks", in Gabriella Pusztai (ed.) *Education and Church in Central and Eastern Europe at First Glance*, (Debrecen: University of Debrecen—Center for Higher Education, Research and Development; Hungarian Academy of Sciences & Religion and Values: Central and Eastern European Research Network, 2008), pp. 179–192.

11. Comparative data are taken from five researches conducted on the representative sample in Croatia (1984–2009): *Social Structure and Quality of Life* (1984, 1989); *Social Structure and Quality of Life in the Period*

of Transition (1996); *Social Structure and Quality of Life: Social and Religious Changes* (2004); *International Social Survey Program—Module Religion* (2009).

12. Dinka Marinović Jerolimov, „Nereligioznost u Hrvatskoj 1968–1990.", in Štefica Bahtijarević (ed.) *Prilozi izučavanju nereligioznosti i ateizma 2* (Zagreb: Institut za društvena istraživanja, 1993), pp. 87–136.

13. Ibid.

14. Constitution of the Republic of Croatia, in *Narodne novine (Official Gazette)* 41, May 7 and June 15, 2001.

15. Siniša Zrinščak, Dinka Marinović Jerolimov, Ankica Marinović, Branko Ančić, „Church and State in Croatia: Legal framework, religious instruction, and social expectations".

16. Ankica Marinović, Ivan Markešić, „Vjerske zajednice u Hrvatskoj pred europskim izazovima"; Ivan Padjen, „Church and State in Croatia", in Silvio Ferrari and W. Cole Durham Jr. (eds.) *Law and Religion in Post-Communist Europe*, (Leuven, Paris, Dudley, MA, 2003), pp. 57–80; Siniša Zrinščak, „Religion and Society in Tension in Croatia: Social and Legal Status of Religious Communities", in James T. Richardson (ed.) *Regulating Religion, Case Studies from around the Globe*, (New York: Cluver Academic Plenum Publishers, 2004), pp. 299–318; Siniša Zrinščak, Dinka Marinović Jerolimov, Ankica Marinović, Branko Ančić, „Church and State in Croatia: Legal framework, religious instruction, and social expectations".

17. Ankica Marinović, Ivan Markešić, „Vjerske zajednice u Hrvatskoj pred europskim izazovima"; Ivan Padjen, „Church and State in Croatia"; Srđan Vrcan, „Bog i državna batina"in *Feral Tribune*, 2.2.2002.

18. That is one of the most contested provisions by the critics from civil society.

19. The State authorities were often criticized by the actors of civil society because of neglecting to monitor the contents and quality of religious instruction.

20. The third item provoked some controversies in the public, especially among civil society actors and scholars.

21. Ankica Marinović Bobinac, Dinka Marinović Jerolimov, „Catholic Religious Education in Public Schools in Croatia: Attitudes towards Other Religions in Primary School Textbooks".

22. Ankica Marinović Bobinac, „Comparative Analysis of Curricula for Religious Education: Exemples of Four Catholic Countries"*Metodika*. 2(2007), pp. 408–424.

23. Grace Davie, *Religija u suvremenoj Europi: Mutacija sjećanja*.

24. Zdenko Kodelja, Terrice Bassler, *Religion and Schooling in Open Society: A Framework for Informed Dialogue* (Ljubljana, Open Society Institute, 2004); Ankica Marinović Bobinac, „Comparative Analysis of Curricula for Religious Education: Exemples of Four Catholic Countries".

25. The first programme of Catholic religious instruction for primary schools was published in 1998. As a comprehensive and renewed document it was re-published in 1998.
26. Ankica Marinović Bobinac, Dinka Marinović Jerolimov, "Religious Education in Croatia"; Siniša Zrinščak, Dinka Marinović Jerolimov, Ankica Marinović, Branko Ančić, „Church and State in Croatia: Legal framework, religious instruction, and social expectations".
27. Ankica Marinović Bobinac, „Comparative Analysis of Curricula for Religious Education: Exemples of Four Catholic Countries"; Ankica Marinović Bobinac, Dinka Marinović Jerolimov, "Religious Education in Croatia".
28. Ankica Marinović Bobinac, „Comparative Analysis of Curricula for Religious Education: Exemples of Four Catholic Countries". That aspect provoked a lot of protest of different actors, mostly those from the civil society, because of the intention to interfere the whole public education with Catholic values.
29. Ankica Marinović Bobinac, „Comparative Analysis of Curricula for Religious Education: Exemples of Four Catholic Countries"; Ankica Marinović Bobinac, Dinka Marinović Jerolimov, "Religious Education in Croatia"; Ankica Marinović Bobinac, „Images of the Religious Other in Religious Instruction Textbooks in Croatia", in Christian Moe and Zorica Kuburić (eds.) *Images of the Religious Others*, (Novi Sad: CEIR i Kotor Network, 2008), pp. 201–217.
30. "Vjeronauk – nova ideologizacija?" in *Slobodna Dalmacija*, September 23rd, 1990.
31. Ankica Marinović Bobinac, Dinka Marinović Jerolimov, "Religious Education in Croatia"; Siniša Zrinščak, Dinka Marinović Jerolimov, Ankica Marinović, Branko Ančić, „Church and State in Croatia: Legal framework, religious instruction, and social expectations".
32. Ibid.
33. In the next Contract on the Catholic Religious Instruction in Public Schools and Religious Education in Public Pre-school Facilities this wording was supplemented as follows: …"what shall be taken into account in the Croatian educational system."
34. Ankica Marinović Bobinac, Dinka Marinović Jerolimov, "Religious Education in Croatia"; Siniša Zrinščak, Dinka Marinović Jerolimov, Ankica Marinović, Branko Ančić, „Church and State in Croatia: Legal framework, religious instruction, and social expectations".
35. That argument became relevant for different actors that criticized confessional instruction in public school.
36. The same demand PROTAGORA sent to President of the Croatian Government, Ombudsman, Ombudsman for children, Office of the UNICEF in Croatia and The Head of EU Delegation in Croatia.

37. http://www.protagora.hr/WebSuite/UserData/Dokumenti/PDF/
    zahtjev_mirno_rje%C5%A1enje_spora-finall.
38. http://www.protagora.hr/Clanak/Tuzba-presuda-i-zalba-u-slucaju-
    Protagora-protiv-diskriminacije-ucenika.
39. http://www.protagora.hr/Clanak/Priopcenje-o-podnosenju-ustavne-
    tuzbe.
40. Stručni katehetski kolokvij, 2000 (Ankica Marinović Bobinac, Dinka
    Marinović Jerolimov, "Religious Education in Croatia")
41. Srđan Vrcan, *Vjera u vrtlozima tranzicije.*
42. Branko, Ančić, Tamara Puhovski, *Vjera u obrazovanje i obrazovanje u
    vjeri: stavovi i iskustva nereligioznih roditelja prema religiji i vjeronauku
    u javnim školama u Republici Hrvatskoj* (Zagreb: Forum za slobodu
    odgoja, 2011).
43. Ankica Marinović Bobinac, Dinka Marinović Jerolimov, "Religious
    Education in Croatia"; Siniša Zrinščak, Dinka Marinović Jerolimov,
    Ankica Marinović, Branko Ančić, „Church and State in Croatia: Legal
    framework, religious instruction, and social expectations".
44. *Pozvani na slobodu/Invited to freedom/*(textbook for 6th grade) (Zagreb:
    Kršćanska sadašnjost, 2003).
45. Programme for Catholic Religious Instruction in Primary Schools,
    Narodne novine (Official Gazette) 156 (3 October, 2003).
46. The textbooks authors present monotheistic religions (Christianity,
    Judaism and Islam) and Oriental religions (Hinduism, Buddhism,
    Confucianism and Taoism) respecting the principle of "ecumenical open-
    ness". Non-Catholic religions have been treated systematically and tol-
    erantly with present limitation that is inherent to confessional approach
    (Ankica Marinović Bobinac, Dinka Marinović Jerolimov, „Catholic
    Religious Education in Public Schools in Croatia: Attitudes towards
    Other Religions in Primary School Textbooks".
47. Tolerant and dialogical approach gives up in the case of new religious
    movements whose authenticity and distinctness was denied. New reli-
    gious movements are presented as a consequence of different shortcom-
    ings of society and the Church. The use of the term 'sect' in the context
    of new religious movements was negatively connotated ('the youth is
    often victim of the sects', 'sects—alienation from the own roots', 'ado-
    lescence as a time of escape', 'making god to one's own desire (golden
    calf)', 'non-critical interpretation of the Bible'...) Evangelical goal is
    emphasized in the textbooks of religious instruction. It is visible from
    many titles in the textbooks contents: 'Jesus Christ is a fulfilment of the
    longing present in all world religions"; "Jesus set me free from idols—
    power, pleasure, dependence, different religious movements and sects"...
    (Ankica Marinović Bobinac, Dinka Marinović Jerolimov, „Catholic

Religious Education in Public Schools in Croatia: Attitudes towards Other Religions in Primary School Textbooks"; Ankica Marinović Bobinac, „Images of the Religious Other in Religious Instruction Textbooks in Croatia".

48. *S Kristom u život/With Christ in life/*(textbook for 8th grade) Zagreb: Kršćanska sadašnjost, 2005), p. 38.
49. Ibid.
50. *Zajedno u ljubavi/Together in Love/*(textbook for 7th grade) (Zagreb: Kršćanska sadašnjost, 2003), p. 28.
51. *S Kristom u život/With Christ in life/*(textbook for 8th grade) (Zagreb: Kršćanska sadašnjost, 2005), p. 40.
52. *S Kristom u život/With Christ in life/*(textbook for 8th grade) Zagreb: Kršćanska sadašnjost, 2005), p. 38. In a daily preparation for religious instruction class relating to the lesson on atheism, one of the teachers set questions: In what extent are we—believers responsible for existing of atheism and religious indifference? How can we influence on "conversion" from the atheism? As a goal of the lesson on atheism, a teacher states: Students should know to recognize atheism and they should, as believers, intercede for truth about men and God (http://katehetski.rinadbiskupija.hr/upload/2010/OS/Ateizam%2520i%2520vjerska%2520 25 March, 2012).
53. *S Kristom u život/With Christ in life/*(textbook for 8th grade) Zagreb: Kršćanska sadašnjost, 2005), p. 38.
54. Ibid, p. 39.
55. *Dijalog s onima koji ne vjeruju* (Zagreb: Kršćanska sadašnjost, 1968).
56. Silvije Tomašević, *Papa Franjo* (Zagreb: Profil, 2014).
57. Ibid.
58. The letter was published on 19 October 2014, at Internet portal INDEXHR.
59. *Protagora* started legal procedure against the Ministry of Science, Education and Sport for the identification of discrimination of primary school students not attending religious instruction.
60. *Guide for confirmands* fosters intolerance towards atheists in a similar way: „ Some people are atheists because they consider that it is nice to think about one's self as a kind of „god" who can determine what is right and what is wrong. The second name for a person for whom his EGO is the centre of the world is an egoist. Egoists are, all of us have sometimes experienced that, pretty uncongenial people. Logically, egoists are atheists because their image of the world does not imply anybody bigger, more beautiful, smarter, more sacred or more valuable of respect than they are" (Tportal.hr, 30 October 2014).

61. The Ombudsman for children confirmed in public that she receives a lot of complaints concerning primary school problems connecting with religious education: problems with organization and implementation of religious instruction—for non-attendants of religious instruction concerning timetable, because there is no alternative subject, the set of problems which coerce some parents to register their children to religious education—to be safe that children are under a teacher's surveillance, to avoid segregation of their children... .
62. Tportal.hr, 30 October 2014
63. Ibid.
64. Ibid.
65. Ibid.
66. Ibid.
67. Ibid.

CHAPTER 8

Politicization of Religious Textbooks in Slovenia

Maca Jogan

INTRODUCTION

Religious education of (young) people is undoubtedly necessary condition for the lasting existence of any religion. Therefore it is one of the key activities also of the Catholic Church (CC), which is the greatest church in Slovene society. Generally, the way of religious education and its effectiveness depends on the church's position within the social structure and its power (and authority) distribution. The degree of church's social power depends on the complexity of the institutional support that varies in regard to the inclusion or exclusion of the church from the (socially recognised, legitimised) public sphere. The historic dynamics of the Slovene society in the twentieth and the twenty-first centuries, designated by the early socialism and post-socialism can be considered as a case of the CC adjustability to the changeable social circumstances. During the socialist era, CC activity was mainly determined by the sharp separation from the state and through its installation into the private sphere (of family), but by the post-socialist changes it really

M. Jogan (✉)
University of Ljubljana, Ljubljana, Slovenia

G. Ognjenović and J. Jozelić (eds.), *Education in Post-Conflict Transition*, Palgrave Studies in Religion, Politics, and Policy, https://doi.org/10.1007/978-3-319-56605-4_8

entered (by the main door and also supported through its own activity) the public space with explicit wishes to achieve the monopoly position on all levels and spheres of society (lost by "totalitarian" socialism). This desired goal (realisable by the new evangelisation) is justified by the necessary completion of "unfinished" democratisation and through the CC conviction that order and peace would prevail when trust as related by it is accepted in its entirety.

This chapter will be focused on the question, of how, in this modern age, religious instruction has been included in the formation of active Christians and in what way the content orientation of teaching instruments (printed religious textbooks) changed according to the shifting position of CC in the Slovene society; we shall be interested in how some great social changes, different turning points, have been reflected in the content orientation of these textbooks, i.e. whether they contain religious teachings as universal without any special additions regarding their implementation in the given circumstances, or whether to these instructions that describe the social community in which the faithful people should take part as active citizens, there are also attached specific interpretations regarding the social reality.

This question is all the more important because religious socialisation is not a part of general education and upbringing in Slovene society, which still remains the goal of the CC for the improvement of democratisation.

> The arrival of democratic government also brought certain changes to the education system. However, they were not such that are most ardently desired by the Church, namely religious classes or catechesis in public schools and historical objectivity in general classes in public schools.[1]

RELIGIOUS INSTRUCTION AS AN INSTRUMENT FOR ACHIEVING THE CHURCH'S POLITICAL GOALS

Religious socialisation is undoubtedly a prerequisite for the preservation of religion of any kind, while its implementation is one of the key concerns and responsibilities of the Church. The scope of responsibility for religious education, the orientation of its content and the manner of its implementation change according to the external conditions of the Church's functioning. The more all of these educational activities (and the operation of the entire social structure) are carried out as self-explanatory, 'natural', the greater their efficiency is and the easier it becomes for 'God's people' to self-regenerate through religious education; the structural coercion of religious education is concealed behind outward naturalness, normalcy and (the proper, socially recognised) morality. Whenever the Church is structurally threatened, excluded from the public arena, its responsibility as an institution for the survival of the faith grows, so the focus of its (pastoral) activity shifts more towards religious upbringing and education.

Due to the changing environment, it is also the approach to catechesis that changes, together with catechetical instruments. Religious textbooks, whose role is to form the kind of personality traits in individuals that fit 'God's commandments', have been the foundation of the comprehensive implementation of religious instruction for decades. However, as the goal of religious education is not aimed at metaphysical spaces but instead the practically detectable social environment, the degree of correspondence of the Church within this context (its socially recognised role) also depends on the way this environment is represented. Given the material and spiritual heterogeneity of the environment and its contesting political orientations, this begs the question of which political orientation is either covertly (implicitly) or expressly (explicitly) adopted as the measure of choice for the clarification of the main traits of the immediate social context. Here, we wonder about the (possible) politicisation of textbooks, namely what political orientation, and in what way, is accepted as the indisputable ingredient of teachings about the 'truth'.

The research interest in the politicization of religious textbooks of the CC, which is the dominant church in Slovenia,[2] builds on the following working hypotheses, presuppositions:

1. The degree of politicization of religious textbooks depends on the extent of the institutional support of the entire social system.
2. When the religious value orientation is seen as something 'natural' and the activity of the Church as self-explanatory, traditionally completely ensured and protected through institutions, the content of (explicit) political ingredients is lower or even non-existent, and its textbooks are narrowly focused on the dissemination of religious truths.
3. In the case where religious orientation is only one of the (private) options, not a compulsory part of regulating life and the work of

all public institutions, religious textbooks are potentially open to politicisation, the extent of which is determined by the primary goals of the Church and its survival strategy.

4. When the primary goal of the Church lies in nurturing religiousness in the limited private sphere while at the same time superficially conforming to the secular (state-regulated) institutional order as a whole, there are no obvious signs of politicisation in textbooks, or they are negligible (and interwoven with the patterns of morality as determined by the religion).

5. In the case where the entire institutional order is secular by definition, while the Church's strategy (with acknowledged autonomy and increased economic power of the Church) hinges on the goal of restoring its monopoly over regulating the spirituality of society members, the politicisation of textbooks becomes manifest and clearly oriented towards the goal of the formation of 'active citizens', depending on the need for building the power (or authority) of the Church.

The validity of these presuppositions will be verified through the CC's religious textbooks in Slovenia from three periods, which follow the chronological order of the changing status of the CC, from monopoly, to institutional marginalisation and again to the potential, modified monopolist status. The particularities of each status are set in specific time frames, starting with the period up until the Second World War, followed by the area of the socialist social order (1945–1990) and ending with the period of 'democratic' Slovenia. In revealing the potential characteristics of the politicisation of religious textbooks, the main attention is focused on the last, post-socialist era of the Slovene society in comparison with the prior phases.

Subject to the qualitative content analysis are textbooks for the religious education of children in the age category of 6–15, reflecting the sequence of primary school years/grades (in the 8th-year primary school, later 9th-year primary school), or in an way educating students in religion from their initial introduction to religious teachings to preparations for their confirmation.[3]

As the main indicator of the politicisation of textbooks, the breakdown of social context is taken into consideration, especially for those watershed historical periods of the twentieth century that resulted in drastic changes in the position and role of the CC, which include the

Second World War with the national liberation struggle, early socialism (with the leading communist party and gradual democratisation) and post-socialism (with its restoration of the multiparty political system and capitalism). The decision for this indicator makes sense because it is the opposition against the 'social evil', which in twentieth century Slovenia manifested itself in socialist (communist) revolutionary changes, which is the basis of the comprehensive efforts of the CC for the acquisition of social power (and authority).

Catechesis: From Compulsory to Optional

As established by theologian Peter Kvaternik,[4] in the post-Second World War period, pastoral workers particularly strongly engaged in the field of catechesis, which is understandable, if we take into account both the Church's historical rootedness in Slovene society as well as its standpoint regarding the measures of the socialist state. Slovene catechesis, which from the Theresian reforms of the eighteenth century onwards evolved in synchrony with the European heartland, grew particularly strong at the time of the first re-catholicisation at the beginning of the twentieth century.[5] Up until the Second World War, catechesis was a compulsory subject with 2 h weekly. One of the first secularisation measures of the socialist state right after the war was the demotion of catechesis to the level of a non-compulsory subject, which could then for a few years still be taught inside public school buildings (even though the teachers of these classes faced various obstacles)[6]; in February 1952, this option was statutorily abolished.

It was this measure that prompted the CC to decide that it is necessary 'to start teaching [catechesis] on new bases'. First, priests were called to introduce religious education in presbyteries or churches everywhere; at the same time, parents were addressed to send their children to catechesis at least for an hour a week. Priests also received very exact instructions regarding the implementation of catechesis, which should not take place 'according to the students' school year but instead in groups formed according to knowledge'.[7] Tensions eventually decreased, and in 1953, the leadership of the CC assured the state authorities that religious classes would not be exploited for ends outside education on faith. In 1956, Škofijski katehetski svet ('Diocesan Catechetical Council') was founded, which was supposed to help attenuate the post-war crisis of catechesis and promote its renewal with its own assorted activities (stimulations, directives, plans). An important role in the renewal of catechesis was also played by the new catechetical curriculum Year first to eighth, which was published in 1958 and followed by a number of textbooks for religious education. Furthermore, the leadership of the CC paid great attention to the organised training of catechists, especially through organising catechetical courses from 1965 onwards. The content of these courses focused on all the crucial aspects of religious education in regard to children's developmental stage, the inclusion of parents and family, and active participation in Christian communities.[8]

'CHURCH IS A GOOD SHEPHERD …'

Bearing in mind the CC's loyalty assurance to the authorities, it is relevant to be interested in any potential departures from instruction on religious teachings in select religious textbooks that were used by the catechists in the socialist era. Compared to pre-socialist catechists who were strict and usually disseminated the teachings of the Christian faith and the Commandments of the CC with no special approaches, textbooks in socialist times stress, in their instructions for the catechist, that the biblical story which is at the heart of every learning unit, should be delivered in a way that is age-appropriate for the child, as it is only in this way that the story will be able to wholly involve the child, 'his or her imagination, mind and heart'; the internalised lesson, the recognition of religious truth, 'must enter into the child's will and life, which should then turn to prayer as "a conversation with God"'. The textbook also includes prayers at the end.

Religious textbooks show that they are meant as preparatory to learning 'religious truths' already with their titles: *Krščanski nauk* ('Christian Teaching', 1973); *Cerkvena zgodovina, vzori in boji* ('Church History, Exemplars and Fights', 1977); *Življenje po božjih zapovedih* ('Life according to God's Commandments' 1987). The textbook for beginners (1973) in its 26 learning units (lessons) discusses religious teachings without any special additions; however, it is at the beginning that the child must already pledge to regularly attend mass. The significance of this obligation is gradually reinforced through increasing the appeal of the good deeds of the 'Saviour' whose work is continued through bishops and priests by the apostles who 'gather people to Holy Mass' where they are also taught. In each learning unit, the conviction about how much good is connected to the faith and love in accordance with God's commandments is laden with the commandments of the Church, which direct all individual students in their practical behaviour. Their goal is to reinforce adherence to the church through an incessant contact with the Church via mass and other rituals but also outside the Church with the observance of church holidays. And even though entering matrimony is yet nowhere in sight for children around the age of eight, the Church's commandment is resolute: 'You shall obey the laws of the Church concerning Matrimony.'[9]

This commandment attempted to instil in children the resistance against secular, lay marriage, and enforce the conviction on what marriage leads to true happiness. The anti-laic (anti-secular) orientation is even more apparent in the next textbook, which is directed at the children of about 14 years of age.[10] After encouraging obedience and loyalty to the CC through a story on the exemplary life of the first Christians, the advocacy of disobedience in lay matters (hence also the option of choosing to accept secular patterns of living) reads very convincingly:

> There is, however, one thing that Christians do not listen to: if someone wanted to deter them from the faith, they prefer to choose death. Their faith is dearer to them than life.[11]

This is followed by a determined refusal of laicism, and the substantiation of the anti-laic stance:

> The greatest and deepest tragedy of Laicism is that it spreads the spirit of division: it wants to separate the supernatural from the natural, God from human, religion from life, then denies the former and overly emphasises the latter. Laicism is in stark contrast to what Christ taught, that is why we reject it.[12]

Together with the examples from the Church's history, the series of learning units also features unambiguous warnings against all lay explanations of different (social and natural) phenomena and the consolidation of those truths that the CC is the guardian of, since its supreme teacher is infallible, as the Holy Spirit protects him from error. This is exactly why, in times when also the students had increasingly more questions on the different kinds of Church violence in history (e.g. Crusades, Inquisition, silence on the Holocaust, the impeding of science), this textbook, too, in addition to minimising[13] problematic past actions of the CC, repeatedly stresses the primacy of the Church because:

> The Church is the homeland of hearts. In it, human finds happiness and peace, truth and virtue. ... it leads the strong, comforts the sad, nourishes the weak and gives the souls blessed peace. The truth of Christ's teaching frees the human from sin and servitude to Satan's. ... The youth is obliged to raise itself, while the adults should do everything to help it do so and to remove all corruption from it.[14]

Given the many changes in Slovene society (and beyond in the second half of the twentieth century), especially in terms of great expectations regarding the changes after the Second Vatican Council, the textbook states the perspective clearly:

> There are some things that the Church can change, while it must keep and protect the others as unchanged and untouched as it received them from Christ ... [This is especially true of] the indissolubility of matrimony, which represents such a great good for the human society that it is impossible to pay regard to some sorry cases of individuals: it provides the couple and the family with those foundations that represent the haven of peace and family happiness, a strong wall against human fickleness and a guarantee for the well-being of children.[15]

The selective attitude of the CC towards its own role in changing 'some things', especially those that refer to its power and 'the God's people' is very clearly expressed in the learning unit of *Slovenski katoličani v najnovejši dobi* ('Slovene Catholics in the Most Recent Age'). Although the victorious national liberation struggle was *conditio sine qua non* in the existence of the national community, it is not even mentioned; neither are any of the achievements of the socialist order (such as a decrease in social inequality, free education, ensured social safety, medical care, etc.). An extremely simplified image of the Second World War[16] that could be set anywhere on Earth serves as a starting point for the justification of endeavours for maintaining the CC, which, through quietly omitting its collaboration and the highest authorities of the Church, suddenly appears with God's help:

> It was then that God's providence sent a man to the Slovenes who started everything anew: he preserved for the Slovenes their faith in God, eternity and the value of sacrifice. This was Archbishop Anton Vovk.

In the second half of the 1970s, when most people lived in (relative) prosperity within the socialist system, this textbook already features the unmistakable settled status of the CC as a victim, which as a (very strong) common thread carries on and strengthens until the present day. This status has been tied to communism, which was the trait of the federal country (SFRY), and this is why the abolishment of 'communism' and the establishment of the independent state (for which the CC's leadership fought in many ways within the state borders and beyond from the end of the Second World War onwards) constituted a goal, which was in a slightly obscured form already written in this textbook alongside the conclusion that 'the social organisation has matured in its national and political aspect to the degree where the Slovenes have become an autonomous unit, joined together with the other republics in a joint country.' The idea of the independence of the Republic of Slovenia, which was also made known to students through this religious textbook (without it being in any way 'contaminated' with the CC's efforts for regaining authority), is, in the last learning unit ('Our Perspectives on the Present, Future and Eternity') set in the framework of 'the modern Church', which

> bravely defends Christian life against everything that could smother, disfigure or dishonour it, while striving to adapt it to those modern features which are not contrary to Christian faith and morals with the intention to purify them, refine them and consecrate them. ... It is strongly convinced that all the theories that deny God are in essence erroneous, depart from the latest demands of sound thinking and take away from the rational order in the world its real and fruitful foundations. This is why it condemns them ... [but hopes for a change] so that life which is more lively and flexible than the fixed systems will overcome the theories.[17]

It is no coincidence that these types of explanations, with a clearly included political orientation, were placed in the textbook for students in their last year of primary school.[18] At this age, students were at the end of their compulsory education and started to turn in the different directions of education for their future professional work. Earlier religious education had already solidified the spiritual foundations, what it only added now is the 'guidelines' for diversified activities basically against everything that was socialist or a fruit of plod 'delusional ideologies'. Religious instruction did not encourage engagement in the many forms of activities that gradually developed and spread under the self-governing socialism, instead, it prompted the young to follow the CC as the only true leader in the chaotic modern world. In regard to the system, religious instruction according to thus oriented textbooks, therefore elicited a passive stance, while the catholically driven active role of the young, or all faithful, was encouraged.

WALKING WITH CHRIST IN THE FIGHT AGAINST COMMUNISM

Religious textbooks, which were prepared by groups of experts, theologians and catechists in independent Slovenia, are in the spirit of the 'modern time' from a didactic as well as design perspective, which has increased their attractiveness in informing children with 'God's word' and for strengthening 'personal faith'. Compared with the socialist-era textbooks, the textbooks after 1991 are visually more animated, as the (old)[19] contents of individual units are illustrated with all the available pictorial additions: photographs that seem familiar to children, depending on their age, in terms of content and experience; art reproductions of local and world renowned foreign painters or sculptors (such as P. Picasso, M. Chagall, or A. Dürer, etc.), together with fresh illustrations by Slovene artists, colourful (and changing) fonts with accentuation and boxes.

The layout of learning contents and the approach to carrying out learning units is in accordance with the newest findings of didactics and prominently targeted at achieving children's active engagement in catechesis. Once self-contained Biblical stories which children were required to learn by heart (e.g. during the Second World War, but also later), feature in modern textbooks as 'wrapped' in pleasant stories, either of peers or famous people (e.g. different stars). Once 'God's word' enters a child's mind and heart this way, the (rather playful) instruction on God's Commandments follows, and then finally the introduction into acquiring new realisations and truths.

These textbooks were gradually complemented with workbooks, while the instructors could, in progressively greater detail, get acquainted with systematic and comprehensive handbooks for catechists,[20] the increasing responsibility of which has also been to ensure that all activities, which now go far beyond the hours of the direct teaching of the Christian faith, actively and wholly include the parents. This is how complex religious education is ensured, and its efficiency can be additionally enhanced by encouraging the celebration of a multitude of religious (imposed and other) festivities, in the public arena (primarily with active participation at the 'Holy Mass and 'Holy Confession', with their membership in their parish community through extremely varied possibilities of participation in target partially oriented activities in the fields of culture, sports, etc.), as well as at home (e.g. through praying several times a day, setting up little altars and keeping their light lit etc.).

Simply put: the religious textbooks radiate the new (economically considerably increased) power of the CC and the conviction of its leadership that now, finally, are able to work publicly and (completely) free, and that there is no limit which would hinder 'God's children' from actively partaking in all political processes. Therefore, it is so much easier in 'the democracy' to carry out their work for catechists, who act as mediators of 'Jesus's love and redemption'[21] for both children and parents in their spiritual growth and who impart on them that one must always and everywhere follow Jesus, even on holidays.[22] This is understandable, as the children have to realise early enough that it is the omnipresence of the divine that is the precondition for the moral behaviour of everyone and always. 'The Holy Bible assists us in this. It tells us how we can further get to know and love God who made a special covenant, or friendship, with people.'[23] The additional appeal for the religious student is presented by this statement: 'even if we don't understand everything, we trust in God',[24] since it equips the student with a sense of security.

> Belief in Jesus begets faith. To have faith in God means to rely on God, as he is credible. Because he is worthy of trust, we remain loyal to him.[25]

This kind of wholesomely, 'in God's image' morally formed student, equipped for life, should amount to an active believer who is expected to be 'in the closest relationship to Christ who remains the same yesterday, today and for ever and ever ... as the path, truth and life.'[26] This is how a person's identity gets completely imbued with the image of Jesus because

> Having faith in Jesus means getting to know him and love him increasingly with a vivid desire. To have faith means to encounter Jesus in prayer, the Holy Bible, at Holy Mass, and also other events of our daily life.[27]

This kind of faith is presumably also a requirement for happiness, which is why God actually created a human.

We are led to happiness by faith and love. God always leaves them for us
on 'the tree of the knowledge of good and evil'. ... That is also why our
life plans acquire the real meaning only when they are intertwined with
real faith and love, and lead us towards God. Thus, our life starts with God
and returns to him.[28]

Near the end of the 9-year primary school (in 8-year 8), a firmly religious
student is also informed of the standpoints for balancing his or her life
and life in this country. Important for true knowledge on one's own life
is a claim that has been deeply internalised by various civil initiatives in
Slovene society in their practical fight against abortions:

God is the master of life from its beginning until its end; nobody under
any circumstances can appropriate the right to directly destroy and innocent human being.[29]

For social activity in independent Slovenia, the emphasis on God's assistance in the creation of the state of this textbook, to which also the
'disdained' Slovenes (from Argentina) were able to return, is important
in this textbook, all of which is indirectly mentioned here:

God is most certainly happy that we have been able to fulfil the longing of
our forbearers. In addition to us who live in Slovenia, other faithful rejoice
as well, especially Catholics, as Pope John Paul II was one of the first to
recognise Slovenia as a sovereign state.[30]

In the textbook, additional justification of the active role of the CC in
public political life relates to information about the separation of religious communities and state, which also holds true for the 'Church', but
which does not mean

that Christians are not equal citizens. It only means that the Church does
not provide for the clergy to hold political office, even though the state
laws allow them to do so. Nevertheless, the Church is bound to raise just,
proud and mindful citizens, and in its own way strive for just, fair, quality
life.[31]

By the end of primary school, before embarking on different educational and professional journeys, students also learn about the essence
of the Church's 'unique own' involvement in political public life at all

levels, from the top level (of archbishops and bishops to priests) to the Church's community. It is what they become acquainted with particularly in the learning units 19 and 20 of the religious textbook for Year 9 of primary school, encouragingly titled *Gradimo prihodnost* ('Let Us Build the Future').[32] In the unit of *Vzpon človeka in padec ideologij* ('The Rise of the Human, the Fall of Ideologies'), Marxist ideas are charged with the greatest evil in recent history, and communism follows right after:

> These kinds of ideas lead to the cruellest kind of totalitarianism in the of humankind, called communism. ... Even before the Second World War, totalitarian systems emerged, led by ideologies. These were Fascism, Nazism and communism. The Slovene nation also suffered tremendously under them. Nazism, Fascism, and communism are those ideologies that have inflicted the most pain and woe on humanity... In order to achieve their goals, they used all means, including devious, violent and also illegal means, this is why they are called ... totalitarian systems or totalitarianisms. ... Much suffering was caused by the communism that spread expansively after the Second World War. Tens of millions of people died in communist camps. Under communism, it was the religious who suffered in particular, as the communists wanted to completely uproot the faith and Church. ... /Highlighted in a box: When military operations ended, the death sentences of Catholic priests had not stopped./ ... For the Church in Slovenia, the times right after the Second World War were therefore difficult. A lot of priests were killed, banished or wrongly imprisoned. Thousands of Slovene refugees fled communism to the four corners of the world. The Church's activity was greatly limited. ... Christians were neglected and shamed due to their faith ...[33]

Students also become acquainted with examples that allow Christians to participate in removing all injustices experienced by the CC; these examples are presented in Learning Unit 20, *Svetniki nas spodbujajo k pogumnemu življenju* ('Saints Encourage Us to Live Bravely').[34] Also included among these role models 'who can assist us in some way due to their close relationship with God', is Martyr Lojze Grozde (1923–1943) who was, before his 20th birthday, 'tortured and killed by communists ... because he had been loyal to Christ and had not hidden it ...' This is the kind of spiritual 'Godspeed' with which the young at the end of the primary school embark upon life, educated that everything begins and ends with God ... In addition, of course, to the included explanation of

the CC, on how to understand history and what to do in order to elimi-
nate the neglect suffered by all the victims of the worst totalitarianism,
communism.

At the end of the presentation of these two learning units in the religious textbook for the Year 9 of primary school from the perspective of
content-related political views, let us draw attention to the manner of
explanation within the two, which follows the generally used pattern of
the battle between good and evil, which is an inextricable part of historical revisionism. On the one hand, there is this amassment of radically
misanthropic evil embodied in 'communism'; 'the communist regime'
after the Second World War is only portrayed as a hostile and destructive system for the Church and its believers, without a word of its contribution to establishing conditions for greater justice and equality. On
the other hand, there is (the self-image of) the CC, always polished to
its highest shine, as an institution (together with the believers, religious
community) which supposedly sees justice, honesty, love for one's neighbour, freedom and democracy as its first duty; and which, as a victim of
'communism', can carry out its humanitarian work for the 'suffering and
neglected' only now, in democratic Slovenia (the credit for which should
go almost exclusively to the CC).[35] And it is for its role, filled with love,
that it trains the future active citizens on time, also through catechesis.

Conclusion: Multidirectional Politicization of Textbooks for Catechesis in Slovenia as the Factor of Survival and Strengthening of the Social Power of CC

Based on the content analysis of religious education textbooks that were
used by the CC in Slovenia in its struggle for survival at the time of socialism, and the textbooks it has used in the context of the multiparty political
system in post-socialism, the following can be established with certainty:

1. These textbooks have never been only intended exclusively for religious education and upbringing, but have instead included major
   or minor, apparent or less apparent traces of political orientations
   and affiliations, yet have always been embedded in the most general biblical discourse on the 'truth' of human engagement and
   draped in the omnipotence and omnipresence of 'God's love'.

2. At the time of the socialist social order, this politicisation was more or less cloaked and woven especially into those topic that related to the CC's existential losses (in comparison with the monopolist 'directing of souls' in the pre-socialist order) and had a clear goal, which is informing the young on the dangers of the secular management of the world while at the same time consolidating the conviction that the CC is the only true 'savour'; it was a politicisation through silence on the existing socialist system, and with a loud NO to working towards the well-being of this system or to active participation in the 'atheist' forms of association.

3. The politicisation of religious textbooks in post-socialism has been completely evident and pointedly one-dimensional with one main goal: an all out fight against the 'worst totalitarianism', which is communism; this is why it reaches its pinnacle in those teaching modules that prepare young people (of about 15 years of age) for a comprehensive and multilayered active participation within the society; in the foreground here is the politicisation with a loud YES for the existing ('democratic') system, the active participation of all its believers in varied forms of associations in all areas so as to (finally) consolidate the 'new morality'.

4. Religious teaching has served particularly as the instrument of gaining and reinforcing the power of the CC, to which also religious textbooks have been subject as indispensable devices for religious socialisation; this is why, in the post-socialist era, emphasising catechetical education in charitableness (which in itself is undoubtedly important for humane human relationships) with Jesus Christ as the supreme example is one of the factors of growing power in the CC, as it is this very institution that opposes structurally ensured social security and welfare for all community members in Slovenia.[36]

The two main directions that have been revealed in the planting of political goals and patterns for the regulation of actual life, so in the direction of the politicisation of the CC's religious textbooks in Slovenia, show extreme ingenuity and adaptability of the CC[37] to the changing social circumstance, in order to remain 'old but forever young'[38]; simultaneously, these findings confirm that the mutatis mutandis CC, even at the beginning of the twenty-first century, sticks to the old rule: 'do not look at me, just listen to me' and that its endless possibilities of the application of God's love and truth enable, here and now, the reproduction of its bigotry (hypocrisy) while at the same time it continually vows to be the holder of the true morality.

The avant-garde in the moral sense should ensure the capacity of the Catholic Church in Slovenia to dispose of even those most painful injuries that were inflicted on it by the socialism, which is the CC's exclusion from publicly ensured childcare and education, and from the regulation of family life. It is these two activities that are constitutive for the existence of the Church and (through it directed) active citizens. On the one hand, there is the patriarchal family ('church in miniature') which is based on the 'holy' matrimony between the (superior) man and (subordinate) woman and where the natural self-regeneration of the population (also 'God's children') takes place and which, due to the original sin, is also responsible for the very earliest recruiting of (future) religious persons. However, since people are not born religious, they are formed through a systematic upbringing in faith and towards faith, the second existentially crucial factor for the unimpeded existence of the CC is religious education; this kind of education is all the more efficient, the more the different socialisation factors coincide, this is why it is necessary to ensure that all the contents (rules and patterns of behaviour and operation of the individual) disseminated by all socialisation factors and forms, and representing the cultural self-regeneration of the social community, are imbued with religion.

In order for the CC to truly carry out its role of the holder of 'new morality' in the 'democracy' of post-socialism in its totality, this 'holy' and 'eternal' institution must conquer two obstacles that were put in front of it by the 'criminal communism', for its proper incarnation and service as the bastion against 'pagans'[39]: it must achieve the equality of the validity of the church matrimony (sacrament) with the civil one, and the inclusion of catechesis in the public school system.[40] These are the two existentially essential tasks, which are included in the strategy of the CC's work in twenty-first century Slovenia and more or less openly,[41] independently or by means of the civil initiatives of (the already 'properly' religiously raised) active citizens,[42] gradually and consistently implemented within the presently given limits of its possibilities and the political support of the holders of key legislative and executive political bodies in the country.[43]

The convincingness of these efforts is increased by the perpetual recalling of the CC's position as the victim of the 'godless' (which equals immoral, criminal) communism and by the consolidation of the idea that communism does not coincide with human rights,[44] in case of the attempts restricting its independent and generally useful activity in the future. This is why it is extremely beneficial for the CC that historical revisionism is also building up in the community outside the Church,[45] and has already firmly carved its path in public education[46] and the activities of the media.

Indirectly, what additionally contributes to the lessening of the resistance on the secular (lay) side, is the extremely cordial and friendly addressing of all people while constantly emphasising that it is only God's love that is the right one, one that brings happiness to people and that everyone must carry God within themselves and only do good. This kind of practise is present not only on the occasion of the most important of religious holidays or only during religious instruction, it has already become a 'normal' part of everyday communication, which, bearing in mind the multitude of saints and patrons, there are as many opportunities as there are days in a year. Bearing in mind that the entire Slovene national community has been handed to Virgin Mary for protection, it is understandable that there is an effort for all the people to actually look up to this figure the way they (especially women) did in the past.

This is how, gradually, the circle of action, supposedly having all the characteristics of true morality, is created (not through magic but recurrently consciously): God—Catholic Church—Catechesis—God's children—God, or, as written in religious textbooks, 'God is the beginning and the end' of all doing. The politicisation of religious textbooks shows that the CC in Slovenia (with God's help) has already almost made it full circle: from open domination to seeming adaptation and now the (almost) open domination not only in its management of souls but human beings as a whole.

NOTES

1. This is claimed by theologian Peter Kvaternik, *Brez časti, svobode in vesti*, 2003, p. 229, who further suggests that the CC after the introduction of optional subjects in public schools (1991) failed to adequately engage in ensuring this; his reproach claiming that even today's catholically organised teachers fail to assume a 'more considerable influence over the formation of the school' has become less and less valid over the past decade, as the Association of Catholic Teachers has proved very active, and the

'objectivity in general classes' (where the subject, e.g. history, allows for it) is getting very close to the CC's standards (later on this). However, an 'unhealed injury' also remains for the CC, which is the conquering of religious instruction in primary and secondary public education, the wound that has already been successfully 'healed' in many a post-socialist country. The following lament of P. Kvaternik still remains current: 'while most other former communist countries have already introduced catechesis in their schools, the authorities in Slovenia do not allow it.' id., p. 230.

2. The position of the CC in other, religiously plural environments (and/ or where the Church is even in a minority position situation) is probably different.

3. The analysis included the greatest number of textbooks from the last period (17), 3 from the time of socialism and one pre-Second World War textbook. In addition, four workbooks and three reference books for catechists from the post-socialist period have been examined.

4. Id., (2003), p. 196.

5. The Association of Slovenian Catechists, founded in 1907, had 356 members already at its very beginning. Peter Kvaternik, id., p. 196.

6. For more on tensions between new state authorities and the CC leadership, which relied on the encyclical of Pope Pius XI on the Christian education of youth, according to which this kind of education has 'priority over any other right of human society', see Kvaternik, id., pp. 197–202.

7. There were at least three groups prescribed, namely of children before their first communion, children after their first communion to 9 years of age, and children age 10 and older when they learn through Catechism. Kvaternik, id., p. 202.

8. The effects of courses can also be linked to the increase of religious instruction among pupils (from 54.3% in 1965 to 68.7% in 1973), which later decreased till 1984 (56.3%) when secularisation was particularly strong. (Similarly in Kvaternik, id., pp. 204–211.) The data on the number of confirmation candidates also indicates noticeable secularisation: in 50 years (from 1951 to 2000), the number of confirmation candidates decreased by 22.7% and dropped below average in 1970, however, it has not significantly decreased in the decades that followed—P. Kvaternik, id., pp. 170–273.

9. *Krščanski nauk*, (Ljubljana: Zadruga katoliških duhovnikov SFRJ v Ljubljani, 1973), p. 83.

10. Compiled by Franc Mihelčič, *Cerkvena zgodovina, vzori in boji*, (Ljubljana: 1977).

11. Ibid., p. 6.

12. Ibid., p. 7.

13. The learning module of *Cerkev se širi med pogane* ('Church Spreads among Pagans') shows this unequivocally through its interpretation of

the very essence of the Church: 'The Church is comprised of two indelible elements: the divine, which is holy, and the human, which is sometimes sinful. ... It is true that stains can sometimes be glanced on the face of the Church. But let us not transgress. Let us be aware that it is still our Mother. Let us not extinguish the Sun only because we can sometimes observe spots and stains in it', Ibid., p. 20.

14. Ibid., pp. 45, 50. The importance of religious education and frequent 'Holy Communion' is again emphasised along with the encyclical *Acerbo Nimis* of Pope Pius X., p. 106.

15. Ibid., pp. 72, 73.

16. The Second World War is only mentioned as having 'left a sad aftermath of material and spiritual devastation in the [previously] flourishing religious life of the Slovenes'.

17. Ibid., p. 113.

18. The religious textbook for the Year 7 of elementary school pupils (*Življenje po božjih zapovedih*, (Ljubljana, 1987)) is oriented towards the individual, pure moral formation of 'God's children' who should strive for perfection, which is achieved when we 'strive to increasingly love God and our neighbour.'

19. A good example of enhancing old contents with new 'wrappers' is offered by a religious textbook entitled *Znamenja na poti k Bogu* (Janez Ambrožič, Stanko Gerjolj, Alojzij Slavko Snoj et al. (Celje: Mohorjeva družba 1991), then for Year 4 of elementary school) that in 2015 already saw its 7th reprint (ed. A. Slavko Snoj, among the authors listed appears a new, female name—B. Jelič).

20. Great attention is devoted to the quality of work of catechists, as this is the person that is the 'co-worker of the Truth', 'in the service of objective truth' and 'mystery', and in itself an 'non-exhaustive source of mystery', which is why it must be a 'strong religious personality', 'credible witness of faith', and at the same time a friendly fellow traveller to the religious student. Niko Tunjič, 'Veroučitelj kot sopotnik veroučencem', *Bogoslovni vestnik* 69 (4), 2009, pp. 494, 503, 504.

21. Janez Ambrožič et al., *Hodimo z Jezusom, veroučni učbenik za 2. razred*, (Ljubljana, Celje: Mohorjeva družba, 1998), Foreword. In this textbook, in the context of promoting charity work, the CC's organisation Karitas is mentioned several times (e.g. pp. 12, 71, 88), while the much older organisation of the Red Cross is omitted. This is how a seemingly trivial mention presents as a reflection of the exclusion of everything (even if charitable) that is not Catholic. The 6th reprint of this textbook (ed. dr. A. Slavko Snoj, (Celje: Celjska Mohorjeva družba, Društvo Mohorjeva družba)) was published in 2009.

22. Ibid., p. 90.

23. J. Ambrožič, Stanko Gerjolj, Alojzij Slavko Snoj et al., *Pot v srečno življenje, Učbenik za 3. razred*, (Ljubljana, Celje: Mohorjeva družba, 1998), Foreword. This textbook was first issued in 1991; in 2015, with minor amendments and additions (in view of the current state of affairs) the eighth reprint was published. The last reprint also mentions the Red Cross as one of humanitarian organisations alongside Karitas. However, the rejection of everything that functioned (well) during the time of socialism was apparent in the first edition of this textbook (1991) where the Red Cross is not even mentioned (while Karitas was still at the beginning of its work and had not yet earned credentials for its entry in a teaching instrument), even though it had more than a century of charity work under its belt by then (from 1863 onwards). Pupils (about 9 years old) were only generally informed by this textbook that: 'Humanitarian institutions are active in the parish, our home country and around the world', p. 19.

24. Stanko Gerjolj et al., *Skupaj v novi svet, Veroučni učbenik za 5. razred*, Pilot edition, (Ljubljana, Celje: Mohorjeva družba 1998), p. 7. All explanations in this textbook are imbued with the praise of God (from Creation to just society).

25. ed. Dr. A. Slavko Snoj, *Hodimo z Jezusom*, 6. reprint, (Celje: Celjska Mohorjeva družba, Društvo Mohorjeva družba, 2009), p. 11.

26. *Krščanski nauk 4*, 15th improved edition, (Ljubljana: Salve, 1998), p. 90.

27. Stanko Gerjolj, A. Slavko Snoj, Janez Ambrožič and Petra Žagar, *Kdo je ta? Veroučni učbenik za 6. razred osemletke*, Pilot edition (Celje: Mohorjeva družba, 1999), p. 43. In 2015, the 9th reprint of this textbook was issued already (for Year 7 of the 9-year primary school) without major changes, except in the title of the 5th learning unit, which in the last reprint reads 'Science and Culture Lead to God', while the 1999 reprint discussed scientific feats under the title of 'Wonderful Life Achievements'. The last edition also features musical notations to songs.

28. *Kdo je ta?* 2015, p. 18.

29. Stanko Gerjolj et al., *V življenje, Učbenik za 8. razred devetletke*, 9th reprint (Celje: Društvo Mohorjeva družba: Celjska Mohorjeva družba, 2015), p. 70.

30. Ibid., p. 101. Incidentally, Pope's recognition was not among the first ten, but even so, his near-primacy has been stressed continuously (which is undoubtedly no coincidence).

31. Ibid., p. 104. The textbook has had inserted current phenomena in appropriate places, for instance (e.g. under 'Beatitudes'), it touches on the non-payment of workers for accomplished work: 'Blessed are all who strive for workers to have enough work and to receive just payment for it,' p. 125.

32. Stanko Gerjolj et al., 3rd reprint, (Celje: Društvo Mohorjeva družba, Celjska Mohorjeva družba, 2009).
33. Stanko Gerjolj et al., *Gradimo prihodnost,* 3rd reprint, (Celje: Društvo Mohorjeva družba, Celjska Mohorjeva družba, 2009), pp. 138–141. Let it be mentioned at this point that nowhere in the textbook is there a mention of even an approximate number of victims that were caused in Slovenia during the time of the occupation by the occupiers or their home-grown collaborators (first with the systematic deportations of Slovene people, then directly in fighting against partisan units, and especially with telling on people and sending them to concentration camps), which considerably surpasses the number of refugees produced by communism. The first mass victims were the Slovenes who were forcibly deported to labour camps (the majority already in 1941—around 80,000), later to Italian and German concentration camps (around 60,000); if all the fatalities of the war years combined are taken into account, they amount to 28,472 partisan fighters, 14,000 Home Guard, and 29,459 civilians. Božo Repe, *S puško in knjigo,* (Ljubljana: Mladinska knjiga, 2015), p. 331.
34. Ibid., pp. 150–156.
35. Initially, emphasising the CC's merits for the country's independence was not too open, even though the CC was one of the key organised forces of independence efforts, where this independence meant freedom from socialism. After almost a quarter of the century of the independent Slovenia, the CC is economically and politically powerful enough, and practically involved in all social life to the extent that its highest representatives declare this proudly to the most general public (e.g. theologians Jože Plut and Janez Dolinar in a conversation at the 25th anniversary of the plebiscite (23/12/1990) for the independent country—in the 'Sledi večnosti' broadcast on Radio Slovenia (Channel 1, 27/12/2015). Regarding all the negative consequences caused by the capitalist neo-liberalist order (with the abundant blessing of the CC), it is held that this is a result of people being too materialistically oriented and failing to work enough 'on themselves'. This was clearly conveyed in the addresses by the Archbishop of Ljubljana, metropolitan Janez Zore, for Slovene citizens at the 25th anniversary of the plebiscite when he stressed that 'it is on the inside where we must work for the good', so we have to transform our consciousness, spirituality, but of course not in any way towards any patterns of the socialist order. Incidentally, if it was only about the believers, this message could have been communicated to the faithful during religious rituals; it was, however, addressed at the general public in various printed and electronic media. It can be reasonably assumed that (for now still partly disguised) the goal of the CC to achieve unity among

the national community (which all the politicians mention as a lost virtue compared with the homogeneity at the plebiscite) would be right up its alley.

36. This is clearly conveyed in the short term action plan of the CC (from 2013 to 2018), *Pridite in poglejte*, 2012, pages 32 and 33, that on the topic of compassion and justice reads: 'Instead of [people] being closed off and transferring [the task of] solidarity to institutions, we will promote the spirit of servitude and compassion, and enliven the sharing of goods among people, material as well as social and spiritual goods... The Christian outlook on the creation of the society of solidarity is irreplaceable, since its advantage lies in the fact that it treats the human being wholesomely. This perspective of human and society is also called the social teaching of the Church. In the future, we must get better acquainted with it and connect it to the practice of charity. Christian charity has its advantage and privilege of support in prayer.'

At the same time, this document stresses that the CC must be counted among those institutions that need special compassion, which is already starting to show, as established by its own people: 'Solidarity and justice are shown in relation to church property. ... The aspiration of the Church in Slovenia to be economically independent is its obligation and a reflection of needs. Slovenia today is one of those countries where the calling of the Church can be wholly realised and carried out without material assistance from abroad,' p. 33.

37. This is actually how the CC is, in a way, discursively secularising in order to colonise the public sphere, 'clericalise' the society, as argued by Roman Kuhar in "Playing with science: Sexual citizenship and the Roman Catholic Church counter-narratives in Slovenia and Croatia," *Women's Studies International Forum* March/April 49, 2015, pp. 84–92.

38. Among the advantages of the CC in present day Slovenia (with the rift in its society), the pastoral plan has established that the CC is strongly present in education ('primary school catechesis is attended by the majority of Slovene children') and, moreover, it has the advantage of the most important force which 'holds the entire church structure', i.e. 'the everyday prayer of many men and women'. It is prayer that reflects devotion to Christ, 'who has a living exemplar in Mary, the mother of Jesus. Mary's stance that is present in our people ... is the primary guarantee for pastoral restoration in the following years'. In: *Pridite in poglejte* (2012), p. 17.

As a rule, religious instruction takes place in church buildings, only in exceptional circumstance (dangerous road conditions etc.) the Ministry of Education, Science and Sport allows for exceptions, which are not even that rare, as in the academic year 2015/16 children take religious classes in 57 school rooms in 45 public school buildings (according to the data of the Ministry of Education, Science and Sport, Pre-School and Basic Education Directorate, 22/12/2015). Furthermore, the Pastoral Plan also includes the following appraisal: 'Primary school catechesis is attended by the majority of Slovene children. A lot of children and young people benefit from educational activities such as the scouts and "oratories". The *Stična mladih* festival … has no parallel in the area of Central Europe. Catholic kindergartens and schools are respected and sought after among people, and could be more numerous. The majority of people appreciate and accept the educational efforts of the Church,' p. 16. These efforts are also organisationally well supported, e.g. the Slovenian catholic Girl Guides and Boy Scouts Association (founded on 31/3/1990, has about 4500 active members) publishes an appealing newsletter called *Skavtič* (with the circulation of 3700 copies, Dec. 2015), which is co-financed by the Ministry of Education, Science and Sport of the RS.

39. Something that both the CC and historian Jože Dežman, "Preseganje travmatskih bremen titoizma," *Bogoslovni vestnik* 74 (4), 2014, pp. 611–638) are aware of is that this system still persists and that 'the liberation from the criminal recent past is far from over yet', and that it is especially the 'crimes of the victorious party' that should be denounced.

40. The CC wishes 'for Church weddings to have civil law effects' (*Izberi življenje*, 2002, p. 187); as for the catechesis, it is convinced that 'religious upbringing and education should be seen and treated as an integral part of the upbringing and education of religious children and adolescents, which the national education programme should take into consideration, not ignore if it wants to respect the religious freedom of children, young people and their parents' (ibid., p. 149).

41. This happens particularly through the attempts of preventing the free regulation of childbirths or, more specifically, in the attempts to prohibit e.g. abortions or artificial insemination of women, or at least to make it more difficult.

42. One of the last very aggressive and successful actions was carried out by the civil initiative called *Za otroke gre* ('It is about Children'), which (at the referendum of 6th December 2015) with the straightforward support of the CC achieved the rejection of legislative possibility for achieving equality between the same-sex and opposite sex marriages.

43. During his first press conference after his nomination for the Archbishop of Ljubljana, pater Stane Zore accentuated that he wished for the fundamental dialogue between the State and the Church, in order to promptly resolve 'all open issues', one of which is the issue of religious instruction in particular. 'There are many children who attend catechesis, but

also there are many high school students [who do so], and nowhere is this evaluated. ... It seems to me that this activity, too—parish religious instruction—can be evaluated and with it the time that is invested in it by both the children, or adolescents, and their parents.' As second come 'initiatives and sometimes also problems regarding the military vicariate, the activity of the Church in hospitals and prisons.' In the article by Matija Grah, 'Temeljni programski dokument je evangelij', *Delo*, 11th November 2014, p. 3.

44. Here it should be added that the CC (not for the first time in history) has been slowly taking credit for heading the efforts for achieving individual social rights (e.g. gender equality). This kind of inclination is also seen in the religious textbook for Year 9, where the *Universal Declaration of Human Rights* is presented as if it has been derived from the efforts of Ten God's Commandments and with the support of the Church.

45. Jože Dežman (already cited article, 2014); Ivo Žajdela, "In Slovenia, there was no civil war. The term "civil war" only clouds the blame of communists and their revolution, "*Slovenski čas*, priloga *Družine* (6–7), February 2015: 'Since it was about defence against the ruthless violence of communist partisans, this collaboration was in no way depraved. ... In Slovenia, one party (the communists with their military organisations) was always attacking and destroying the other party; in the first phase the members of democratic parties and the Church, respectable civilians, and in the second phase the relatively weak units of counter-revolution in the form of village guards, and lastly the Home Guard who had their hands tied due to the presence and demands of the third party, which were the occupying forces. One party was destroying the other, the other only defended itself, weakly and only here and there successfully,' p. 7. Regarding the weakness of the collaborationist party, numbers should be mentioned: up until September 1942 there were about 4000 members of the Anti-Communist Volunteer Militia part of Italian military units in the Province of Ljubljana (Mario Cuzzi, *L'Occupazione italiana della Slovenia*, Roma, 1998); from autumn 1943 until the end of the war, there were about 13,300 Slovenes organised in Home Guard units (Boris Mlakar, *Slovensko domobranstvo 1943–1945*), and additionally about 5500 in other units; this army had a complete material and military support and operated together with German units or independently. In comparison, by the end of the war, there were about 37,000 fighters that were part of partisan national liberation units, while in total about 100,000 took part during the war years (*Enciklopedija Slovenije 7* (Ljubljana: Mladinska knjiga), p. 324).

46. This can be seen in the changing of the contents of textbooks for history classes in public primary schools, especially for Year 9. For instance, the history textbook for the Year 9 of primary school *Raziskujem preteklost 9* (Jelka Razpotnik and Damjan Snoj, 2nd reprint, (Ljubljana: Rokus, 2010), pp. 81–91) indeed starts with the summary of violence inflicted by the occupiers but goes on to present the camp that was 'loyal' to occupiers and 'intolerant of communists' first, and later states that 'it was also the Liberation Front who, from its foundation on, organised resistance activities.' After the listing of certain Liberation Front actions it is mentioned that it was these actions that triggered the aggression of the occupying forces over the civilian population; this is why they shot hostages, imprisoned people, or sent them to 'internment camps'. In the meantime, the bourgeois camp 'gradually prepared for resistance'.

CHAPTER 9

Religious Education and the Large Group Identity

Dženana Husremović

Introduction: All people are God's children, but We are the best

A quality upbringing and education are the foundations of economic and social development of every society. Educational system is a place where social values, aspirations and vision of the future are best presented. Education in post-conflict societies is, however, a focal point of determining the long-term development and stabilization after a conflict. In such a society, education may initiate reconciliation, mutual understanding, tolerance and acceptance, but it may also deepen segregation, intolerance and division. This double role of education—constructive and destructive—is described as "a two-faced education".[1] When considering educational goals, it should be kept in mind that the goal of education is acquiring and developing essential competences necessary for work and employment, as well as for active social and civil activities. The main argument of this article is that education forms individual and collective identities, as well as the feeling of belonging to certain groups

DŽ. Husremović (✉)
University of Sarajevo, Sarajevo, Bosnia and Herzegovina

© The Author(s) 2018
G. Ognjenović and J. Jozelić (eds.), *Education in Post-Conflict Transition*, Palgrave Studies in Religion, Politics, and Policy,
https://doi.org/10.1007/978-3-319-56605-4_9

that Vamik Volkan named "large group identity".[2] Large group identity is the result of historical continuity, geographic reality, myths about
common ancestry and other events. Large group identity is neither good
nor bad in itself; it is a normal phenomenon recognized as an important
educational goal in documents. For example, the Framework Law on
Primary and Secondary Education in Bosnia and Herzegovina states that
the general objectives of education result from generally accepted, universal values of democratic society, as well as its own value system based
on specific qualities of national, historical and cultural tradition of ethnic
groups and national minorities living in Bosnia and Herzegovina. The
objectives include developing awareness of commitment to the State of
BiH, one's own cultural identity, language and tradition, in a way appropriate to the legacy of civilization, as well as learning about the other and
the different by respecting the differences and cultivating mutual understanding and solidarity among people, peoples and communities in BiH
and in the world.[3]

Large group identity is very strong because that individual perception of ethnic, religious and national identity is an inseparable part of
the basic, individual identity as a perception of oneself and one's own
being through time. Although different large group identity classifica-
tions are found in literature, depending on the main element of identity
formation, Volkan[4] argues that the most important categories are those
based on (1) ethnicity, (2) religion and (3) language, where the **ethnicity** is the privileged category. As Stein wrote,[5] ethnicity is not a natural category; rather, it is a mode of thought. Ognjenović[6] explains the
constructed nature of ethnicity using Bauman's description of ethnicity
as a liquid by external ascription and internal self-identification. Ethnic
groups are not discontinuous cultural isolates or logical a priori to which
people naturally belong. Ethnicity includes also feelings and convictions
that form the group's "We-ness" and ethnic identities are the result of
intergroup relations. **Religion** is also connected to the basic ways of
human experience and not only does it connect an individual with God,
but it also provides the feeling of collective or togetherness with other
fellow worshipers. Religion is less specific as the basis of a shared identity,
but it can also be found in the very foundation of defining ethnicity. For
example, Serbs, Muslims and Croats in Bosnia and Herzegovina share
the same ethnic background (South Slavic), but religion divided them
into three groups. And finally, **language** is also an element of large group
identity formation. It is also a rudimentary part of ethnicity. In Bosnia

and Herzegovina today, the issue of language has been set on a pedestal as the issue of survival. Ethnic groups in Bosnia and Herzegovina that used a single name for the language spoken in most parts of Yugoslavia (Serbo-Croatian or Croatian–Serbian) today speak Bosnian, Serbian or Croatian, insisting threat on the language purity within ethnic groups.

The story about ethnic/national groups in Bosnia and Herzegovina deserves the special attention. By Dayton agreement, there are three constitutive people in BiH—Serbs, Croats and Bosniaks. There are also national minorities (like Roma as biggest minority group), but their position is marginalized due to the unresolved problems among the three majority groups. Although these three groups are named Serbs, Croats and Bosniaks, they are fundamentally citizens of Bosnia and Herzegovina and should be seen as Bosnian Serbs, Bosnian Croats and Bosnian Bosniaks. All three groups are almost completely identified with religious affiliation. Bosnian Serbs belong to Orthodox religion and are members of Serbian Orthodox Church, Bosnian Croats are Catholics and Bosnian Bosniaks are Muslims. They also have their (national) native language— Serbian, Croatian and Bosnian (which is usually declared as a native language by citizens who see themselves as "others" and do not belong to any major group). The data from 2013 census show that individual identities within the three groups are completely based on symbiosis between religion, language and belonging to national group. This was the overarching goal—to separate groups and make them exclusive based on religion and language. To be certain that people would not forget how to declare themselves, nationalistic leaders did not rely only on memory of recent war and earlier historical process. They organized campaigns in which the citizens were persuaded that they should declare themselves in accordance to this symbiosis (national group membership, religion and native language). One of those campaigns was named "It is important to be Bosniak" in which the members of Bosniak groups were instructed to declare as Bosniaks, Islamic religion and Bosnian as a native language. Table 9.1 shows how people declared to those three census questions:

As already mentioned, the symbiosis of religion and national group membership is not only the result of the recent events in Bosnia. It started a long time ago and was intensified in the last 30 years. The goal was and is to create collective identities without the possibility for common elements between. Ognjenović in her essay "Quo Vadis, Vlachs?"[6] described brilliantly the process of melting the ethnic group with religion

Table 9.1 Religion and large group identity

	Category 1 (%)		Category 2 (%)		Category 3 (%)	
National group membership	Bosniaks	50.7	Serbs	30.75	Croats	15.43
Religion	Islamic	50.11	Othodox	30.78	Catholic	15.19
Native language	Bosnian	52.86	Serbian	30.76	Croatian	14.60

using the example of Serbian Orthodox Church and Serbs as ethnic group. Very similar process, but within the different historical contexts, happened also for Bosniaks and Bosnian Croats. Ognjenović wrote: "..when we look at the Orthodox part of the population in Southeastern Europe, the mixing of the religion and ethnicity has a long tradition". The process of melting nation and religion started in thirteenth century when Serbian Orthodox Church was organized. The members of SPC were ethnic Serbs and members of other ethnic groups, but this connection of nation and religion, in the long run, resulted in the identification of Orthodoxy as Serbism. By explaining the reorganization of Orthodox Church in Croatia and assimilation of Croatian Orthodox people (Vlachs) in the identity of Serbs, Ognjenović clearly explained how the process of nation–religion symbiosis had developed. Today, in Bosnia and Herzegovina, major groups call themselves Serbs, Croats and Bosniaks and not Bosnian Serbs, Bosnian Croats or Bosnian Bosniaks. There is no doubt that there are people in Bosnia and Herzegovina who are Serbs (from Serbia), Croats (from Croatia) or Bosniaks (from other countries, not from BiH), but the majority of the population are first Bosnians and Herzegovinians. In the examples given in this article, the terms Serbs, Croats and Bosniaks are used all the time. This shows that the major problem for this country is the fact that the first and major identification for people is not with common identity (citizens of Bosnia and Herzegovina), but with national identities. Hence, religion as a demarcation line marks the ethnic identity of groups in Bosnia and Herzegovina and therefore has played one of the key roles in national/ethnic policies in the last 30 years in these areas.

How is the large group identity formed? Without any pretences of touching upon the developmental psychology, I will only provide a framework of Volkan's taxonomy of large group identity.[4] According to this model, there are seven threads that form large group identity:

1. Shared, graspable reservoirs of ideas and images connected to the positive emotions.
2. Shared positive identifications.
3. Absorption of negative characteristics of others.
4. Absorption of inner worlds of the transformational or charismatic leaders of groups.
5. Chosen victories and celebrations.
6. Chosen traumas.
7. Forming symbols that develop an autonomy of their own.

Children begin to develop individual and group identities around the age of three and they become intertwined as the child's internal world begins to increasingly get in contact with the outside objects and experiences that bear cultural and historical importance to their parents and immediate surroundings. For example, "The one who does not like grilled minced meat (cevapcici) is no Bosnian". Although the formation of large group identity initially depends on the outside elements, the socialization process in which a child internalizes (adopts that what belongs to the outside as his/her own) and the increase of cognitive capacities leads to a more sophisticated perception of the membership to a certain group. Even in preschool period, a child is going through an identification process with adults and with the surrounding and that process of identification inevitably includes those common perceptions, images and behaviours determining the large group identity (for example, parents wear a religious symbol on a necklace, a child also receives his/her own little necklace with the symbol, everyone is thrilled while the child internalizes the positive emotions and images and identifies him/herself with the surroundings and with the relatives). Going to school and identification with teachers, religious teachers, children of the same age, additionally instigate the child's investment into large group identity development, as well as the feeling of being different from those who are not a part of that group. Volkan argues that, after the first two threads of group identity formation become incorporated in the sense of self (in the adolescence period), it is very difficult, even impossible, to change that feeling of commonness connected to the large group identity.

Still, group identity cannot exist for its own self. It can be solely formed if there exist Those who are not We, that is, other groups. One group can identify itself only if it prescribes negative characteristics to the other group and, thus, in this game of interdependence, it distinguishes itself from others. On the contrary, if a group fails to find and incorporate or absorb negative characteristics of the other group, that the Others are in fact us. For example, in Bosnia and Herzegovina, some Bosniaks will say that all Serbs are "a warlike, genocidal people" in order to incorporate the characteristics of Bosniaks as "peaceful and noble" into their own group identity.

The fourth precondition for forming group identity is a charismatic leader who successfully transmits his own inner world to the group. Such leaders are celebrated; their speeches are remembered and read because in that way the essential components of the group identity are preserved. Thus, in Bosnia and Herzegovina, every ethnic group has its own leaders, celebrated champions, while others are considered criminals at the very least.

The chosen victories and selected traumas are of equal importance for the formation of identity. In essence, those are important events experienced by a group at some point in history and that are taught to the new generations so that they integrate them into their own identity and thus preserve them as key markers of the large group identity. The selected traumas, transferred from one generation to the next, carry potential energy for mobilization of the group and for that reason they play an important role in the education of the future generations.

Finally, large group identity is visualized through symbols. Symbols are a distiller of large group identity, "telling" the surrounding what that person believes in and with which group he/she is affiliated. Avoidance of symbols of the other, "enemy" group becomes very important so that the surrounding environment would not suspect that individual and his/her loyalty to the collective. For example, the author of this text (a Bosniak) came to work one day wearing a scarf that had a pattern resembling a cross. Several times that day she was warned that "the scarf has crosses" and why would she choose to wear that particular scarf with crosses among all other scarfs.

Why Is This Particular Story of Identity Important for Understanding Problems in Education in Bosnia and Herzegovina?

Prior to the 1990s, Bosnia and Herzegovina were considered "a mini Yugoslavia". Different peoples lived together on its territory and it was an example of Tito's idea of brotherhood and unity. Moreover, the dominant identity of the largest number of people was that of Yugoslavian. Religion was considered a very private thing and one could realize a significant professional promotion through membership in the Communist Party and avoidance of showing religious feelings. Before the war in Bosnia and Herzegovina, there were over 30% mixed marriages. Everybody named language the same, everybody celebrated common state holidays and neighbours would celebrate religious holidays together. With no intention to discuss historical reasons or the very course of the bloodiest conflict in Europe since World War II, what is important in this story is that the war has caused a terrible division of the society into groups that had shared the language and the alphabet of the selected victories and traumas, as well as symbols and all other elements of large group identity. One can freely state that the war and the post-conflict period in Bosnia and Herzegovina are dedicated to the construction of threads of the ethnic identities of three large groups— Bosnian Bosniaks (mainly Islamic religion—Muslims), Bosnian Serbs (mainly Orthodox religion) and Bosnian Croats (mainly Catholics). Religion, language and cultural heritage have been granted the status of differentiation along the ethnic lines. Nationalistic policies knew all too well that the division, created by a fierce war, would not last because the older generations remember the life before the war, unless the new generations raised the way to strengthen their group identity as much as possible, separated from other groups' identity to the largest extent. In that sense, formation of ethnic identities as the large group identity in Bosnia and Herzegovina has become The project of nationalistic policies. Geographical layering and creation of ethnically pure territories at the state level have significantly helped the process.

The education system in Bosnia and Herzegovina is a peculiar mixture of decentralization and centralization. The state of Bosnia and Herzegovina and its administrative apparatus does not have any strategic executive authority in education. Besides, regulation of education differs largely in the two entities the country has been divided into (Republika

Srpska and the Federation of Bosnia and Herzegovina). In Republika Srpska, education is centralized and the main executive decisions are uniquely passed by the ministry and its institutions (the RS Pedagogical Institute) and the curriculum used in the Republika Srpska is called the Curriculum in the Republika Srpska. In the Federation of Bosnia and Herzegovina, two curricula are implemented—the Curriculum in Croatian Language and the Curriculum in Bosnian Language. Brčko District has its own system that is most similar to the former Yugoslav system. So, there are currently 12 instances in charge of education, as well as two more (a ministry at the level of the Federation of BiH and a sector for education at the State Ministry of Civil Affairs), that have a coordinating and advisory role—mostly unimportant, as well as four curricula which differ not only in language, but also in the content. Essentially, the main differences are related to the language, the selection of writers, interpretations of literary works, as well as interpretations of historical events and positioning of Bosnia and Herzegovina (and some other geographical locations) in geography. That is the contents of the so-called "national group of subjects"—mother language and litera- ture, history and geography. Such a complicated structure of education management disables to a large extent the synchronization of reforms, strategic investments and rational use of human and material resources. However, the main issue of such an education is that it supports a physi- cal and psychological distance between children of different ethnic groups and in that way deepens the feeling of enormous, insurmountable differences between the collective identities.

For the purpose of synchronizing education in the entire territory of Bosnia and Herzegovina and under pressure by the international com- munity, a framework agreement on synchronization of three parallel systems of education was achieved in May 2000. A coordination mecha- nism was initiated and the Framework Law on Primary and Secondary Education in Bosnia and Herzegovina was passed in July 2003. Institutions that register in accordance with the current laws in Bosnia and Herzegovina for providing services in the field of preschool, primary and secondary education, as well as education of adults and other institu- tions in the field of education, are obliged to implement and respect the principles and norms determined by the framework law and to ensure equal education for all students. By this law, aims of education stem from the generally accepted, universal values of democratic society, as well as its own value system based on specific qualities of national, historical, cultural and religious traditions of nations and national minorities living in Bosnia and Herzegovina. The objectives include developing awareness on commitment to the state of Bosnia and Herzegovina, one's own cultural identity, language and tradition, in a way appropriate to the legacy of civilization, as well as learning about the other and the different by respecting the differences and cultivating mutual understanding and solidarity among people, peoples and communities in BiH and in the world (www.aposo.gov.ba, 2003). This law states that every child has a right of access and equal possibility to participate in the appropriate education process, while the school is responsible for contributing to the creation of a culture, which respects human rights and fundamental liberties of all citizens in its area, as set forth in the constitution and other international documents from the field of human rights, signed by Bosnia and Herzegovina. It is also the responsibility of the school to promote and protect religious freedom, tolerance and dialogue in BiH. The school cannot discriminate children's access to education or their participation in the educational process based on race, colour, gender, language, religion, political or other beliefs, national or social origin, on the basis of special needs status, or on any other basis. The school promotes equal opportunities for all its students, teachers and other employees, taking into consideration and at the same time promoting the right for differences among them. By this law, languages of the constituent peoples of BiH in all schools shall be used and all students shall learn scripts that are officially used in Bosnia and Herzegovina. The language and culture of any significant minority in BiH shall be respected and accommodated within the school to the greatest extent practicable, in accordance with the Framework Convention for the Protection of National Minorities. [7] The law also provided the basis for the common quality standard in the entire territory of BiH and set conditions for the common core curriculum. The common core curriculum lays down the content that should be incorporated into all curricula in the BiH territory, but 30% of content may be outside the common core in order to meet the specificities of the ethnic groups. Upon reading this Framework Law, a naïve reader could be lead into thinking that in the past 10 years important structural changes have occurred in equalling the rights of students and promoting cohabitation and tolerance. However, one should by no means forget interpretations of the law within the paradigm of nationalistic policies and a strong need to maintain and deepen segregation. Thus, the syntagm "developing awareness on commitment to the state of BiH, one's own cultural identity, language and tradition" has been used for dividing one curricula into three curricula—the Curriculum for primary schools in the Republic of Srpska, the Framework Curriculum for the Federation of Bosnia and Herzegovina and the Croatian language curriculum. The methodology and structure of those curricula are the same, but the main difference is in the content of so-called "national group of subject". The national group of subject consists of native language and literacy, history and geography. Depending on the curricula, children are taught in Serbian, Croatian or Bosnian language, historical interpretation from the perspective of the ethnic group and geographical terms is important for developing the attachment towards regions or countries in which that particular ethnic group is the majority. Ethnic interpretations also helped in institutionalizing the segregated schools, popularly called "two-schools-under-one-roof", where children of two ethnic backgrounds are physically completely separated. In the field of language and literature, this syntagm resulted in children reading "their own" writers, that is, writers belonging to their own ethnic background, while classical writers have been removed from the list because they are not "ethnically" suitable. Research and additional reviews of textbooks have shown that the poems originally belonging to one dialect have been translated into the dialect of a certain people, so that a child is not even in that way exposed to the "other" language.

Religious Education

Religious education is not a part of the "national group of subjects". Religious education in Bosnia and Herzegovina has been promoted as an electoral subject in the early 1990s as a response to the general national and religious awakening initiated by the dissolution of former Yugoslavia and a strong need for the development of ethnic identity which would later be exclusively defined by religious affiliation, in addition to the language and culture.

Introduction of religious education in those turbulent times for Bosnia and Herzegovina was not seen an important issue to be contemplated, nor was it high up on the agenda of citizens and institutions. War and war trauma had awakened ethnic identity with people who until then identified themselves as Yugoslavs. That means returning religion as the cornerstone of individual and group identity in Bosnia and Herzegovina. That is how religious education entered schools.

When the conflict ended in Bosnia and Herzegovina, the process of clear and exclusive categorization of people into ethnic groups continued. War trauma and the feeling of being threatened by other ethnicities is still the main instrument nationalistic currents are using to homogenize the citizens and to assemble them within a collective ethnical identity, under the guise of need "for defence of national interests, culture and religion" from the other and from the different.

Awoken and encouraged religious institutions and nationalistic parties (whose rhetoric and politics have dominated Bosnia and Herzegovina for 25 years already) recognized education as a strategic place for the transmission of nationalistic ideologies and as the best way for the additional widening of the gap between national groups in Bosnia and Herzegovina. Towards that end, they have, by interpreting laws, especially the Framework Law on Primary and Secondary Education in BiH (Article 9: "...Having in mind diversities of beliefs/convictions within BiH, pupils shall attend religious classes only if latter match their beliefs or beliefs of their parents. The School cannot undertake any measures or activities aimed at limiting freedom of expressing religious beliefs or meeting other and different beliefs.") positioned religious education as a guaranteed right of parents and children to receive education in public schools on matters of faith as well.

MODEL OF TEACHING RELIGIOUS EDUCATION AND WHO CONTROLS IT ALL?

The model of teaching religious education in Bosnia and Herzegovina is confessional [8] and exists as a separate subject in both public and private schools. Status of religious education in the Federation of Bosnia and Herzegovina is diverse. If a child attends school using the Croatian language curriculum (which is the case in the predominantly Croat regions), the subject is "obligatory elective". That means that parents, upon enrolment of the child to the first grade of the primary school, state whether he/she will attend religious education. This subject has no alternative. If they give a positive answer, religious education becomes an obligatory subject until the end of the child's primary education. If the child attends the school in which Bosnian language curriculum is implemented and does not want to attend religious education, they choose between alternative subjects such as Society, Culture and Religion or Healthy Lifestyle (which subjects are offered and under what title depends on the administrative unit in charge of education). In Republika Srpska, this subject is also "obligatory elective" for students from second to eighth grade of primary school and has no alternative. That means that there will be no alternative to attending religious education, even if a student does not want to.[9], [10] It is also important to emphasize that the grade in religious education is a part of the grade point average and is thus equally important as any other subject, e.g. mathematics, science, foreign languages, etc. Training for religious education teachers, instructional design (curriculum of the subject), as well as contents of the textbook fall under the competence of religious communities, although advisories for religious education are employees of the pedagogical institutes (that are a part of the education system). It can be said that the official education system has no real competences regarding the content and teaching methods of religious education. Officials granted these competences to the religious institutions by signing fundamental agreements.[11] For example, on 19 April 2006, the Fundamental Agreement was signed between the Holy See and Bosnia and Herzegovina. The state signed this agreement on the grounds of the constitutional principles and the Holy See on the grounds of the Second Vatican Council and on the grounds of the canon law. This agreement also regulates the issue of religious education.

> However, Article 16 is of special importance as it establishes thatBosnia and Herzegovina, in the light of the principle of freedom of religion, recognizes the fundamental right of parents to see to the religious education of their children; and it guarantees within the framework of the academic programme and in conformity with the wishes of parents or guardians, the teaching of the Catholic religion in all public schools, elementary, middle and higher, and in pre-school centers, as a required subject for those who choose it, under the same conditions as other required subjects. In collaboration with the competent Church authorities, the educational authorities will allow parents and adult students the possibility to avail themselves freely of such teaching at the time of registration for the academic year, in such a way that their decision does not give rise to any form of academic discrimination. The teaching of the Catholic religion will be carried out by teachers who are suitable, with the canonical mandate of the local diocesan Bishop, and in possession of the qualifications required for the particular level of school by the laws in force in Bosnia and Herzegovina, with respect for all the rights and duties pertaining thereto. In the case of

withdrawal of the canonical mandate by the diocesan Bishop, the teacher will not be able to continue teaching the Catholic religion.[11]

The same competences granted to the Catholic Church by the Fundamental Agreement have been given to other religious communities—the Islamic Community and Serbian Orthodox Church. In that way, the decision makers have limited the possibility of influencing the content and processes related to this subject and have thus essentially disabled possibility of non-religious authorities to help in positioning of religious education as a subject through which values and knowledge important for bringing together ethnic/religious groups in Bosnia and Herzegovina are developed.

Analysis of the Content of Textbooks from the National Group of Subjects and of Religious Education—What Do We Teach Our Children?

As has been emphasized several times already, education in post-conflict societies is a strategic place for either development or further disintegration of social cohesion. An education system is an ideal place where a society can either decide to deepen social traumas and segregation or to again turn to rebuilding coexistence and respect of universal values and guaranteed human rights that belong to all individual members of the society. For that purpose, the international community, primarily the OSCE, has been involved in the development of an educational system aimed at initiating reconciliation and cohabitation through active defining of textbook content and curricula. Although their efforts were significant, and in some aspects even crucial, ethnic segregation continued. Many factors contributed to that, but one of them is certainly the content of what children have been studying, especially in the group of national subjects and religious education, for those are the subjects containing the crucial content for the formation of large group identities and for increasing the differences between the groups. The curriculum (and textbooks) is never a pure assortment of knowledge that somehow appears in texts and in classrooms in a country. It has always been a part of the selective knowledge, the result of somebody's choice, a vision of a group about legitimate knowledge.[12] For that purpose, the Soros Open Society initiated a research entitled "What Do We Teach Our Children:

Analysis of Textbook Contents for National Subjects"[13] and the crucial question was **do and to what extent the textbooks promote social cohesion and initiate a positive attitude towards one's own country, that is, to what extent do textbooks truly meet the conditions and tasks of education prescribed by the laws in BiH, and how much do they initiate the development of universal values necessary for life in an open society**. The conceptual framework for this research was developed in accordance with the basic principles of the open society education. The term "open society" means "a society based on the acknowledgment that no one holds a monopoly on the truth, that different people have different views and interests and that there is a need for institutions that will protect the rights of all people so that they could live in peace. An open society is characterized by its reliance on the rule of law, on the existence of an elected government and a diverse and vibrant civil society, and the respect of minorities and minority views." The importance of investing into an open society especially comes to light in post-conflict societies in which ideas and interpretations of conflict differ among groups, such as the case with Bosnia and Herzegovina.

Education for life in an open society is based on the following principles:

- education as a public domain: quality education places a student and his/her needs in the focus and is at the same time striving to promote the entire society;
- interculturalism: educational content and teaching methods initiate a full understanding of oneself and of the others, develop the feeling of solidarity with other people of respect for a pluralistic society;
- social justice: ensuring a quality education for all with full acceptance of different educational needs, especially of the marginalized, threatened and deprived persons in the society and
- respect of human rights: educational institutions guarantee group and individual rights of all members of the society and promote through integration processes the respect of universal values and diversity.

The main tasks set in this research were:

1. To identify (map) the content of textbooks from the national group of subjects, including religious education, that positively

or negatively influences preparation of students for life in an open society and

2. To develop recommendations on the basis of the analysis of the content for the development of future textbooks.

In the process of analysing the content of the textbooks and identifying examples, researchers were aware and paid close attention to the fact that religious education is a confessional subject aimed at structural teaching of religion and they did not in any way problematize the content determined by dogma, doctrine and convictions. The analysis focussed on the views and interpretations of textbook authors that were approved by the religious communities. In this research, all textbooks for higher grades of primary school and for secondary school used in religious education that year in the territory of Bosnia and Herzegovina were analysed. Four Islamic religious education textbooks analysed were used in primary schools (for children from 11 to 15 years of age), and of the six Catholic religious education textbooks, four were used in primary and two in secondary schools, and of the five Christian Orthodox religious education textbooks, four were used in primary and one in secondary school.

The methodology for the analysis required that the content of a textbook be analysed by a group of relevant experts (five of them), whereby one textbook would be analysed by at least two experts to achieve the inter-rater agreement on whether the identified content truly meets the criteria defined by the research. Here, we will show the content that was identified as an example of good practice, but also the content that has no place in an open society education.

Positive Examples Promoting the Respect of Diversity Within BiH Themes

Residents of the World[14]

Ana, Sanela, David and Chen live in the same neighbourhood, in the same city. They often meet in the street, in shops, especially at school. Their parents come from different places. However, now they all live in the same city and contribute to the better and more beautiful life of this society and of this city. They want to live in peace and develop a happier future. Like many other people, the parents of these children also ask themselves – What is it that we need to do to be happy? How can we build a more just and happier world? What values do we need to teach our children? They all ask the same questions, they are all looking for answers.

Our friends' parents are believers and in their religions they are looking for guidance on how to live well and right. Sanela's parents often remind her of the teachings from the Quran.

David has learnt from his parents the Ten Commandments that are familiar to you too: "I am the Lord your God…" Ana too has learnt those commandments from her parents.

Chen's grandfather repeats Buddha's messages to his grandson.

This is an example from a Catholic religious education textbook where names typical of certain ethnic groups in Bosnia and Herzegovina are mentioned at the beginning. The text further emphasizes the parents' desire for their children to live together and build a just world, and to teach their children the universal postulates of every religion promoting equality of people before God. In this way, students are sent a message that human communities should not be ethnically homogenous, that diversity is wealth and that there are universal values that initiate respect for one another as human beings.

A CRITICAL REFLEXION OF ONE'S OWN ROLE

Catholic religious education textbooks contain sections that have been identified as examples of good practice because they show that the religious community itself does not idealize its role through history and areas.

Dark Pages of the Church in the Middle Ages[15], [16]

Alongside all these great achievements of the Church in the Middle Ages, there were, sadly, events and activities that cast a negative light on the Church and its Christian teachings. By that we mean the Crusades, enormous wealth and luxury in the Church, inquisition and the crisis of the papacy.

The Conquest of Jerusalem (1099)[17]
Already in Antioch, the crusaders left a trail of horrible destruction; they mercilessly killed and pillaged both Muslims and Christians. What happened after the conquest of Jerusalem cast a shadow on all prior violence of the crusaders. The Muslim and Jewish population of the city was almost entirely killed.
J. Heidrich

Such (self)critical reflection enables the students to understand that politics and activities of the religious community have not always been completely right and that it is important to reflect upon them in order not to repeat the mistakes from the past. By such examples of critical thinking and education, the possibility of using events from the past for setting additional triumphs and traumas as the pillars of large group identity is significantly limited.

EQUALITY OF RELIGIONS

We already stated in the introduction that religion is one of the fundamental elements upon which large group identity rests. In that sense, examples in which different religions, especially religions of groups that were involved in a conflict until recently, are brought together are very important for accepting the other and the different and for the development of the ability to live a quality life and to act in religiously heterogeneous communities. Raising students on the idea of equality of religions and respect for every human being, as well as an equal treatment towards everybody (not only towards members of one's own religious community) decreases the potential of forces that strive to maintain religious animosity and prejudice.

Different but Connected[14]
Human community consists of different religions, different languages and peoples. Customs, faces and clothes are different. We

call God by different names, we warship Him differently. That is our wealth and our future.

Dialogue, friendship and mutual understanding should replace division and discrimination among people.

Muslims believe in Messengers of God and their names are mentioned in the Quran. We also believe that there have been other messengers of God. It is a duty of a Muslim to treat members of other religions with full respect and consideration.[15, 16]

Christians are aware that all people, regardless of their belief or disbelief, race or skin colour are worthy of equal respect, because they are people.[18]

Thus, a Muslim is obliged to create conditions for general peace and prosperity. He is not to commit injustice to neither another Muslim, nor to a non-Muslim, for Muhammad PBUH warned us:

"Beware of injustice so that you do not get cursed by the one you did injustice to, for Allah will hear his prayer and sigh, even if he were a non-believer."[19]

A man is obliged to treat other people the way he treats himself and according to the words of Christ: Do unto others as you would have them do unto you (Mt 7,12).[20]

Examples promoting peace and peaceful resolution to conflicts in Bosnia and Herzegovina are especially important. In that sense, these examples have been selected as good practice in order to show the way to create contents in future textbooks, for the purpose of minimizing the potential for ethnic conflicts.

War and a ruthless arms race are also against the Fifth Commandment. It is a duty of every man to promote peace and love amongst people and nations. Peace is built on the grounds of a just society, on equality of all peoples, solidarity and on helping poor countries materially.[15, 16]

These examples show that religious education in the confessional model can be a subject promoting internalization of universal values like equality of all people, respect and solidarity, peaceful resolution of conflicts and it in a way prevents the absorption of negative traits of other groups as foundations for the formation of a group ethnic identity in Bosnia and Herzegovina. We could even say that if we want to strengthen individual identity and prevent membership in a group from completely determining individual identity, these examples help us as educators because they maintain the boundary of group identity open and flexible, instead of rigid, closed and unchangeable under the influence of the context.

Still, examples that do not initiate social cohesion and equality of all people have been mapped in the religious education textbooks. Moreover, examples contributing to further segregation and promoting the development of large group identity have been mapped as well. The ratio between positive and negative examples was 1:5—to one positive example, five negatives were mapped per textbook. Further in the text, we will try to show what it is that discourages social cohesion and open society development.

CHARACTERISATION OF ONE'S OWN RELIGION AND OTHER ETHNIC GROUPS

Religious education textbooks, although prepared for the confessional model of teaching, contain texts which deal with more "worldly" topics that concern peoples and historical events in Bosnia and Herzegovina, which shows that in Bosnia and Herzegovina religious affiliation also implies affiliation to a certain ethnic group. For example, if you are a Muslim, you are a Bosniak and if you are a Catholic, you are a Croat. So, these are the examples of symbiosis of religion and ethnic groups.

Thus, religious education textbooks emphasize certain characteristics of an ethnic group in order for children to adopt the positive characteristics of their own group and to see the differentiating elements through examples related to other groups.

That is why Muslims are known as a compassionate people, forgiving and able to suppress anger quickly.[19]

This is an example of an autostereotype that presents to children certain individual characteristics as characteristics of an entire group.

In the following example, we also find an interpretation of a historical event in the light of a great sacrifice that one ethnic group endured to defend Christianity. The way the text was written (in the confessional narrative) adds to the romantic undertone of this sacrifice.

With Courage and Faith against All Troubles[21]

Numerous calls to the European rulers to help Croats in the fight against the Ottoman conquest were to no avail. On several occasions the Popes encouraged the Christian rulers to jointly resist the Ottoman policy of conquest. Once they realized that the Christian West was closing its eyes before the troubles of Croats because of the lack of unity, selfishness and discord, they themselves financially and organisationally helped the defence of the Croatian areas.

During the most intense Ottoman attacks, when they lost all hope of receiving help from the powerful European countries, Croats had only to rely on the power from above. "They are convinced", Marko Marulić wrote, that "only God can save them". In those dramatic moments, they showed an unbreakable and impressive strength of the spirit. Owing to their numerous victims, further Ottoman penetration into Europe was prevented. For that victory, history gave them a title: "the bulwark of Christianity".

CHARACTERISATION OF ONE'S OWN AND OTHER RELIGIONS

In the basic postulates, Abrahamic religions contain the same messages and we have seen in the positive examples that religious education textbooks recognize that. However, there are examples where the power of one in comparison to the other faith is emphasized, so it can be said that these polarizations send a message to children: "We are all equal, but we are the best."

Only Islamic fasting is perfect and fully beneficial.[19]
As there is only one Christ, so there is only one Body of Christ, and only one bride of Christ: "one Catholic and apostolic Church".[17]

Although the following text, i.e. hadith, concerns all neighbours regardless of their religious affiliation, the introductory part of the text, as well as the interpretation following the hadith, underlines helping Muslims.

A Muslim is obliged to take care of other Muslims and help them in the time of need. Muhammad PBUH warns:
"It is a haram for a Muslim to dine if he knows of a neighbour who does not have dinner." (Hadith)
We can see in this hadith how greatly a Muslim is obliged to take care of another Muslim.[19]

Selected Traumas, Victories and Sacrifice in the Name of Religion and Ethnic Groups

As was mentioned in the introduction, a group needs its own selected victims, traumas and victories to be able to constantly remind itself of the importance of the large group identity. Religious education textbooks play a significant role in the construction of this side of the group identity, for they contain contents glorifying historical events where struggle, war and death are shown as an expression of the deepest patriotism and loyalty to one's own group.

Fierce persecution of Christians began. They invented the worst possible torture for them. They would let hungry beasts from Africa in a huge circus to tear them apart, men women and children. Christians in Rome suffered many a torture but they never gave up on Christ.[22]

This example lets children know that the first Christians were unremitting and that they endured great suffering, which implies that sacrifice in the name of religion must be taken as a heritage that is never to be abandoned.

The following poem was published in a textbook for children aged 11–12, and in it, birds are used as a metaphor for the members of an ethnic group that are being killed by unspecified villains. Those birds are peaceful and, in general, loved for their beautiful song. The message that can be conveyed is that the group is a victim of others who are constantly trying to eradicate it and that this happens whether one wants it or not (while you are sleeping...). Thus, do not fall asleep and do not trick yourselves into thinking that the Other wants good for you.

From Mashriq to Maghrib[23]
From Mashriq to Maghrib, and everywhere where ezan calls, they kill your flock, your skylarks and nightingales.
Our village has fallen silent and the skies stand in sorrow!
The more we bleed, the more we love Thee, the stronger we move and new dawns we see...
Now – as you sleep – they slit the throat of one bird? They kill – for nothing! – tender sisters and brethren!
Now – as you sleep – they set nests alight. Tonight they freeze – for nothing! – little bird's eyes forever shut tight!
Now - as you sleep – a new flock flies out – We hug and we watch: who tomorrow will we be without?!
Demaludin Lati

In the following examples, we can see how the emphasis is being placed on self-sacrifice (giving one's life) as the highest form of loyalty towards religion and country—glorification of death and war.

In our proud country of Bosnia and Herzegovina there were many soldiers who testified the greatness and truthfulness of Istishhad. If need be to defend Religion and Country, Bosniaks are willing to accept Istishhad even today. There are many such Muslims in other parts or our planet as well.[15], [16]

....to sincerely share joy and sorrow, the fortunes and misfortunes of our fatherland and our people and, if necessary, give our life for it as our Lord Jesus Christ said "Greater love hath no man than this, that a man lay down his life for his friends" (John 15:13)[20]

A Muslim must not submit to the enemy of his faith and country; his response must be calculated and decisive. He fights until victorious, to live free on his own, to live in safety and with dignity. To fight in the path of Allah is therefore an important part of Islamic life. A Muslim must always be prepared to guard freedom and protect the truth if he wishes to be consistent to the right path.[15], [16]

Relationship Towards Other Beliefs

Examples from religious educationv textbooks explaining different beliefs, including atheism, to children are very interesting. It could, in fact, be asserted that these interpretations in the textbooks of all three religions are consistent and even somewhat paradoxically they unite "worshipers" (of the Abrahamic religions) against other beliefs and disbeliefs.

Relationship Towards Different Beliefs

Sectarians do differ between themselves, but they also have something in common. They all desire to destroy the basic elements of human existence, such as FAMILY and STATE. The word sect is of Latin origin and means to follow.

The sect therefore designates a community of people following their founder. Fully aware that the family is the pillar and cornerstone of every society, sectarians endeavour to destroy the family and to create conflict within the family based on their principle: "the worse it gets, the better it is". In most cases sects order their members to beak all ties with their families and relatives. Sects propagating overt Satanism go even a step further. The following can be heard as part of their prayers: "Rip the mother out of your heart and spit your father in the face". We must be aware that these sectarians are, in fact, fake teachers and that their science is aimed primarily against Christ as the Saviour of mankind. They are described as "wolves in sheep's clothing" and we therefore need to avoid them. The consequences of "collaborating with them" are painful and deeply scar both the individuals involved and their families.

All sects are equally dangerous to the soul of every Christian. Their founders are in most cases persons with certain emotional or psychological disorders. Because of these disorders they imagine that God has selected them to spread his word. They think that everyone else is deluded and they are the only ones treading on the right path.

They forget that there is only one true path leading to eternal life and that path has been shown to us by the founder of our church, our Saviour Lord Jesus Christ: "I am the way and the truth and the life" (John 14:6).

The goal of these sectarians is to rip man from the embrace of Christ's Church and to win him over for their heretic teaching. They cannot win over a stable person. Their efforts are therefore aimed at those with weak personalities, those with big problems, those experiencing a difficult transitional period (losing a job, divorce, conflict with parents). Such persons are their prey and they skilfully use that. To avoid that we too become prey of these "wolves in sheep's clothing" we need to take precautions to avoid their traps. These measures include: knowing well the teachings of our Church, attending service in our Church, contact with our priests and respecting the church commandments. "Do not read heretic books". We need to know the names of these sects and their false teachings so that we can timely avoid them and getting in contact with them.[20]

Negative Attitude Towards Atheists

Faith in God is a precondition for happiness and salvation. A man without faith is like a ship without a compass. Just like a ship cannot find its harbour without a compass, so man without faith cannot reach the silent harbour of salvation. Losing faith is the greatest misfortune that can happen to a man. This sin against faith is called atheism or godlessness. This sin is great and unforgivable and different circumstances, such as bad behaviour, negative examples in the youth, one-sided and superficial education, can lead a man to it.[20]

Atheism means godlessness, or an upbringing without God. They claim this to be an expression of progress. We know from the experience of recent events that noble-minded persons cannot be brought up without God and against God, in fact, it often creates people such as those who established Auschwitz.[21]

Science and technology can foster the strengthening of practical atheism, especially if a man delights excessively in his knowledge and technological progress. When he gets carried away by scientific success to such an extent that he forgets all ethical and moral principles, to such an extent that he no longer needs God, then he begins to behave like an atheist.[21]

In the "modern world" people spend years living door to door in the same building without getting to know each other. This is a habit imported from the godless West. A result of such behaviour is depression, the most widespread illness in the West. In most cases it is a result of a feeling of loneliness and helplessness.

Loneliness and helplessness go hand in hand. This illness is practically non-existent in the Muslim world and suicides are rare. We know that the standard of living is high in the West, yet people are still unhappy.

Why?

It does not take great wisdom to answer to this question. Man is a social being. He has the need to share both good and bad with others. Only then is he happy and safe.

The war in BiH showed vividly the importance of socialisation. In this, the bloodiest war in contemporary history, Bosnians preserved their mental health.

> Psychiatrists from the West predicted that we would suffer from depression during and after war. This did not happen because we shared everything with our neighbours during the war, and now we go out to the street and rejoice over every surviving Muslim. This enriches our lives. We feel strong and resilient.[19]

All these examples pertain to interpretations and views of the authors and, as such, their aim is not to educate children in religion (in the sense that they learn the basic principles of their faith, religious rituals, etc.).

REALISTIC VIEW AND ACTION FOR THE FUTURE—RELIGIOUS EDUCATION IS HERE, HOW TO USE IT FOR SOCIAL COHESION

Religious education has become a right enshrined in several state laws and international agreements. Despite ongoing debates in favour of and against religious education in schools, it is possible to note that even the most ardent proponents of throwing religious education out of schools are coming to terms with the fact that it will remain a part of school education. It also needs to be noted that of all the subjects introduced in the education system after the war, only religious education underwent comprehensive development, including curriculum development, while other alternative subjects were in most cases inadequately developed with teachers lacking formal education to deliver them, as they are teaching them as supplementary subjects.

Furthermore, the religion has become an important component of individual identity for a large number of citizens in Bosnia and Herzegovina. The communist era during which worshipers were system- atically discriminated against left bitter memories and strong emotions, especially among worshipers and priests who oppose any changes to the status of religious education. They consider calls for the introduction of Culture of Religions and Religious Studies subject a manifestation of fundamentalist secularism or "fundamentalist enlightenment" which is again trying to marginalize religion and push it to the sidelines.

In addition to that, as Alibašić[11] explicates *"differences do exist in Bosnia and Herzegovina and they cannot be erased. BiH can only survive if these differences are accepted and recognised and if there is teaching on how to deal with them"*. The cited positive examples from the contents of the religious education textbooks show that this subject can have an important educational role in the development of a multi-ethnic Bosnia and Herzegovina by promoting diversity as wealth and unity in diversity.

However, textbooks also contain material which is disturbing and could have a negative effect on social cohesion, i.e. could lead to further segregation of the ethnic groups.

The cited negative examples illustrate how the content of religious education textbooks shapes the development of the identity of a large group. All such contents do not represent direct religious dogma or quotes from religious books, it is rather in the form of interpretations inserted into textbooks, confirmed by an authority and (often) presented without critical scrutiny. As such, they become facts just like $2 + 2 = 4$ in the phenomenological framework of students. Use of generalizations in describing the characteristics of an ethnic group, positive auto-stereotypes and the glorification of successes leads to the inclusion of children into a set or group that shares common reservoirs of concepts linked to positive emotions and positive identification with the respective ethnic groups. To prevent this "romantic" conviction about the beauty and positive traits of one's own ethnic group from being shattered, it is also necessary to add content which will be roused by the image/belief of others as significantly more negative than one's own ethnic group. This process of education is the most effective in childhood when children form their identity and everything that is done during this period remains a part of the heritage.

A large number of students attend religious education, either because it is a compulsory subject in certain areas, or because parents and children chose religious education from a list of other offered subjects. 85% of students chose religious education as a subject during the 2014/2015 school year in Sarajevo Canton as compared to 15% of students who chose Society, Culture and Religions or Healthy Life Styles. Therefore, parents want their children to attend religious education and children do attend. In an attempt to examine the reasons why children attend religious education in such high numbers, the Soros Open Society and pro-MENTE Social Research[25] conducted a research on how a decision is reached with regard to which subject the child should attend and reasons that were taken into account as important in making the decision. The results showed that 50% of parents included in the sample responded to the question "who made the decision on which subject the child should attend?" as them being the ones who made the decision, that in 37% of cases it was the children who made the decision, and that teachers and the education system had practically no influence in this process. In 37% of cases, the parents stated that the main reason why they chose religious education for their child was because they wanted their child "to be a better person". 19% stated the practical reason of wanting their children to "apply in everyday life what they have learned", 18% stated that they wanted their children to have "better relations with others" and a further 18% stated that they wanted their children to "adopt important life skills". These reasons were also cited by the children with 46% of them stating as the chief reason for their decision, the desire "to become a better person".

It can truly be stated that religious education as a subject teaching children spirituality and educating them in the light of universal values such as equality of all before God and in the world, justice and honesty possess a strong potential of becoming a point of cohesion. However, the question remains whether this can really be achieved with a subject positioned in such a way. It is therefore necessary in Bosnia and Herzegovina to constantly monitor the content of teaching, not only of religious education but of all subjects dealing with national issues in order to prevent abuse and further dissolution of the already sensitive and fragile BiH society. Religious education as a subject currently has a specific status as compared to all other subjects because it is under the sole competence of religious institutions. On the other hand, although religious institutions are the greatest authority for the preparation of the religious education curriculum viewed as an exclusively confessional subject, the content of textbooks and the teaching of religious education need to be in accordance with the commitment of education serving the purpose of reconstruction of the society. It cannot be exempt from efforts that the content of the textbooks should promote tolerance, understanding, solidarity with all (not only with members of one's own religion) and respect of human rights. Positive values and characteristics must be presented as universal values typical of people in general. The content of the textbooks must not suggest that certain values belong only to "true" worshipers or worshipers of one's own religion, but that they are universal values typical of every human being regardless of religious affiliation. The content of the textbooks must not support the view of a group being at constant risk, as this increases social distance within the society. If suffering of one group is presented, then students also need to be presented facts about the suffering of other groups which should allow for a critical analysis of events and the position of different ethnic groups under different historical circumstances.

Furthermore, regardless of the complete integration of religious education into the education system of Bosnia and Herzegovina, it is necessary to continue with a serious consideration of alternatives that could really be interesting to students and which they would perceive as possible options. Universal values such as equality, justice and solidarity continue to be particularized in Bosnia and Herzegovina and viewed as a buffet where everyone can pick and choose what best suits them by saying "all people are God's children, but we are the best".

NOTES

1. Kennet D. Bush, and Dianna Saltarelli (eds.), Two faces of Education in Ethnic Conflict: Toward the Peacebuilding Education for Children. UNICEF Innocenti Centre: Florence (2000).
2. Vamik Volkan. Bloodlines: From Ethnic Pride to Ethnic Terrorism. Colorado: Wastview Press (1997). www.aposo.gov.ba. 30 June 2003. Accessed 2015.
3. Vamik Volkan and Blind Trust, Large Groups and their Leaders in Times of Crisis and Terror. Charlottesville, Virgina: Pitchstone Publishing (2004).
4. Howard F. Stein, International and Group Mileu of Ethnicity: Identifying Generic Group Dynamic Issues. Canadian Review of Studies in Nationalism 17 (1990): 107–130.
5. Gorana Ognjenović, Quo Vadis Vlachs? Project Čarnojević into Twenty-First Century. In Politicization of Religion, the Power of Symbolism, ed. G. Ognjenović and J. Jozelić, 7–27. New York: Palgrave Macmillan (2014).
6. Council of Europe, 1995. Available: www.coe.int.
7. Zdenko Kodelja, and Terrice Bassler, Religion and Education in Open Society, Sarajevo: Open Society Institute (2007).
8. Nebojša Šatara, Vjeronauk u Srpskoj nema alternativu, 12 December 2014. Available: www.mondo.ba.
9. Davud Muminović. Available at: www.nezavisne.com. 3 May 2015.
10. Ahmed Alibašić, A Problem that Does Not Have to Be: Religious Education in Public Schools in Bosnia and Hercegovina. Religion and Education in Open Society: Questioning the Model of Religious Education in Bosnia and Hercegovina, 11–34. Sarajevo: Open Society Institute (2009).
11. Michael W., Apple, Cultural Politics and Education. Columbia University: Teacher College Press (1996).
12. Dženana Trbić, Dženana Husremović, Stephen Powell, Ajla Šišić, and Aida Dolić, Education in Bosnia and Hercegovina: What Do We Teach Our Children. Sarajevo: Open Society Institute (2007).

13. Ružica Razum, I am the Way: Religious Education Textbook for 5th Grade. Zagreb-Sarajevo: Kršćanska sadašnjost (2004).

14. Josip Perišić, Together in Love: Catolic Religous Education for Seventh Grade. Zagreb-Sarajevo: Kršćanska sadašnjost (2004).

15. Viktorija Gadža, Nikola Milanović, Rudi Paloš, Mirjana Vučica, and Dušan Vuletić, Courageous Witnesses: Catolic Religious Education for Second Grade of. Zagreb-Sarajevo: Katehetski salezijanski centar (2004).

16. Viktorija Gadža, Nikola Milanović, Rudi Paloš, Mirjana Vučica, and Duško Vuletić, Seekers of the Sense: Catolic Religious Education Textbook for the First Grade of Secondary School. Zagreb-Sarajevo: Katehetski salezijanski centar (2004).

17. Muharem Omerdić, and Fahira Kalajdžisalihović, Islamic Religious Education for Seventh Grade, Sarajevo: El Kalem (2005).

18. Mensura Ćatović, Islamic Religious Education Textbook for the Sixth Grade. Sarajevo: El Kalem (2003).

19. Slobodan Vrhovac, Orthodox Christian Religious Education Textbook for the Ninth Grade, Banja Luka: Katihetski odbor (2004).

20. Josip Perišić, Mirjana Vučica, and Duško Vuletić, With Christ into Life: Catolic Religious Education for Eight Grade. Zagreb-Sarajevo: Kršćanska sadašnjost (2005).

21. Niko Mojsilović, Orthodox Christian Religious Education Textbook for the Sixth Grade, Banja Luka: Katihetski Odbor (2005).

22. Group of authors, Islamic Religious Education for the Fifth Grade, Sarajevo: El Kalem (1997).

23. Ivona Čelebičić, Sidik Lepić, and Andrea Soldo, Religious Education/ Society, Culture, Religion/Helathy Life Styles: The Effects of Implementing Alternative Subjects in Canton Sarajevo, Sarajevo: Open Society Institute (2014).

CHAPTER 10

Religious Education in Serbia as a Litmus Test for Church–State Relations

Bojan Aleksov

Fifteen years after its introduction, religious education (RE) in Serbia hardly arises any more public interest and most students, parents and

I acknowledge that I use a metaphor already used by Zorica Kuburić i Milan Vukomanović in theirs, "Religious education: The Case of Serbia", in Zorica Kuburić and Cristian Moe (eds.), *Religion and Pluralism in Education* (Novi Sad: CEIR in cooperation with the Kotor Network, 2006), pp. 107–138. It led to the subheading title in a wider study by professor Milan Vukomanović of the University of Belgrade entitled "Ecclesiastical Involvement in Serbian Politics: Post-2000 Period," in Gorana Ognjenović and Jasna Jozelić (eds.), *Politicization of Religion, the Power of State, Nation, and Faith* (London: Palgrave Macmillan US, Palgrave Studies in Religion, Politics, and Policy, 2014), pp. 115–149, here p. 118. While we arrived to this conclusion independently I am most indebted to Prof. Vukomanović for many insights on the topic of religion in Serbia derived from his numerous studies cited below as well as from private conversations. My differences in analysis will be spelled out towards the end of this article.

B. Aleksov (✉)
The School of Slavonic and East European Studies,
University College London, London, England, UK

© The Author(s) 2018
G. Ognjenović and J. Jozelić (eds.), *Education in Post-Conflict Transition*, Palgrave Studies in Religion, Politics, and Policy,
https://doi.org/10.1007/978-3-319-56605-4_10

teachers seem to have come to terms with it.[1] A couple of years after first classes began, I conducted an evaluation and in the meantime many other authors have done research, providing valuable insight, analysis and criticism of many of its aspects as well as recommendations for its improvement.[2] In the past years, some technical issues raised have been resolved while other problems remained. However, going beyond technicalities there is a scant evidence and limited pedagogical methodology to demonstrate whether and what impact RE had on those enrolled and the Serbian society in general. So what is there more to say on the subject that would draw attention, especially that of English language readers? It is only in the larger context of its introduction and continuous amendments it underwent that RE provides useful hints for scholars of contemporary Serbian society. As already suggested by Milan Vukomanović, RE is a litmus test, a prism through which Church–State relations in Serbia is studied since 2000.

What lends importance to the topic of Church–State relations is the association of the Yugoslav crisis in 1980s and the tragic wars that followed its dissolution in 1991 with country's multiconfessional demographics and more importantly, the detrimental role played by religious hierarchies and clergy in hate mongering and victimisation.[3] The body of literature on this topic is growing but it is less known that during the period of open conflict and wars, when Serbia was under the leadership of Slobodan Milošević, there was hardly any change in Church–State relations. Religious communities and most notably the biggest of them, the Serbian Orthodox Church (SOC), were certainly not repressed any longer.[4] They gained access to media and became more prominent in the public sphere but these important symbolic changes were not reflected on the legal/constitutional level. In fact, Milošević vetoed any attempt to change the position of the SOC or begin the process of return or compensation for Church property nationalised after the Communists took power in Yugoslavia in 1945.[5] The real transformation only ensued after Milošević was ousted from power and was actually linked to his arrest and deportation. The first step was the introduction of RE in schools which opened the door for many other changes. Teaching RE and other pastoral and clerical roles for which State financing was acquired allowed for a manifold increase in the number of clergy and lay persons in the mission of the SOC. With the prioritised return of confiscated property, financial aid from the state on multiple levels and increased donations or emoluments, the SOC has become a powerful institution in Serbia. Allegedly, the Church is the third largest income taker in the country after state electricity and oil companies though this is difficult to measure and confirm given that its monetary transactions remain outside the financial system. At the same time, the SOC is entrusted with providing an ideological framework and value system for state institutions ranging from schools to armed forces and penitentiary institutions. These developments make Church–State relations a valuable topic as the following pages will attempt to demonstrate.

In lieu of conclusion, I will offer criticism of the existing interpretations and propose a somewhat different view of the changes. Acknowledging that the initial decision in 2001 to introduce confessional RE in Serbian schools might have been driven by sheer pragmatism of the government of Zoran Đinđić, that wanted to appease the Serbian Church after the extradition of Milošević to the International Criminal Tribunal (ICTY), all developments to date indicate that it set a pattern for future Church–State relations in Serbia. As numerous subsequent concessions demonstrated, the hasty introduction of RE paved the way for the unprecedented role of the SOC in the history of the modern Serbian state. Yet, the concessions to the Church were arbitrary more often than not. Moreover, it is the state that makes the concessions and still holds the upper hand in this relationship, heavily determining its outcome. Therefore, my conclusion will dismiss the notion of clericalisation of the Serbian society, which is often used, though admit some clericalism within the SOC itself. There is also little evidence for the thesis of de-secularisation or countersecularisation. Taking a stock of RE 15 years after its implementation and assessing some other developments in Church–State relations, my article will nevertheless underline the enormous political role given to the SOC in Serbia's post-conflict and post-socialist transformation in times of post-democracy. This larger context determines the growing importance of the SOC a development already described in much more detail in neighbouring Romania and further away in Russia, to mention but two countries with Christian Orthodox majority and great role assigned to their respective churches.[6] The following undertaking is based on previous research of others and my own as well as press and electronic media survey and field observation.[7] Unfortunately, neither the government nor church officials in charge were available for comment.

Introduction and Amendments to Religious Education Over Last 15 Years

As already indicated the government's decision to introduce RE in public schools in Serbia took place outside of the then existing legal framework, without prior public/parliamentary discussion and bypassing the Ministry of Education. Many civic organisations objected its constitutionality and legality as it licenced only seven so-called traditional religious communities to perform it and because the decision contradicted the existing education laws. Their arguments were rejected by courts and subsequently, the government passed the necessary regulations and amended the Laws on Primary and Secondary Education. Aside from legal lacunae, the key issue was the selection of confessional model of RE, which was designed and instructed by the above-mentioned traditional denominations. In reality, the SOC provides 90% of RE in Serbia with Islamic Community and Roman Catholic providing for the rest with a small number of children attending Hungarian Reformed and Slovak Lutheran Churches' classes. For smaller religious communities, it is much more difficult to organise RE provision because of higher dispersion of their potential attendees. Educational experts warned strongly against the model of catechism as it is usually known but the government sided with the SOC, whose request for confessional model was also backed by other denominations involved. Initially, the government envisaged RE and its counterpart Civic Education as optional subjects but because of weak interest and upon the insistence of religious denominations in 2002–2003 the subject became compulsory with the only option being the two subjects.

Given that the educational dimensions of confessional model were discussed widely elsewhere, this article, focusing on Church–State relations, will look at few other implications the new subject in state schools brought about. In terms of financing and human resources introducing RE meant that the state was accepting and taking over the payment of salaries or parts of salaries to hundreds of priests (and few imams) and lay religious teachers appointed and supervised by their confessional hierarchy alone. Because of sheer numbers of students and teachers involved, the SOC was an overwhelming beneficiary of the model applied. The next important government's decision was in 2004 when the Theological Faculty of the SOC was reassociated with the state-financed University of Belgrade, 52 years after it was removed by the former Communist-led government.

In the meantime, the Faculty was fully governed and financed by the SOC. Despite the State's takeover, the Church's full control of the rules of admission and promotion was maintained which many deemed discriminatory.[8] In logistic terms, accepting to finance the Theological Faculty of the SOC, the state effectively undertook the cost of training of RE teachers but also of the rest of SOC clergy too. Clearly, introducing RE sets the pattern of the state overtaking important shares of church finances. But let us pose for the moment and take a stock of some of the other issues raised by the research on RE.

The problem with this kind of research, and Belgrade's Institute for Pedagogic Research conducted two surveys on behalf of the Ministry of Religion, is that they could only capture personal subjective perceptions of students and RE teachers.[9] There is no control group to assess how much of proclaimed tasks and aims were fulfilled. Furthermore, these tasks and aims are not clearly defined and teachers and students have quite different expectations as indicated by Vladeta Milin, one of the researchers from the Institute.[10] An undisclosed research by the Ministry of Education among teachers of RE from 2014 singled out the uneven quality of programmes and stressed they were the most problematic in early grades where topics, contents and methods were not correlated with the age of pupils, which in turn affected their motivation. In Catholic RE too, some topics were singled out as excessively difficult for students while a particular problem was the lack of programme for 3-year high schools which simply did not teach the fourth year without any adjustments.[11] RE teachers also stressed that they expected more support from their superiors in the promotion of the subject in their own professional training and in terms of more quality textbooks and teaching material.

There has been little clarity about popular demand for classes and the issue was made somewhat redundant when the RE/CE was made compulsory. Year after year the Ministry of Education repeats that approximately 50% of students opt for the Religious and consequently similar number for Civic Education. The lack of precise data implied in this 50–50 figure reminds of when white wine is mixed with soda in a so-called spritzer, as it is locally known, where the exact ratio is not so important because of poor wine quality.[12] Fragmentary evidence suggest that more students (or their parents) opt for RE in rural areas and in South Serbia but this is just a speculation as long as the Ministry does not disclose concrete figures and trends over years.[13] More significantly, the conflict and division within the Islamic community in Serbia led to the boycott of RE taught by imams and teachers from the opposite side of the divide exposing all the vulnerability of confessional model.[14] Namely, if there are conflicts within religious communities or among their leadership, this immediately reflects on state provision of RE.

Despite the problems only sketched above RE continued with the unequivocal support of all post-Milošević governments in Serbia. Nevertheless, towards the end of 2015, a big shock erupted when the Education Minister Srđan Verbić publicly expressed doubt in educational aims and outcomes of RE, stressing that it creates divisions and segregation instead of building unity and harmony.[15] The problem, according to Verbić, is especially acute in multi-ethnic (multiconfessional) areas where students split into Orthodox, Islamic and/or Catholic catechism and those who opt for Civic education. Furthermore, Verbić stressed the lack of competent staff and students being overburdened, suggesting that in the future RE should be taught in 4 instead of all 12 years of schooling (8 years of primary and 4 years of secondary education). None of these arguments was new and has been pointed out in all previous evaluations mentioned above. The only new argument raised, and a rather valid one given that it was raised by the Minister of Education himself, was about the cost of RE. Verbić's cost reminder makes all the more sense knowing that Serbia has been in uninterrupted recession since 2008 and salaries (and pensions) of all state employees including teachers were slashed. However, his initiative came as big surprise and remains an enigma given that Verbić was brought to the government by the so-called Progressive party or SNP, which won two previous elections with an overwhelming majority. The Progressives ruled for years and cemented the model of quasi-pluralist Church–State relations described above which was built around the confessional model of RE.

Not surprisingly the barrage of attacks against the Minister came from the SOC. Rev Dragomir Sando, coordinator for RE with SOC accused Verbić of the lack of professionalism and morality (sic).[16] Nevertheless, the topic soon got buried amidst more pressing issues. After the elections in April 2016, the new government was formed without Verbić as the Minister in charge. Yet during the same summer for the first time since RE was introduced in an appeasing statement, the SOC (its Commission for RE) accepted some criticism made by the Institute of Education (Zavod za vrednovanje vaspitanja i obrazovanja). It promised to work on new plans and programmes and produce a new set of textbooks which would be in accordance with the existing Law on textbooks, indirectly admitting previous ones were not.[17] In an unusually compromising announcement bishop Irinej of Bačka, who wields the most power in SOC concerning education matters, also foresaw a new set of criteria and expertise for RE teachers and promised that new teaching materials would be more related to everyday life and more accessible to students.[18] The very same coordinator for RE with SOC who previously attacked the Minister and all criticism on behalf of educational experts announced that new textbooks will be done via open competition as with other school textbooks (previously they were all written by a single bishop Ignjatije of Braničevo). It was the state's turn, according to the SOC, to respond by fully equalising the status of RE teachers, allowing them other benefits available to full teaching staff such as housing credits, etc.

Despite the anticipating rhetoric the long-term observers or political life in Serbia and Church–State relations doubt if there will be any change on the horizon. Textbooks were little used before and two issues at the core of Verbić's criticism—division of students and costs associated with confessional model of RE—were not addressed. This last episode of discussion on RE once more exemplifies the nature of Church–State relations shaped by arbitrariness and concessions the government is granting to the Church for political and symbolic gains. RE has been introduced and is still driven by the state and ruling party's political interests rather than the educational needs of students and the Serbian society. This approach has been vindicated in all subsequent state dealings with the SOC.

Church and State in Serbia Since 2000

The codification of the new model of Church–State relations in Serbia, which institutionalised seven "traditional" religious communities, happened with the new Law on the Churches and Religious Communities in 2006. Again all objections to this law, like to previous government's decisions regarding RE, were rejected by the Constitutional Court. Withholding the official state church status to the SOC, the Serbian authorities applied the so-called "quasi-pluralist" model of Church–State relations, as described by Stan and Turchescu in Romania.[19] This approach ensures informal precedence of the Serbian Orthodox Church by government agencies on all levels. Moreover, it was immediately followed by the Law on the Restitution of Church Property which foresaw, with regard to religious communities, the complete restitution of their nationalised property while the return of nationalised property to private individuals is still pending. There are more than 3000 claims with the SOC claiming more than 90% of the property for return according to the official report.[20] The process of return is extremely complex and slow and so far less than half of the property has been returned. Nevertheless, righting the previous injustice not only cemented the primacy of SOC among religious communities but its political importance for the state as other victims such as private persons or endowments are still left behind.[21]

After education, the most important breakthrough for the SOC was its association with the Army. Previously, the bastion of Yugoslavism and Communism, after 2000, the Army found itself in an ideological vacuum and the SOC was enthusiastic to fill it with its own version of Serbian nationalism vaguely defined as *Svetosavlje*.[22] Excursions to monasteries were followed by mass baptisms of officers and soldiers and RE was duly introduced in military schools. The mutual rapprochement eventually culminated with the Agreement on Military Chaplaincy between the Ministry of Defence and seven traditional religious communities in 2011, that envisages paying chaplains the same salaries as officers (depending on their rank), reduced service years for retirement, housing help and other benefits.[23] Again the overwhelming beneficiary was the SOC with most chaplains, military chapels and close association between the two institutions, clearly visible at every religious celebration or military anniversary as men (and now women soldiers too) parade in military uniforms and church vestments side by side.

Over the years and especially by way of the return of property and taxation policy (or lack of it) the central government became the main financier of Churches.[24] Since 2004, the government is funding salaries for priests and monks in Kosovo and some other areas of Serbia considered remote. From 2012, it is also paying the retirement contribution to all active priests. Special stamps were introduced to finance the building of the monumental St. Sava Church in Belgrade, to which the State already contributes in various other ways. It is difficult to estimate or calculate the amount of financial aid from state funds to the SOC as it takes place on many more levels than central government contributions and subventions.[25] After the Army built churches in its major headquarters and barracks, state hospitals, social care and penitentiary institutions followed suit, engaging a number of priests to officiate in them. Furthermore, most local communities provide land and infrastructure for church building free of charge and contribute in various other ways. State utility companies are also among the major donors. Last but not least, the SOC was given initially a place and then a chairmanship of the Serbian Radio Broadcasting Council, a media regulatory body.

CLERICALISM, DE-SECULARISATION OR ELSE?

Acknowledging the recent rise of SOC prominence and its close ties to the state, the question remains what to make of it and here is where analysts disagree. First of all, one must recognise the fundamental ontological differences in analysing a church and other secular institutions in terms of their mission, influence, outcomes. Not withholding that a church is most interested in the other world by definition, this article only evaluates its strengthening in this world. Nevertheless, it questions the conclusion by some observers that due to the unprecedented growth of the SOC in terms of clergy and associates' numbers, accumulation of financial power and influence as well as its privileged position secured through legal changes Serbia is in danger of Clericalism.[26]

Clericalism like Fascism is an often (mis)used notion rendering it hardly viable and explanatory. Historically, the term Clericalism was coined to describe a political tendency for influence or domination of the Catholic Church and its clergy. It was developed in relation to political Catholicism in the late-nineteenth-century Europe and signified the drive of Catholic Church leadership and ordained clergy to impact or decide matters of political and sociocultural importance in an increasingly secularised world. In majority Orthodox countries, there was no equivalent force. For centuries now in Orthodox countries, the state was subjecting and controlling the Orthodox Church and often state rulers chose or removed bishops and patriarchs. State domination of the Orthodox Church in Serbia too has also had two centuries of long uninterrupted tradition. Clearly, the notion of clericalism in Serbia does not apply in historical perspective but what about today?

Looking closer at the most recent developments in Serbia, there is an evident tendency from political elites, mostly leaderships of recently formed political parties, to manipulate the SOC for their own ends, mostly as a political legitimacy tool. This tendency is somewhat reminiscent of the interwar and earlier periods. In addition to this historical predisposition, contemporary Serbia undergoing post-socialist transition, like neighbouring Romania and more distant Russia, is facing a huge ideological gap. In all three countries, we can observe political elites filling this void with the help or in close association with the Orthodox Church. What is more, being late or the latest country to transition from conflict and socialism, Serbia's recent developments coincide with European-wide questioning of the direction or end station of this transition. Throughout Europe but also elsewhere there is a widespread negation of democracy. In fact, our age is already described by Colin Crouch as post-democracy, where elections and decision-making are no more than a spectacle run by spin doctors and where the mass of citizens plays a passive, quiescent, even apathetic role.[27] It is this post-conflict, post-socialist, post-democratic context that provides a fertile backdrop to Church–State relations in Serbia.[28] The rise of political extremists and anti-democratic political options throughout the region, or simple dismissal of democratically elected governments of Italy and Greece, relativize the actions of the Serbian political leadership and relieve them of any scrutiny including Church–State relations. International partners, primarily the European Union, which Serbia aims to join ever since it ousted Milošević in 2000, are too busy for pettiness of democratic proceduralism and sees relations with the SOC as a side show to more important issues. Facing the lack of political expertise, economic recession, loss of territory (Kosovo) and widespread popular distrust Serbian (also Romanian or Russian) secular elites need allies and rely heavily on symbolic rewards that close associations with the SOC provide. Thus, once again in Serbian history, the state became the chief financier, supporter but also regulator of the Orthodox.

The SOC has generally and willingly accepted the close relationship for financial and other benefits, which nearness to real power brings. Over the last decade and a half, Church–State relations have not been a one-way road but in most instances the state has been determining the direction. Criticism or initiative from the Church is limited to few issues. On several occasions, prominent bishops and the entire hierarchy of the SOC expressed their discontent and fierce opposition to state policy towards Kosovo to no avail. The two most remarkable occasions were in 2004 when the then Serbian President Boris Tadić clashed with the Patriarch and the Church over voting in Kosovo, which nevertheless took place. In 2013, protesting the signing of the so-called Brussels Agreement between governments of Kosovo and Serbia, Metropolitan Amfilohije and bishop Atanasije held a prayer for death [molitva za upokojenje] of government and parliament members of Serbia for what they deemed was a state treason. The SOC considers Kosovo as its Holy Land or Serbian Jerusalem and condemns any move of the Serbian government to reconcile with the Albanian rule of the country since it unilaterally declared independence in 2007. Nevertheless, Patriarch Irinej later condemned bishop Atanasije as enfant terrible and the SOC reconciled with the government. Similarly, anti-EU position of many bishops never became official SOC's position and never threatened state policies of EU accession.[29]

The second most important concern for the Church is the abysmal and declining birth rate among Serbs and it uses all possible means to condemn the right to abortion, which it deems a crucial factor for low fertility. Yet an initiative from the SOC to change the law regulating birth control was immediately dismissed by the Health Minister.[30] The Church has also been the fiercest opponent of non-discrimination of LGBT and their right to demonstrate. There are many studies on the issue of the gay parade in Belgrade and most rightly stress that behind the Church opposition stood the attempt to de-secularise public sphere and re-traditionalize social relations.[31] Yet after a period of harsh protests from the Church and severe violence employed by some para-church organisations to stop it, previously reluctant Serbian government now secures the LGBT parade year after year. Similarly, the opposition to decriminalisation of homosexuality by the Orthodox Church in Romania was quashed by its government and in Orthodox Greece, where the Orthodox Church has much more power and privilege than Serbia, the Parliament recently approved of gay partnership let alone the right to march despite massive protests from the Church.

Finally, it is not only in terms of key policies that the state seems to distance itself from the SOC. Stories, often half-truths or rumours, about sexual and other (mostly financial) scandals involving priests and bishops are freely circulating in Serbian media, most of whom are linked to the state or stakeholders close to the government. Clearly, the clergy has no special media immunity awarded to politicians or businessmen and are easily exposed to ridicule. The SOC in turn never ceased cherishing an inimical attitude to media and for years has been attempting to circumvent them by creating its own radio and TV stations alongside print and electronic media. These Church media however still struggle to gain a wider audience.

In conclusion, the position of SOC improved massively compared to repression or marginalisation during Communist-led Yugoslavia and some clergy managed to translate it into financial gain. Yet there is very little evidence that they are able to affect government's foreign or economic policies or change basic tenets of parliamentary democracy in Serbia, thus emptying any possibility of Clericalism in its original definition. On the other hand, Clericalism as a term has also been used to describe the cronyism and cloistered political environs of denominational hierarchy. Again it appeared mainly in connection to the Roman Catholic Church, where for centuries the hierarchy and/or clergy dominated over believers in all matters before some important changes were made to the Second Vatican Council. This understanding of clericalism has more reference with the Orthodox Church which is, like its Catholic counterpart, episcopalian, hierarchical and authoritarian by definition and has not succumbed to any reforms. Furthermore, the numerical and financial growth of Orthodox Churches in post-socialist countries inevitably saw an accumulation of power behind the scene by few bishops, priests or even laymen.[32] More and more sons of priests follow in their footsteps, a practice which was a norm in the Russian but nonexistent in the Serbian Church. It is also rumoured that Bishops who cannot marry surround themselves with family members.

Despite these clearly "clericalist" developments, the SOC remains vulnerable as an institution if not becoming even more so with the recent changes. Here are some illustrations: Although canons proscribe that one is a bishop for life, or in canonical terms wedded to his bishopric, the Constitution of SOC allows for "retirement" in exceptional circumstances and requires the majority in the Bishops' Assembly to vote so. In the last few years, more Serbian bishops were "retired" for financial, sexual and other violations than in entire Church's history.[33] Processes among several other bishops are well under way and some owe their continuous status only to divisions between various lobbies or groupings among the bishops. With the rise of financial stakes, these inner conflicts are only set to rise. Among the lower clergy and SOC Patriarchate staff too, there were already a number of well-documented cases of fraud and the so-called financial mismanagement despite the attempts to keep them hidden from the public.[34] Outside its ranks, the SOC has been awarding medals and praising its donors even though some of them were accused of smuggling, privatisation frauds and economic criminal.[35]

Besides internal personnel issue, the Serbian Church and its bishops are fraught with their links/dependencies on Russian and Greek (Ecumenical)

Church. The divide among Orthodox Churches was best exemplified in the refusal of the Russian Church (joined by churches of Antiochia, Bulgaria and Georgia) to attend the pan-Orthodox Council in Crete in summer of 2016. For the SOC, this perennial division is crucial given the disagreements of two camps about the future of the Orthodox diaspora, which is one of the biggest financial resources for the SOC. So far the Serbian Church was pretty successful in its balancing act between the two powerful centres of Orthodox Christianity. This is because most powers and decisions over foreign relations are concentrated in the hands of two Irinejs. One is Patriarch and bishop of Belgrade, the other is bishop of Novi Sad. Presiding over two biggest and richest dioceses, they also hold most power within the Church and traditionally make sure to keep good relations with both Orthodox powers as well as with secular powers in Serbia. But sometimes the balancing act gets out of control. Recently, the news agency of SOC in a Freudian twist mistakenly transmitted the information on a traditional meeting of Serbs and Greeks with the title "Serbian-Russian friendship".[36]

Relations with other Orthodox Churches are fraught with difficulties and the SOC faces many challenges in what it sees as its canonical territories adding to the above-mentioned vulnerabilities. Romanian Orthodox Church, for example, tonsured its own priests in East Serbia, the first step in establishing its own diocese on the territory the SOC sees at its exclusive domain or canonical jurisdiction.[37] For years there has been no solution to this problem and negotiations involving Serbian and Romanian secular authorities only worsened the situation. In Montenegro, for many years, the Serbian Church is confronting the opposition and attempts by those who ethnically identify themselves as Montenegrins to establish their own national church. Last but not least is the issue of the Orthodox Church in Macedonia, unresolved for half a century. As it was discussed elsewhere, here it is only mentioned to underline the weakness of the SOC. Orthodox Christian principle of one state-one church simply does not resolve the problem of jurisdiction of the Orthodox diaspora in countries with non-Orthodox majorities or in the countries emerging after the dissolution of the Soviet Union and Yugoslavia. In conclusion, the Serbian Church remains vulnerable as an institution making it more difficult to impose its will on Serbian state or society as definitions of clericalism would require despite the favourable Church–State relations.

The best analyst of the rapprochement of the state and church and increasing clerical involvement in Serbian politics Milan Vukomanović rightly saw the main impetus for changes in the SOC ambition for de-secularisation. In a recent study, Vukomanović provided a detailed and damning picture of the SOC rejection of democracy, ecumenism, human rights, European Union and many other aspects of modernity and glo-balisation.[38] Yet we found little evidence of important SOC impact on state policies besides securing privileges for itself as an institution and its clergy or RE teachers for that matter. Namely, the criticism that senior figures in SOC so frequently direct at European Union accession crite-ria or policies of non-discrimination create for the Serbian government much less headache and threat than economic recession, vile criminal groups, corruption or foreign interference in Serbian affairs.

We still need to investigate whether and what change the SOC impacts in the society or among the majority of citizens who declare as Serb and Orthodox. The political organisations, mostly Youth groups, that are favouring Church's anti-European, anti-modernist stance do not count a massive membership and only in the last elections, the strong-est of them, *Srpske Dveri*, managed to climb electoral census and enter the Parliament with 5% of the vote. Another telling evidence is the 2010 research concerning the attitude of the citizens of Serbia towards the European integrations with traditional believers being the most support-ive of the Serbian accession (89%) despite the anti-EU stance and from SOC[39] while almost all citizens of Serbia declare as believers, sociolo-gists interpret this as national identification rather than adhering to the faith let alone moral or political precepts of the Church. Levels of church attendance remain very low despite hundreds of new churches being constructed and other public or personal displays of easily visible markers of Orthodox identity (crosses, prayer ropes, icons, etc.).

On the other hand, in Serbia, just like in Romania or Russia, sur-veys show that their dominant churches (and the army) enjoy highest degrees of popular trust, by far higher than democratically elected insti-tutions such as parliaments. This too should come as no surprise given the widespread disillusion with the so-called democratic transition and especially the neoliberal model of capitalism, most notable in the policies of privatisation, which made few very rich and vast majorities poorer. In Serbia (and much of former Yugoslavia) not only well-being but personal security was under threat for a decade with wars raging from Slovenia to Macedonia with various intensity. The political instability continues to this day, which renders great appreciation for solace, tradition and stability, all values associated with the Church. No wonder political elites extend to churches for legitimacy and an illusion of stability that is so hard to come by. Together with the hierarchs, political leaders and opinion makers in Serbia nourish the image of the SOC as an embodiment of national unity and purpose which implies constructing its role in history, privileging its position in the present and sticking to an illusionary vision of the future.

The SOC cherishes the current situation and thus prefers to deal with the state rather than society at large. Its caritative, developmental, environmental or Youth-related mission are still in their infancy although there have been no obstacles for such work for a quarter of century now. As this is a topic for another study let me only give two examples. During last year the SOC started its first ever programme for prisoners and had 10 (ten) attendants out of more than 10,000 incarcerated in Serbia.[40] The SOC was more active in the rehabilitation of drug users but here again with mixed results, having established some good practice but also had to confront the murder of one inmate by the priest in charge.[41] To invoke the parallel with neighbouring Romania again and Stan and Turcescu's condemning verdict of the Romanian Church's failure to fulfil its social mission, which could be applied to the SOC too: "The Church's most serious enemy is itself."[42]

The case study of RE was used to illustrate recently transforming Church–State relations which defy existing terminology and standardisation and can be understood only within Serbia's post-conflict, post-socialist and post-democracy context. Recent traumatic experiences make both sides in this uneven relationship unwilling to clash over any disagreements. Quite the opposite they have found common interests and share similar agenda of speaking or preaching for unity, purpose, solace and stability in times when these are completely lacking. More specifically, pressing with RE the SOC showed it was not only a puppet in state's hands and it managed to impose its own agenda and lay the ground for its own future. As a result of the informal precedence by government agencies on all levels, direct state aid and popular support, we are witnessing an unprecedented growth of the Serbian Church. Yet its concrete influence in Serbia in many spheres from how to run the economy to youth sexuality remains limited if any at all.

NOTES

1. Jelena Jorgačević,"Đaci su zadovoljni", *Vreme*, 05.08.2010.
2. Bojan Aleksov, *Veronauka u Srbiji* (Niš: JUNIR,2004) [Abbreviated version in English: Bojan Aleksov "Religious Education in Serbia,"*Religion, State and Society* Vol. 32/4, 2004, pp. 341–364]; Jana Baćević, "Veronauka i(li) evronauka: kritika elemenata reforme obrazovanja 2000–2003" (Beograd: Filozofski fakultet, 2004); Zorica Kuburić i Milan Vukomanović, "Religious education: The Case of Serbia," in Kuburić and Moe (eds.), *Religion and Pluralism in Education*, pp. 107–138.
3. For brief analysis of pre-war developments, see Klaus Buchenau, "What went wrong? Church-State Relations in Socialist Yugoslavia," *Nationalities Papers* 33 (2005) 4, pp. 547–567. For more on the role of churches, see ibid, *Kämpfende Kirchen. Jugoslawiens religiöse Hypothek* (Frankfurt a. M.: Peter Lang 2006, Erfurter Studien zur Kulturgeschichte des orthodoxen Christentums, 2).
4. This article will concentrate on the relationship between the state and the Serbian Orthodox Church given its dominant position among the religious communities in the country. Furthermore, the introduction of RE institutionalised seven "traditional" religious communities who among themselves account for more than 95% of declared believers and who in dealings with the state mostly act in unison.
5. The only exception is some 60 acres of land used by an apiary cooperative during the Communist ruled period that the Government of Serbia in 1997 returned to the Monastery of Dečani. This decision has long been contested by local Kosovo Albanians though it was on several instances confirmed by European authorities in power in Kosovo during the transition European rule after NATO occupied Kosovo in 1999. Earlier this year, the Kosovo Constitutional Court confirmed it in final instance. See Roksanda Ninčić,"Varanje Crkve. Bogu božje - caru imovina," *Vreme* N. 429, 9.1.1999. For the Decision of the Kosovo Constitutional Court in English see http://www.gjk-ks.org/repository/docs/KI132-15_ANG.pdf.
6. For Romania, see Lavinia Stan and Lucian Turcescu, *Religion and Politics in Post-communist Romania* (Oxford: Oxford University Press, 2007). The literature on Church and State in Russia is too rich to note here. Book volumes include: Wallace L. Daniel, Peter L. Berger, Christopher Marsh (eds.), *Perspectives on Church-State Relations in Russia* (J.M. Dawson Institute of Church-State Studies; 2008); Katja Richters, *The Post-Soviet Russian Orthodox Church. Politics, Culture and Greater Russia* (London: Routledge, 2012). For other case studies in the region see Ines A. Murzaku (ed.), *Quo Vadis Eastern Europe? Religion, State, Society after Communism* (Ravenna: Longo Editore, 2009). For recent

development regarding RE in these two countries, see Lavinia Stan and Lucian Turcescu, "Religious Education in Romania," *Communist and Post-Communist Studies* 38, no. 3 (September 2005), pp. 381–401; See also ElenaLisovskaya and Vyacheslav Karpov, "Orthodoxy, Islam, and Desecularization of Russia's State Schools," *Politics and Religion*, Vol. 3, No. 2 (2010), pp. 276–302.

7. Most important recent studies include: Klaus Buchenau, "Orthodox values and modern necessities", in Ola Listhaug, Sabrina Ramet, Dragana Dulić (eds.), *Civic and uncivic values, Serbia in the post-Milošević Era*, Budapest (New York: CEU Press 2011), pp. 111–142; Ibid, "The Serbian Orthodox Church," in Lucian Leustean (ed.), *Eastern Christianity and Politics in the Twenty-First Century* (London/New York: Routledge 2014), pp. 67–92; Ibid., "From Hot War to Cold Integration? Serbian Orthodox Voices on Globalization and European Integration," in Jerry Pankhurst, Victor Roudometof, Alex Agadagian (eds.), *Eastern Orthodoxy in a Global Age, Comparative Perspectives and Transnational Connections* (Walnut Creek, CA: AltaMira Press 2005), pp. 58–83; Milan Vukomanovic, "The Serbian Orthodox Church as a Political Actor in the Aftermath of October 5, 2000," *Politics and Religion* Vol. 1 (2008), 237–269; Ibid, "The Serbian Orthodox Church: Between Traditionalism and Fundamentalism," in Ulrika Mårtensson, Jennifer Bailey, Priscilla Ringrose, and Asbjørn Dyrendal et al. (eds.), *Fundamentalism in the Modern World* vol. 1, (London: I.B. Tauris, 2011); Ibid and Radmila Radic, "Religion and Democracy in Serbia since 1989: The Case of the Serbian Orthodox Church," in Sabrina P. Ramet, *Religion and Politics in Post-Socialist Central and Southeastern Europe Challenges since 1989* (London: Palgrave Macmillan, 2013), pp. 180–211; and mine "The Serbian Orthodox Church: haunting past and challenging future," *International Journal for the Study of the Christian Church* Vol. 10, No. 2, (2010), pp. 176–191; "The New Role for the Church in Serbia," *Südosteuropa* Vol. 56/3, (2008) pp. 353–375.

8. Potential candidates need blessing from their bishops in order to enrol. Almost all academic staff is male; many are clergy but all have to be approved by the Church.

9. One is published as Snežana,Joksimović (ed.), *Verska nastava i građansko vaspitanje u školama u Srbiji* (Beograd: Institut za pedagoška istraživanja, 2003).

10. Jelena Jorgačević, "Đaci su zadovoljni".

11. "Veronauka bliža deci," *Večernje novosti*, 28.09.2016.

12. The last available data are from 2011 when the Ministry of Religions reported 530,000 students attending Orthodox R, which was taught by 1789 catichets. Islamic RE was taken by 38,000 students and Roman

Catholic catechism was followed by 14,000 and taught by 160 teachers while the smallest group was of the Slovak Lutheran Church with 1170 students. Decenija učenja veronauke,"*Večernje novosti*, 13. february 2011, see http://www.novosti.rs/vesti/naslovna/drustvo/aktuelno.290. html:319096-Decenija-ucenja-veronauke.

13. V. Nedeljković, "Beogradski đaci neće na veronauku," 04.10.2008. Available on http://www.pressonline.rs/info/politika/48341/beograd-ski-djaci-nece-na-veronauku.html.

14. "Lecima u Novom Pazaru poziva se na bojkot veronauke,"*Blic*, 3.10.2012. http://www.blic.rs/vesti/drustvo/lecima-u-novom-pazaru-poziva-se-na-bojkot-veronauke/bpnw8fy.

15. Iva Martinović, "Veronauka u Srbiji na testu: Ministar protiv vetrenjača,"*Radio Slobodna Evropa*, available on http://www.slobod-naevropa.org/a/veronauka-u-srbiji-na-testu-ministar-protiv-vetren-jaca/27489411.html.

16. Among many angry reactions, see "Crkva ljuta na Verbića" available at http://www.informer.rs/vesti/drustvo/47041/CRKVA-LJUTA-VERBICA-Ukidanje-veronauke-bilo-SKANDAL-KAKAV-PAMTI.

17. Jelena Čalija, "Novi nastavni planovi za pravoslavnu veronauku,"*Politika*, 29.08.2016.

18. See the official statement from the SOC, Veronauku pohađa pola miliona učenika available on http://spc.rs/sr/veronauku_pohadja_pola_miliona_uchenika.

19. Stan, Turcescu, *Religion and Politics in Post-communist Romania*, pp. 26–29.

20. Most common form of nationalised property from religious communities is arable land, followed by forest, real estate, industrial and commercial premises. The full list is available at the report by relevant government body dealing with restitution of church property. See http://www.res-titucija.gov.rs/latinica/direkcija-za-restituciju.php.

21. Jelena Čalija, "Crkve favorizovane u vraćanju imovine," *Politika*, 05.05.2011.

22. Klaus Buchenau, "Svetosavlje und Pravoslavlje, Nationales und Universales in der serbischen Orthodoxie", in Martin Schulze Wessel (ed.), *Nationalisierung der Religion und Sakralisierung der Nation im östlichen Europa* (Stuttgart:Franz Steiner Verlag, 2006), pp. 203–232, is the most elaborate attempt to historically trace and define Svetosavlje. See also Maria Falina, "Svetosavlje. A Case Study in the Nationalization of Religion," *Schweizerische Zeitschrift für Religions- und Kulturgeschichte* 101, pp. 505–527 and mine "Nationalism in Construction: The Memorial Church of St. Sava on Vračar Hill in Belgrade," *Balkanologie* Vol.VII/2, 2003, pp. 47–72.

23. The relevant agreements are available on the website of the Ministry of Defence of Serbia. See http://www.mod.gov.rs/lat/4348/verska-sluzba-u-vojsci-srbije-4348.

24. The "traditional" religious communities are freed from property, income, and financial transactions' taxes. All laws governing religious communities are available at http://vere.gov.rs/cir/Siteview.asp?ID=19.

25. More on financial benefits and taxation in Radić and Vukomanović, "Religion and Democracy in Serbia", pp. 194–197.

26. An example is the project publication *Kritika klerikalizacije Srbije* by AFANS, Antifašistička akcija Novi Sad, (samizdat 2007). Also used by the late analyst Mirko Đorđević. See his interview "Klerikalizacija Srbije" available at http://www.slobodnaevropa.org/a/intervju_mirko_djord-jevic/1884601.html. Vukomanović too criticises the use of clericalisation and instead suggests "etatisation" of the SOC in his "Ecclesiastical Involvement", pp. 125, 147.

27. Colin Crouch, *Post-Democracy* (London: Polity, 2012), p. 4.

28. Post-socialist and post-conflict context is the most important framework of analysis for the most recent compendium of studies on Church-State relations in several of Yugoslavia's successor states. See Branislav Radeljić, Martina Topić (eds.), *Religion in the Post-Yugoslav Context*, Lanham: Lexington books, 2015).

29. The report by Helsinki Committee in Serbia details and analyses thoroughly these conflicts and their apparent reconciliation. See Helsinški odbor za ljudska prava u Srbiji,*Ljudska prava u Srbiji 2013. Iskonski otpor liberalnim vrednostima* (Belgrade, 2014), pp. 374–384.

30. Helsinški odbor, Ibid., p. 399.

31. Marek Mikuš, "Faggots Won't Walk through the City": Religious Nationalism and LGBT Pride Parades in Serbia," in Srdjan Sremac, R. Ruard Ganzevoort, (eds.), *Religious and Sexual Nationalism in Central and Eastern Europe* (Leiden: Brill, 2015), pp. 15–32.

32. Three laymen with close relationship to Patriarch Irinej and bishop of Bačka represent the Church in State Media Commission (Dušan Stokanović); run the SOC production of clerical vestments, candles and other accessories (Dejan Nakić); and manage public relations (Dimitrije Stikić).

33. Recently removed are Bishops Artemije of Kosovo, Konstantin of Germany, Georgije of Canada, Vasilije of Tuzla-Zvornik, Filaret of Mileševa, Sava of Slavonija and Jovan of Niš. Temporarily suspended was Pahomije of Vranje.

34. In 2013, the accountant of the Patriarchate Srba Žikić, known for his jet set lifestyle was arrested and accused for stealing over 1 million Euros of church money. The whole case was then buried from public eyes.

See http://www.blic.rs/vesti/tema-dana/opljackana-kasa-patrijarsije-bla-gajnik-spc-ukrao-milion-evra-gotovine/wjtvf64.

35. Ivana Kljajić, "Bože, pomiluj me grešnog: Srpski političari i biznismeni viđeniji ktitori", 19.04.2015, *Alo.rs*.http://arhiva.alo.rs/vesti/aktuelno/boze-pomiluj-me-gresnog-srpski-politicari-i-biznismeni-videniji-ktitori-foto/94189.

36. Seehttp://spc.rs/sr/srpskorusko_prijateljstvo_u_ruti_hilu.

37. Under the leadership of Bojan Aleksandrović, who the SOC previously defrocked, the Romanian Church created the so-called Romanian Orthodox Protopresbyterate of Dacia Ripensis. See http://www.daciaortodoxa.ro.

38. Vukomanović, "The Serbian Orthodox Church: Between Tradition and Fundamentalism".

39. This research and its apparent paradoxical results are discussed in Vukomanović, "Ecclesiastical Involvement", p. 139.

40. Jelena Čalija, "Zatvorenici veruju u biblijska čuda,"*Politika*, 25.10. 2016. http://www.politika.rs/sr/clanak/366326/Drustvo/Zatvorenici-veruju-u-biblijska-cuda.

41. Reverend Branislav Peranović who committed the murder was sentenced to 20 years while the bishop in charge apologised publicly. See http://spc.rs/sr/saopshtenje_za_javnost_episkopa_shabachkog_gospodina_lavrentija.

42. Stan, Turcescu, *Religion and Politics in Post-communist Romania*, p. 39.

CHAPTER 11

The Politicization of Religion and Ethnic Distance in Serbian School Textbooks

Srđan Barišić and Vladimir Jevtić

The process of desecularization in former Yugoslavia is directly linked to effects of previous and/or co-occurring secularization and atheism and it is a kind of reaction to these processes, and it is more appropriate to be interpreted as countersecularization. In the pioneer systematization of this process, Vyacheslav Karpov pointed out the following tendencies of countersecularization: (1) a rapprochement between formerly secularized institutions and religious norms, both formal and informal; (2) a resurgence of religious beliefs and practices; (3) a return of religion to the public sphere ("de-privatization"); (4) a revival of religious content in a variety of culture's subsystems, including the arts, philosophy, and literature, and in a decline of the standing of science relative to a resurgent role of religion in world construction and world maintenance; and (5) religion-related changes in society's substratum (including religiously inspired demographic changes, redefinition of territories and their populations along religious lines, reappearance of faith-related material

S. Barišić (✉) · V. Jevtić
Faculty of Philosophy, University of Belgrade, Belgrade, Serbia

© The Author(s) 2018   231
G. Ognjenović and J. Jozelić (eds.), *Education in Post-Conflict Transition*, Palgrave Studies in Religion, Politics, and Policy,
https://doi.org/10.1007/978-3-319-56605-4_11

structures, growing shares of religion-related goods in the overall economic market, and so on).[1]

Analyzing religious changes in postcommunism, in this "reactionary" character of desecularization in the former Yugoslavia, Milan Vukomanovic pointed out that the revitalization of religion in Yugoslavia was a kind of shift from negative to positive politicization of religion. The "Balkan rebirth" took place in conditions of prolonged economic, social, and political crisis, and after half a century of the process of "religization of politics", i.e., forcing a "hyper-politicization" of almost all aspects of social life, including religion that has been ideologized in a negative sense, there is a change of direction of the same process.

"Return" to traditional religion, even to conservative religiosity, appeared to be a significant factor in the preservation of national identity, whereby the positively valued traditions, national and religious worship of the past led to political abuse of the connection between religion and nation.[2] At the same potential function of desecularization process, among other things, noted Karpov analyzing "regimes of desecularization", pointing to the case when regimes supports countersecular tendencies for nonreligious reason: the conflicted area of the former socialist Yugoslavia, the homogenization of national religious groups, religion as a resource of resistance or defense of an endangered culture.[3] The process of desecularization was often uncritically regarded as exclusively initiated by religious communities, especially the majority one in a society, and the role and interests of the state in the mentioned process, namely the ruling political elite, were often neglected.

As an integral part of social changes in postcommunist societies, the revitalization of religion was primarily carried out through the politicization of religion or, in other words, in the context of the collapsed identity (socialist) framework by reaffirming the old ethnic and confessional patterns with the aim of homogenizing identity within a national framework. The sacralization of national identity has strengthened the power of political elites, while at the same time enabling the long-awaited return of religious elites to the public scene and reinstating at least some of their lost privileges.

After several decades of atheism of the Yugoslav society, the Serbian Orthodox Church[4] made a comeback in the period of blocked social transformation and it was only after October 5, 2000 that it established institutional ties with the state. The processes marking its comeback were politicization of religion and religization of politics: national interests, those of the political elites and the Church and its dignitaries were often treated as the same and discriminated sometimes. The state labeled itself secular from the very beginning of social transformation (transition); however, in the process of democratization launched after October 2000, it was often criticized for developing nonconformist relations with the majority Church—actually for desecularization and even clericalization[5] of the Serbian society.

It was as early November 2000 that the Serbian Orthodox Church and the state established direct communication following the Synod's request for introduction of religious education into public school curricula. Courses of religious education[6] and priests delegated to military institutions by the end of 2000 marked the beginning of close State–Church cooperation.

Over time, the majority church in Serbia on several occasions demonstrated its respectable political influence: obstruction of placing the Statute of Vojvodina on the agenda of the National Assembly in February 2009, withdrawal of the Draft Law against Discrimination in March 2009, participation of church representatives in the negotiating team for Kosovo and Metohija, active participation, even in management positions, of priests in the work of secular institutions (Republic Broadcasting Agency, National Education Council, etc.).

The Serbian Orthodox Church's strong symbolic and normative presence in the public sphere after October 5, 2000 grew to the proportions of considerable social responsibility; it predominantly shaped ideological and value-based structures of secular institutions and organizations, which entailed not only strong influence but also responsibility. In the identity vacuum of the blocked transition, it monopolized the "historical role" in the safeguard of national identity contributing to national homogenization with its powerful ethno-confessional imprint. Hence, it became a benchmark for other social processes. Reestablishment of a forcefully broken tradition and continuity with the pre-communist era reshaped social relations, especially in the sacred–profane context, reaffirming Eastern Orthodoxy as a source of military morality and restoring religious education, religious holidays as national holidays, sanctification ceremonies in secular institutions, etc. Seeing pictures of saints hung on the walls of municipal and national institutions, schools named after saints or public institutions marking the days of their patron saints became nothing unexceptional. At the symbolic level also, national emblems of the Republic, the number of sacral elements at coats of arms of Serbia's towns and municipalities were indicative enough of the change.

"Desecularizing activists" were able to activate all of the tendencies of the process of desecularization, and even to make it dominant over, mostly just nominal, secularism, but "desecularizing actors"[7] responded to establishing "regime of desecularization" mainly in two ways: conversion to the "legitimate" religion or ritually "belonging without believing".[8] Srđan Vrcan once pointed at this traditional and conventional tie to religion and church, and the fact that confessional/religious affiliation is not identical with religiosity.[9] Also, Dragoljub Đorđević sorted almost identical forms of confessional identification: (1) traditional connectivity for a specific religion, without religiosity, but with a clear awareness of confessional background, and (2) recognition of confessional origin, "religion by birth".[10]

COUNTERSECULARIZATION AND EDUCATION

At the institutional level, there is a reaffirmation of Orthodoxy in the education system of the Republic of Serbia. In the early 90s, more precisely since 1993, Saint Sava again becomes the patron of Serbian education,[11] and educational institutions started to mark January 27 as academic celebration (the ritual glorification of school's patron saint). Today, according to the official calendar of the Ministry of Education, Saint Sava is celebrated as a holiday, working but a nonteaching day, marked with the appropriate content. The same religious holiday is also celebrated on the highest state level with the ceremony of St. Sava Academy, when the Ministry of education awards prizes to the most deserving individuals and institutions for the development of education in Serbia.

There were two time periods during which many schools have changed their name to the name of the patron saint of education in Serbia. Based on the modest random sample, it is striking that the first period included the early 90s, for example, elementary schools in Kragujevac (1991), Batočina (1992), Gornji Milanovac, Sremska Mitrovica (1993), Kikinda (1994), or high schools in Požega (1991), Belgrade (1992), etc. The second wave of renaming started after 2000, for example, elementary schools in Bačka Palanka (2002), Čačak (2003), or high school in Kladovo (2005). As might be expected, many schools do not show (on official web presentation) the data when they change the name, but almost all point out that the name change was created by the will of school employees. Of course, there are schools that have been established in the mentioned first wave and bearing the name of Saint Sava, such as the elementary school in Pančevo (1992).

Today, there are two schools that carry the (new) name of Nikolaj Velimirović, one in Valjevo (2002) and another in Šabac (2004). The first one, from Valjevo, proudly insists on the fact that it is the first school in Serbia that bears the name of the (controversial) bishop.

By the Decision of the Government of the Republic of Serbia which the decision on the liquidation of the Orthodox Theological Faculty declared unconstitutional and annulled, from 1 January 2004, the Faculty has reinstated as part of the University of Belgrade. However, the Faculty has remained in the spiritual and canonical embrace of Serbian Orthodox Church and Serbian Patriarch is ex officio chief sponsor of the Faculty.

After adoption of the Law on the basis of the educational system in Serbia, at the end of August 2009, Vladimir Ilić again pointed to "systemic reproduction of unequal access to authorities for religious communities".[12] This law reproduces discrimination, which was launched in 2001 with the adoption of Regulation on organizing and implementing religious education and alternative subject in primary and secondary schools, and again in the sphere of education confirms the privileged position of the majority church in Serbia. The Act provided for the functioning of the National Education Council in charge of pre-school, primary and secondary general and artistic education, which has 43 members elected by the National Assembly for a term of 6 years. Among the members of the Council, in addition to members from the ranks of academics, teachers, university faculty teachers who educate primary school teachers, etc., there is also "a member from the ranks of Serbian Orthodox Church, from the list of candidates submitted by the church", as well as "a member from the ranks of traditional churches and religious communities, except the Serbian Orthodox Church, from the list of candidates which is commonly submitted by the churches and religious Community". These provisions of the Act privilege only one of privileged seven "traditional" churches and religious communities. One place in the Council is planned for a member from the Serbian Orthodox Church, while for second place in the Council agreed the remaining six (later seven) of traditional churches and religious communities. Other nontraditional churches and religious communities, were registered in dispute on the register of churches and religious communities or not, are completely disempowered for participation in the work of this body.

It is interesting that just one of the responsibilities of the National Education Council is monitoring and analyzing the state of education at all levels within its competence and compliance of the education system with European principles and values. The foundations that underpin the work of this body directly contradict to the principles of the OSCE from Toledo,[13] and favoring only one of the seven privileged churches and religious communities and the disempowerment of "nontraditional" churches and religious communities completely deviates from the principle of equality of religious communities before the law and the basic principles of a secular state and lay education.

POLITICIZATION OF RELIGION IN EDUCATION THROUGH TEXTBOOKS

In most countries, the Ministry of Education provides accreditation for the use of textbooks, making them virtually programming state documents. For states and societies, textbooks provide the desired patterns of identity, which are politicized and reflect the political context in which they are incurred. Textbooks have become an important arm of government, the official carriers of memory, and "approved knowledge".[14] They are "a mirror of the society that produces them",[15] and their content may be a good guide as to a society's values; history books, in particular, may reflect the image a human society has of its past and, indirectly, the way it imagines its future.[16]

The meaning of the first change of textbooks in Serbia, in 1993, was the adjustment of history events to current political regimes. The drastic changes of historical consciousness and rapid construction of a new national identity were the basic motive for change of textbooks and the entire curriculum.[17] It was necessary to show that our nation is the oldest and authentic, and also provides a "historical" justification of its territorial claims. During 1990s, this task should be to fulfill by para-historiography that occurs everywhere throughout the Balkans. If my nation is the oldest and biggest victim, then it is very easy to emotionalize and normalize every way of compensation. Para-historiography has quite successfully activated and emotionalized past in the civil war of the 1990s.[18]

The second change of the textbooks after 2000 was aimed at changing perceptions of the Second World War and the socialist period thereafter. This is due to the strong wave of anticommunism, which entered the public scene in Serbia since 2000.[19] "De-ideologization" was in some countries partly used as a political instrument to achieve their own political aims and former interpretations were replaced by new, ethnocentric perspective. Some textbooks which date from that period clearly show influences from everyday politics and public opinion and they present data in a way which is close to political propaganda.[20]

During this social transformation, the collective past was revised, the old myths were replaced either by new or by older ones from the time when the Balkan national states were established. The dominance of myths in the way the past was described and perceived served as the foundation for ethnocentrism and the lack of tolerance.[21]

The main subject of our research is the ethnic distance in textbooks for the secondary schools in Serbia seen as the result or consequence of ethno-confessional identification. This analysis covers the standard textbooks for the second, third, and fourth grades of secondary schools oriented toward social studies and languages, as well as for the third grade of vocational schools and secondary schools oriented toward natural sciences and mathematics. The history textbooks for the first grade of those schools deal with ancient history and do not mention of the national identity and Orthodoxy whatsoever. Accordingly, they have not been analyzed in this paper.

All textbooks for the Serbian secondary schools that will be analyzed in this chapter were published in Belgrade by the major state publishers, the Institute for Textbooks and Teaching Supplies (*Zavodza udžbenike i nastavna sredstva*). Until recently, this publisher had a monopoly on the production of all textbooks in Serbia. These books were approved for use either by the Ministry of Education of the Republic of Serbia or by the Educational Council of the Republic of Serbia. We will consider only those chapters that include topics relevant to our inquiry into the perception of own or other's national or confessional/religious identity.

The liberalization of the market of textbooks in Serbia began only in 2003, in fact 2004 with the implementation of "Sample on the publication of textbooks for the 1st and 2nd grade of elementary school".[22] For economic reasons, "new" publishers have engaged in market competition with the previously monopolistic competitors, the Institute for

Textbooks and Teaching Supplies primarily in publishing textbooks for primary school, due to the number of potential consumers, as well as the implementation of the uniform programs. Market competition for differentiated, and therefore less profitable, high school programs for different educational profiles, started in 2012 when the Ministry of Education approved first books of the "new" or "other" publisher for high school curricula. From a cursory insight into Excerpt from the register of approved textbooks, it is clear that those (approved) editions of the Institute for textbooks and teaching aids dating back to the late 80s (of course in many reprint editions of originally approved), but mostly from the period of the first "systemic" change of textbooks (1991–1993), or from the second wave of change (2002–2005).[23]

History textbooks in the former Yugoslavia, including Serbia, were usually in the focus of various studies on textbook content. The dominant themes of these studies were the problem of the revision of the past, the selectivity of approach and data, images of others in textbooks, etc. Trying not to repeat mentioned studies, we focus exclusively on highlighting ethnic distance in textbooks in the context of the dominant ethno-confessional identity.

One of the key tools of manipulation is the selection of facts, whereby, by emphasizing some and leaving out other facts, it constructs the desired image of the past. Since the extensive material in textbooks should be presented in an extremely confined space, the authors were forced to a rigorous selection and restriction data. This data selection leaves room for manipulation and, by emphasizing some and pushing or "forgetting" other facts, it creates an unbalanced picture of the past with a desirable political message.[24] A representative example of stringent selection of information can be found in the textbook of Constitution and Civil Rights,[25] where in the description of the development of constitutionalism in Serbia there is no any trace about the development of the constitutionality from the formation of the first to the breakup of last Yugoslavia, or even up to 2006.

The linguistic manipulation is also the basis of historical manipulation. It is of great importance the use of certain terms or terms that suggest a certain historical significance. Whether it is a war of liberation or conquest, a rebellion or a war for independence, revolution or counterrevolution will depend on the interpretation and understanding of events. Geographical or personal names can also be the basis of manipulation, especially place names. Of course, there is the use of apodictic language that leaves no doubts and closes the debate and the dilemma.[26]

In history textbooks of secondary schools oriented toward social studies and languages, history of the Ottoman period is largely seen as a time of "slavery under the Turks"; attention is generally paid to the history of the revolt, migrations, and wars, which are interpreted as the result of Ottoman "occupation" and the pressure of the Ottoman "master" on the Serbs to give up of their religious and ethnic identity. In a similar matrix observed the history of Serbs in the territory of the Habsburg monarchy. A result of these pressures was that the Serbs became fewer in number while neighboring nations profited from that. There is a suggestion that they arise from the Serbs: "Serbian society, which until then were mostly Orthodox, became a confessional. It belonged to three religions Orthodox, Roman Catholic, and Islamic. The religious division is the most tragic occurrence in the history of Serbian nation since it destroyed his identity and in the nineteenth and twentieth centuries prevented the unification. Serbian national being left as a three-piece, but while Orthodox Serbs declare themselves as members of the Serbian nation, Roman Catholics and Muslims is increasingly considered themselves as Croats and Bosniaks".[27] A little further is the following: "It is an indisputable discrimination of Christians, and therefore the Serbs in the Ottoman Empire, since they lived in a subordinate position and that it was not advisable to stand out".[28]

Here is the inadequate use of the concept of discrimination, and concealing the fact that the Ottoman Empire in the sixteenth and seventeenth century was the most tolerant society in Europe. In the Ottoman Empire, members of other religions, who did not belong to the ruling Islam, have clearly defined rights and were able to enjoy them. In other countries of Europe at that time, religious minorities are persecuted. For example, the Spanish kings have persecuted Jews from Spain in the sixteenth century, and these were mostly settled in the cities of the Ottoman Empire.

The Ottoman Empire is called Turkey, which is wrong, because it was not a nation-state of the Turkish people; the Ottoman Empire became Turkey only in 1922, with the reforms of Mustafa Kemal Atatürk. For the Sandžak of Novi Pazar (Novopazarski sanžak) we can find the name of the "Raška region", which is also debatable, because the last title came running 90s, and had never used before. The name of the Sandžak of Novi Pazar was in use from sixteenth to nineteenth century as the name of the administrative authorities in the framework of the Bosnian beglerbegluk (pashaluk). In several places, the Albanians are "Arnauts" and "Sh(q)iptars" and Islamized inhabitants of the Ottoman Empire "poturčenjaci (Turkicized)". "The Turkish population in Belgrade pashaluk made real Turks and islamized Serbs, but the Turkicized (poturčenjaka) was little number, much less than in Bosnia and Herzegovina"[29]. Facts about assimilation are shown only from one side, illuminating only processes where Serbs are blending in other ethnic groups, but not the reverse situation.

Processes and events from sixteenth to eighteenth centuries are often seen in the so-called national content, although it is difficult to speak about the national consciousness in history before nineteenth century. The Orthodox Church is called a national institution, and a struggle for the acquisition privilege in the Habsburg monarchy in the seventeenth century is called the "fight for the preservation of national identity".[30]

The modernizing reforms of the Habsburg rulers are shown in a positive light, if they resulted in the reduction of power and influence of the Hungarian nobility and the Catholic Church, or show a strong negative if they touched the acquired privileges and position of the Orthodox Church hierarchy. It is found that the Hapsburgs "from the Jesuits learned to be patient, cunning and theatrical".[31]

History of the Serbs in the Habsburg monarchy has also shown very one-sided, mainly as a history of wars, conflicts with the rulers, Hungarian and Croatian nobility and the Catholic Church, which has sought to force the Orthodox to convert to Catholicism. Very little attention is devoted to the cultural and material development of the Serbs in Austria, despite the undeniable historical facts, which show that just the Austrian Serbs played a key role in the modernization of the entire Serbian ethnic group. There is no question about any interethnic cooperation in the history textbooks and avoids the mention of the name of Croats. There are almost no examples to mention either the name of Croatian national history until the second half of the nineteenth century, except incidentally, meaning conspiracy Zrinski–Frankopan. History of the Ottoman conquest of Central Europe is described in detail, but famous Battle of Szigeth, often described as the Croatian Thermopylae, is mentioned only in passing.

On the territory of the Triune Kingdom and Bosnia and Herzegovina, one generally does not recognize the existence of Croats or Bosniaks, or that their origin is drawn from the Serbs: "The population of Croatian and Slavonia (with Srem) was very ethnically heterogeneous. Of the approximately 1.9 million Catholics, Protestants and Jews, over 400,000 were foreigners. Šokci, whose ancestors were Roman Catholic Serbs, were the most numerous in Slavonia".[32] There is also an interesting reading on the next page: "The Serbs (both Orthodox and Catholic) naively accepted the theory of Croatian state law in the area of so-called Triune Kingdom, supporting, against the Hungarians, Croatian requirements as their".[33]

Victimization is more convincing if independent sources are used: "According to Italian sources, from the mid-nineteenth century in Dalmatia, in the vast majority lived 'Illyrian-Serbian' people of the Orthodox and Roman Catholic faith, punctuated by oases of 'Latin' or the Italian ethnic element. After numerous proselytistic campaigns by the Roman Catholic Church, in the area of Dalmatia remained relatively small number of Orthodox Serbs. A number of Serbs has kept the name, but in religious terms belonged to Roman Catholicism".[34] There was an almost same situation in the territory of Bosnia and Herzegovina: "In ethnic terms, the Serbs dominated in Bosnia and Herzegovina. In Bosnia, in the mid-nineteenth century, there were about 900,000 inhabitants, of which 400,000 Orthodox Serbs, 328,000 Muslims (mainly Serbs of Islamic confession) and about 178,000 Roman Catholics, who are in large numbers represented catholicized Serbs and immigrant aliens. Austro-Hungarian occupation forced the immigration of the Catholic population. Because of the religious identity of Muslims and Roman Catholics, Serbian identity remained distinctly religious stained".[35]

There are many explanations for the importance of religious identity in the preservation of national identity: "Conversion of Serbs to Islam, has resulted in denationalization because leaving the religion meant the abandoning of the Serbian nation. So many Arnauts, according to modern research, were Islamized Serbs. Cities in Macedonia, with the majority of Christian population, had fewer churches than there were Muslim Mosques".[36] Further, there is very important explanation of the forced Islamization of the former Serbian majority areas: "The pressures on the Serbs were various, from forced eviction tribes from Albania, attacking the honor and dignity of the family (attacks on women and children, rape) to the implementation of the Islamisation of entire villages. It is estimated that Old Serbia (Kosmet), Sandžak and Macedonia in the period from 1876 to 1912 left about 400,000 Serbs, despite the efforts of Serbia to protect the Serb indigenous population. Only in this period, there is violated ethnic balance between Serbs and Shiptars in the territory of Kosmet and northern Macedonia".[37]

In the analysis of the First and Second Serbian Uprising and the First Balkan War, there is almost epic narrative. Instead of the date, or in parallel with them, there are the names of Orthodox religious holidays: "on Meeting of the Lord, 2/14 February 1804, they held an assembly in Orašac" or "Battle on Čokešina took place on Lazarus Saturday, 28 April 1804". In the tiniest details are described the most insignificant battles of insurgents against the Turks, for example, the battles on Drlupa and Čokešina and they take up more space than all the battles of Napoleon's epoch. One of the textbook units is titled "Vostani Serbije!", and "Archpriest Atanasije swore them by curse similar to prince Lazar before the Battle of Kosovo. (…)It was a time when the living envied the dead".[38]

It is necessary to note that information about the past can be found in other school subjects. In some cases, the information placed in this way are even more important than those given in the teaching of history, because students receive them indirectly, which can reduce the resistance that they have when they are explicitly imposed on certain facilities.[39]

In the older (third) edition of the still active Sociology textbook, which was in use during the entire 90s, under the heading "The nation and the national question in modern societies", could be found the following: "Serbian medieval state was at the height of his powers at the time of Nemanjić dynasty in the thirteenth and fourteenth centuries, and the historical development of the Serbian nation was suddenly cut off and threatened by invasion of the Turks in the Balkans in the late fourteenth century. After the Serbs lost their country, for further preservation of national spirit is responsible Serbian Orthodox Church, which has shared the fate of the nation and preserved the tradition of St. Sava. National epic legends and mythology of Kosovo also contributed to maintaining the continuity of the national consciousness".[40]

On the same page, there is the following: "…after the Berlin Congress in 1878, the constitution of the Serbian people in the Serbian nation is completed, but it does not resolve the Serbian national question because outside the Serbian national state live more than a third of the Serbian people." In the same article there is a reference to "close neighbors": "The Croats had their own 'Illyrian revival' in the mid-nineteenth century, but the cultural awakening has not led to the creation of Croatian

national state. The Catholic Church has impeded nation-building processes for Croats and Slovenes because the independent state of Croats
or Slovenes was not acceptable for Austro-Hungary and Italy. Creation
of a common state of South Slavic peoples, after the First World War, was
not particularly suited to the Vatican, which was last admitted its existence and first declared its disappearance (after the April collapse in 1941,
and after the secessionist war in 1991). Albanians are also historically late
because they too long tied its destiny for Turkey".[41]

In the section that analyzes the "Christianity" or more precisely
"Serbian Orthodox Church", is the following: "All the time of Turkish
rule in the Balkans, Serbian Orthodox Church was and still is the main
pillar of Serbian unity, its religious and spiritual center".[42] Highlighting
national independence is reinforced by religious component. In explanation of the organization of the Orthodox churches, we may find the following: "Thus, for example, the Serbian Orthodox Church is completely
independent in its decisions, while the Diocese of the Catholic Church in
Croatia obediently executes the decisions of the Council and the Roman
Catholic superiors - the Pope".[43]

In future editions of mentioned textbooks, aforementioned content loses its quantity, but not quality: "All the time of Turkish rule in
the Balkans Serbian Orthodox Church was and still is the main pillar of
Serbian unity, its religious and spiritual center".[44] In several places can
be found explicitly that equalization of national and religious components of Serbian identity is apologetic. Thus, when explaining differences in respect of different calendars, there is the following question:
"Why Catholics - belonging to another wing of Christianity, celebrate
Christmas Eve on 24 December, while the Serbs - Orthodox Christmas
Eve celebrate on January 6? (...) Serbs, Russians and some other
Orthodox churches until their annual, religious holidays and feasts are
calculated according to the Julian calendar, while Catholics do the same,
respecting Gregorian calendar".[45] In the second place, the analysis of
concepts, ceremony, ritual, and cult, cited examples: "celebration of the
'baptismal name' (or slave) among Serbs" or "Serbs Christmas Eve -
when comes to the fore precisely the cult of ancestors - strictly celebrate
on January 6, according to the new calendar".[46]

When explaining the concept of the liturgy, in the section "Schism
in Christianity. The Catholic and Orthodox churches", there is an
interesting selection of examples of important events from the past:
"Liturgy is performed either at the time exactly certain religious holidays

- Christmas, Easter, were some occasions or during evoking memories of the glorious or tragic events of the past, for example, during the celebration 600 anniversary of the Battle of Kosovo (1989), or the consecration of the Temple of St. Sava, the importance of victims in Jasenovac".[47]

Generally, Christocentric discourse dominates in explanation of religiosity and religious elements in social life. For example, "Minaret is typical for a mosque; it is the main characteristic of the Arab church architecture".[48] There is Church architecture rather than religious or sacred architecture. Further, in the typology of marriage, according to the manner of establishing and maintaining relationships between spouses, marriage can be (among others): "regulated by church - marriage within the institutionalized religion that is based from church bodies and sanctioned religious norms".[49] In this case, a church is equal to religion, although many religious communities are not familiar with this type of organizational form or institutional authority. For example, "Religious marriage" can be more appropriate to include all religious forms, institutions and authorities, or religious communities.

Quantitatively, presentation of monotheistic religions is very uneven. Judaism is presented in little more than two pages, Christianity at ten pages, Buddhism in almost two pages, and Islam in almost two and a half pages. Christianity takes up more space than other monotheistic religions together.

Illustrations (Case Study)

Good examples may be found in the text, in particular the marked areas that represent the kind of conclusions, as well as the questions posed to students, and which directly suggest suitable policy conclusions. Significant results can be achieved using photos, which is very suggestive, especially with the help of text explaining the pictures, attach the attention of students and often more compelling than text convey certain messages.[50]

Chapter 5 (Sect. 3) of the Sociology textbook, which explains "Monotheistic religions", has a total of nine illustrations, average two illustrations per presented religion. They are all black-and-white, because the textbook was not printed in color and depict the following motifs: "Michelangelo: Moses" and "Rabin studied the text from the Talmud" for Judaism; "Crucifixion of Christ (Church of the Holy Virgin. Monastery Studenica)", "Christ carries his cross", and "Cologne

Cathedral (gothic style)" for Christianity; "Drawing from the eighteenth century. The sketch is given the proportions that are appreciated when creating a Budha image. Buddha standing for meditation and peace" and "Buddhist temple" for Buddhism; "Sinan Pasha Mosque in Prizren, built of stone desecrated the church of St. Archangel, built by Emperor Dusan" and "In the mid twentieth century 1,186,000 pilgrims undertook the journey to Mecca, and thus complied with the vow of every Muslim ('Obedience to God'), in the course of life make a pilgrimage at least once" for Islam.

Almost all the illustrations are "neutral", except the illustrations for Islam that stands out with strict local (national) character. The selection criteria of illustrations are quite confusing: nor in terms of symbolic content, territory criterion, nor is it an illustration description (quantitative and qualitative) uniform. "Buddhist Temple" is certainly fictitious, although it is a photo of particular temple; "Cologne Cathedral" is selected only from authors' well-known reason; and "Sinan Pasha Mosque in Prizren", which is "built of stone desecrated the church of St. Archangel, built by Emperor Dušan" seems to be the only mosque that the authors could think of.

In Serbia, especially in the area of the Balkan Peninsula, there are a number of authentic Cathedrals, Orthodox churches, synagogues, and mosques, and once even in Belgrade pagoda operated between the First and Second World Wars. A large number of temples were constructed on its own grounds,[51] and a certain number is certainly created by retrofitting or change of purpose of temples of other confessions or religions.

It is interesting that in the first editions of the same textbooks, before 1994, there was no discriminatory controversial content of the same illustration, and says only "Sinan Pasha Mosque in Prizren". The controversial addition is added in one of the later editions, during the period of social transformation.

In general, it is the very intrusive negative attitude toward Islam. For example, the following can be found: Against polytheism Muhammad says in the Koran: "Allah and his Messenger do not recognize polytheists ... And when the sacred months have passed, then kill the polytheists wherever you find them. (Koran, IX, 3, 5)".[52] First, it is a commonplace that the Koran is the word of God, and that Muhammad is a messenger of the God's words. Second, authors quoted only part of ayat from the Koran without the part of the same in which God talks about forgiving and merciful.

Also, "Fundamentalism in Islam" is isolated and bolded in the text about Islam, although it is not mentioned among other religions, even in Protestantism where it was created.

CONCLUSION

In this article, we have tried to find answers to the following two questions: (1) How the role of religious elements of national identity is presented and evaluated in textbooks? (2) How do textbooks present relation between ethno-confessional identity and ethnic distance?

It is significant that the trend of secularization is practically avoided in most Southeast European school systems. The relation between the national identity and the religious one is central in many textbooks,[53] and the confessional identity acted and still acts as one of the major patterns of cultural, social, and/or political identification. Most textbooks, however, still present quite an ethnocentric picture, where national history is in the center of the historical development. In most textbooks, there is still no multiperspective approach to events and people while in some of them the existence of the others is almost completely ignored or even negative picture of the other is created.[54]

Nevertheless, there are some more positive developments in textbook production lately. The emergence of alternative and parallel textbooks and competition among publishers helped to improve the quality of design and appearance of textbooks. The textbooks started to present their subject matter in a more balanced and neutral way, while the textbook design, illustrations, and other supportive materials (including interactive questions and assignments) contributed to their more modern look.[55] For example, compared with the Sociology textbook of the 1990s, the last Sociology textbook published by the Institute for Textbooks and Teaching Supplies[56] is characterized by a much more descriptive, neutral, "politically correct" language. To all presented religions is given equal attention, there is no discriminatory discourse for Other, there is religious marriage instead of church marriage, etc. From year to year, more and more alternative history textbook publisher offers more balanced content, but a systematic approach is needed.

Taking into account the concepts of "hidden curriculum" and "cultural capital" (Pierre Bourdieu), as well as "legitimate knowledge" (Michael Apple), it is necessary to note that the greatest responsibility, as well as the possibility of systemic change, has the state, the creator, moderator, and controller of educational system. Anyhow, the Ministry of Education continues to exercise control, regardless of the liberalization of markets of publishing, and through curricula and textbooks promotes a particular belief system, and establish legitimate political and social order.

NOTES

1. Vyacheslav Karpov, "Desecularization: A Conceptual Framework", *Journal of Church and State*, Vol. 52, (2010) No. 2: 232–270, p. 250.
2. Milan Vukomanović, *Sveto i mnoštvo: Izazovi religijskog pluralizma*, Beograd: Čigoja, (2001) p. 99.
3. Mirko Blagojević, *Vitalnost religije u (de)sekularizovanom društvu*, Beograd: Institut društvenih nauka, (2015) p. 25.
4. This paper treats Serbian Orthodox Church as a church organization the doctrines and sociopolitical stands of which are advocated by its highest institutions and dignitaries (Synod, the Patri-arch, bishops, priests, etc.), and the very notion of the church from the sociopolitical rather than theological or metaphysical angle.
5. The term clericalization usually denotes not only a religion's growing significance and influence—in this case the significance and influence of the majority religious organization of the Serbian society—but also the church's ever stronger involvement in political and national affairs.
6. Introduction of religious education in the educational system was implemented "counterclockwise" to the legal procedure: first came the governmental decree on religious education as an alternative subject in elementary and secondary schools, then the Law on Churches and Religious Communities and finally the Constitution. The influence of theological discourse on the laical educational system of the secular state culminated when Ljil-jana Čolić, the minister of education in the Vojislav Koštunica cabinet, tried to elimi-nate Darwinism from curricula by the means of a "private decree."
7. Karpov distinguishes between activists and actors of desecularization: Desecularizing activists are individuals and groups immediately and actively involved in efforts to reestablish religion's role in societal institutions and culture; Actors of desecularization are larger groups whose interests, grievances, and cultural and ideological orientations are congruent with activists, but who provide a more passive backing to countersecularizing efforts, not participating in them actively, but rather serving as a social and political support base of countersecularizing activities (Karpov, op. cit. 2010, pp. 251–252; Blagojević, op. cit. 2015, pp. 22–24).

8. Karpov distinguishes several types of mass reaction to the establishment and functioning of the regime of desecularization: (1) conversions to "legitimate" faiths, (2) the innovative search for alternative ones, (3) ritualistic "belonging without believing", (4) religious indifference, and (5) a secularist rebellion (Karpov 2010, op. cit., pp. 258–259; Blagojević, op. cit., 2015, p. 26).

9. Srđan Vrcan, *Od krize religije k religiji krize*, Zagreb: Školsa knjiga (1986).

10. Dragoljub B. Đorđević, "Sociološki uvid u kulturu pravoslavlja (Srpsko pravoslavlje i SPC)", *Teme*, Vol. XXIV, Br. 1–2, (2000): 161–175, p. 164.

11. Church holiday of St. Sava was established as patron of all schools in Serbia in 1840 and celebrated until the Second World War.

12. Vladimir Ilić (ur.), *Verske slobode u Srbiji: stanje, prepreke, mogućnosti*, Zrenjanin: Centar za razvoj civilnog društva, (2009), p. 79.

13. *Toledo Guiding Principles on Teaching about Religions and Beliefs in Public Schools*, Prepared by the ODIHR Advisory Council of Experts on Freedom of Religion or Belief, OSCE: ODIHR (2007).

14. Dubravka Stojanović, "Sećanje protiv istorije. Udžbenici istorije kao globalni problem", Beogradski istorijski glasnik IV, (2013), 185–204, p. 188.

15. Christina Koulouri (ed.), *Clio in the Balkans: The Politics of History Education*, Thessaloniki: Center for Democracy and Reconciliation in Southeast Europe, (2002), p. 31.

16. Ibid., p. 32.

17. Dubravka Stojanović, Konstrukcija prošlosti – slučaj srpskih udžbenika istorije, Genero 10–11: 51–61, (2007), p. 52.

18. Todor Kuljić, *Kultura sećanja: teorijska objašnjenja upotrebe prošlosti*, Beograd: Čigoja, (2006), p. 181.

19. Stojanović, op. cit., (2007) p. 54.

20. Snježana Koren, "Yugoslavia: a Look in the Broken Mirror. Who is the Other?", in: Christina Koulouri, (ed.) (2002): *Clio in the Balkans: The Politics of History Education*, Thessaloniki: Center for Democracy and Reconciliation in Southeast Europe, (2002), p. 194.

21. Koulouri, op. cit., p. 25.

22. Sonja Ćirić, "Tržište udžbenika: Šest izdavača traži učenike", *Vreme*, No. 712 (August 26, 2004), http://www.vreme.com/cms/view.php?id=389085&print=yes.

23. Excerpt from the register of approved textbooks—Catalogue of textbooks for secondary schools approved for the academic year 2016/2017 for high schools and vocational schools (general subjects), Ministry of Education, Science and Technological Development: http://www.mpn.gov.rs/udzbenici/.

24. Stojanović, op. cit., (2013), p. 192.

25. Slavko Tadić, *Ustav i prava građana: za 4. razred gimnazije i 3. i 4. razred srednjih stručnih škola* (Prvo izdanje), Beograd: Zavod za udžbenike, (2008), pp. 106; Slavko Tadić, *Ustav i prava građana: za 4. razred gimnazije i 3. i 4. razred srednjih stručnih škola* (3. izd.), Beograd: Zavod za udžbenike, (2012), p. 11.
26. Dubravka Stojanović, op. cit., (2013), p. 194.
27. Radoš Ljušić, *Istorija za trći razred gimnazije opšteg i društveno-jezičkog smera*, Beograd: Zavod za udžbenike i nastavna sredstva, (2007), p. 81.
28. Ibid., p. 82.
29. Ibid., p. 93.
30. Ibid., p. 89.
31. Ibid., p. 100.
32. Nikolić, K., Žutić, N., Pavlović, M., Špadijer, Z (2002): *Istorija za treći razred gimnazije prirodno-matematičkog i četvrti razred društveno-jezičkog smera*, Beograd: Zavod za udžbenike i nastavna sredstva, p. 34.
33. Ibid., p. 35.
34. Ibid.
35. Ibid., p. 38.
36. Ibid., p. 43.
37. Ibid., p. 41.
38. Ljušić, op. cit., (2007), pp. 194–195.
39. Stojanović, op. cit., (2013), p. 187.
40. Milovan Mitrović and Sreten Petrović, *Sociologija za III razred stručnih škola i IV razred gimnazije* (Treće izdanje), Beograd: Zavod za udžbenike, (1994), p. 68.
41. Ibid.
42. Ibid., p. 159.
43. Ibid., p. 157.
44. Milovan Mitrović and Sreten Petrović, *Sociologija za III razred stručnih škola i IV razred gimnazije* (Šesnaesto izdanje), Beograd: Zavod za udžbenike, (2008), p. 170.
45. Ibid., p. 169.
46. Ibid., p. 144.
47. Ibid., p. 164.
48. Ibid.
49. Ibid., p. 68.
50. Stojanović, op. cit., (2013), p. 193.
51. Bajrakli mosque was built on its own grounds and it is one of the oldest buildings in Belgrade, outside of Kalemegdan fortress. In Sandžak and Kosovo and Metohija, there are a number of authentic mosques that are under state protection and are monuments of culture of the Republic of Serbia.

52. Milovan Mitrović and Sreten Petrović, op. cit., (2008), p. 173.
53. Mirela-Luminita Murgescu, "Religious Education and the view of the 'Other'", in: Christina Koulouri (ed.) (2002): *Clio in the Balkans: The Politics of History Education*, Thessaloniki: Center for Democracy and Reconciliation in Southeast Europe, (2002), p. 297.
54. Koren, op. cit., (2002), p. 194.
55. Milan Vukomanović, "Images of the Ottomans and Islam in Serbian History Textbooks", in: Moe, Christian (ed.): *Images of the Religious Other: Discourse and Distance in the Western Balkans*, Novi Sad: CEIR, (2008), p. 34.
56. Dimitrije Dimitrijević (ed.), *Sociologija za III razred stručnih škola i IV razred gimnazije* (1. izd.), Beograd: Zavod za udžbenike (2011).

CHAPTER 12

An Analysis of the Religious Education Textbooks in Serbia

Svenka Savić

INTRODUCTION

With democratic processes in Serbia, at the beginning of twenty-first century, the discussion in Serbian public was initiated and developed related to the introduction of religious education as an elective into elementary and high schools: many intellectuals believed that this step was a concession to the theocratic government, while those that dealt with practical questions of teaching in schools pointed to the educational and didactic difficulties: an absence of textbooks, unpreparedness of schools and teachers for such teaching. Remarks were justified because textbooks were only gradually been published for individual grades within the period of 8 years (2002–2009), and the discussions for and against religious education spread in the public as

I am thankful to Veronika Mitro and Mirjana Čanak for the help they provided during the execution of this research, which is the result of the research project and to Vesna Dragojlov for the translation of this text into English.

S. Savić (✉)
University of Novi Sad, Novi Sad, Serbia

© The Author(s) 2018
G. Ognjenović and J. Jozelić (eds.), *Education in Post-Conflict Transition*, Palgrave Studies in Religion, Politics, and Policy,
https://doi.org/10.1007/978-3-319-56605-4_12

well as the question of the content of such a class in relation to another elective which was introduced at the same time—Civil Education.

Religious education was introduced as an elective in elementary and high schools in Serbia during 2003–2004 school year with the explanation to "offer students a holistic religious outlook of the world and life and to allow them free adoption of *spiritual* and life's values of the church or a community to which they *historically* belong, which is preservation and nourishment of their own religious and cultural identity."[1] In the public the discussion pertained to the foundational goal of this course (because spirituality can be achieved by other means), as well as about the intention that spirituality be deepened within "a community to which the students historically belong" which does not assume a vital dialog with those who are historically (or in any other way) outside that community.

Serbia is a multilingual and multireligious state, and an approval to conduct religious education within the school's curriculum on the territory of Serbia was granted to seven religious communities: Serbian Orthodox church, Catholic Church, Islam community, Slovakian Evangelical church, Slovakian Christian Church, Christian Reformation Church and Jewish community. This implies that some religious communities did not get the approval (for instance, various Protestant communities in Vojvodina which have a long history of its existence and a significant number of followers) and related to this, everything happening within the framework of the organization of religious education teaching is missing for those communities in schools, so their religious education is conducted within their religious communities.

Gender sensitive researchers of religious issues mainly, have been involved in the empirical studies, as follows: Bojana Aleksov (2004), sociologists—Nada Sekulić (2001), Zorica Kuburić and Snežana Dačić (2004), ethnologist Lidija Radulović (2003, 2012), philosopher Janja Bačević (2004); psycholinguist Svenka Savić (2009).

In 2003, *Svenka Savić* and her associates applied a discourse analysis to the textbooks in native language (Serbian) in an elementary schools in Vojvodina (Serbia) and came to a conclusion that in those textbooks the representation of male and female roles was patriarchal and that they are insufficiently sensitive to the gender dimension in the Serbian language. Later on, by applying a critical analysis of discourse Savić demonstrated an insufficiency of a linguistic formation of texts in the textbooks for religious education and made a suggestion for a change of this type of writing in the textbooks.[2]

Janja Bačevićanalyzed gender stereotypes and politics of education in the textbooks for religious education for the first grade of elementary schools of Eastern Orthodox religion (by the author, Ignjacije Midić). She concludes that "true power of stereotypical representations (and specifically in those related to gender roles) lies in the fact that they not only tell us the reality of things, but also how they should look—in other words, they create attitudes, expectations and relationship of an individual toward the world they encounter."[3] It is important to point out here that stereotypes show what is "normal" for how things should look. And, as with every norm, other possibilities are excluded which can also have a potential to be the norm.

Zorica Kuburić and Snežana Dačić[4] found out the need for guidance for a religious education teachers in their practical work so they published the book about the methodology for religious teaching (unfortunately, it was not approved for the curriculum in the schools in Serbia).

Lidija Radulovic[5] in her analysis of the textbooks applied discourse analysis to the representation of a family in the textbooks for religious education in Serbia in elementary and high schools for Orthodox, Catholic and Islamic communities, and concluded that those textbooks legitimize traditional (often conservative) moral values which construct "a patriarchal model of gender relationships and hierarchy in a family, and which are not in accordance with the changed model in which young generations live. Textbooks for religious education are anachronistic, and they inspire a patriarchal model of families, they are not adapted to the contemporary concepts of families and their way of life, so they have little associations with reality."

The goal of this research was to analyze the process of decision-making in the publication of textbooks for religious education and elements (implicit and explicit) of gender and interreligious discrimination in the texts of the textbooks which are used in Serbia in elementary (and high) schools, using discourse analysis.

The hypothesis stated that textbooks reflected Plan and Program adopted by the Ministry of Education, so what appears in the textbooks by individual authors is not a desire of individuals, but rather it reflects the attitude approved by the Ministry of Education in the state of Serbia.

Corpus of empirical data for analysis comprises the following: (1) Data about the approval procedure of textbooks (in accordance with the Ministry of Education and with the bishop/synod's blessing, printed in a state institution, The Institute for Textbooks and Teaching Material in Belgrade); (2) Data about the curriculum of religious education in elementary (high) schools for Orthodox, Catholic and Islamic religions (which is conducted in three languages—Serbian, Croatian, Bosnian—all derived from the former Serbo-Croatian language), and comparative data are from the two Protestant communities (in languages of the national communities—Slovakian and Hungarian); (3) Data from the textbooks texts for the religious education for Orthodox, Catholic, and Islamic teaching, printed in agreement with the adopted curriculum and its application in Serbia.

There are three units of analysis: body text, a sentence, a word. By body text I mean a unit bigger than a sentence which can be in the form of verbal material that consists of the following: a basic (main) body text, a didactic apparatus: questions, the message about religion and various citations and non-verbal elements (drawings, images, photos and other companion to the text). I have analyzed the way a basic (main) text relates to other didactic parts of text. The type of text is either monologs (narrations) or dialogs (interactions according to age groups, gender, familiarity with the material). Smaller units of text are *sentences* (syntactic, units which require a verb). I have calculated the total number of sentences in a text and median length measured by words. The smallest unit of analysis is a *word* (a collection of characters separated by blank spaces in a text).

DATA ABOUT THE PROCEDURE FOR TEXTBOOKS APPROVAL PROCESS

The state company, The Institute for Textbooks and Curriculum is in charge of publishing textbooks about religious education. Though the Law about textbooks was passed in Serbia in 2015, textbooks publishing has been monopolized because The Ministry of Education has approved only publications by The Institute for Textbooks and Curriculum for use in schools. The procedure for the approval of textbooks for religious education has been designed in such a way that the highest ranks in church (synod and bishop) select the author (those are mainly episcopes), they give them blessings, and the Ministry of Education approves it (in each copy for every grade of the religious education at the very beginning of a textbook it writes: "With blessings of St. Archpriest Synod of Serbian Orthodox Church" (that is, for Catholic books: "Msgr. Dr. Janos Penzes, Subotica bishop"), and at the bottom of the same page there is information that says that The Ministry of Education approves the textbook. Synod/bishop are superior to the Ministry of Education in such a way that they select one author they trust for all grades of elementary schools—one episcope writes all textbooks for orthodox religion; one bishop writes all textbooks for catholic religion, and the Ministry just approves the selection. After the author finishes his manuscript of the textbook, it is reviewed by a team comprised of mainly the same persons, people of trust of synod/bishop (for instance, in orthodox catechism, that person is at the same time employed by the Ministry of Education—a state body that approves textbooks, which is an example of a conflict of interest).

Teachers of religious education can become selected people by synod, that is, bishop (if they receive blessing), and they use textbooks for religious education printed at the Institute. Additionally, evaluation data about the teaching are sent to the Ministry of Churches (not to the Ministry of Education) and thus far have not been made public. In short, textbook publishing for religious education is a tightly controlled process and has been monopolized by churches, the Ministry of Education and the Ministry of Churches. It has been estimated that today that in the whole of Serbia around 1300 teachers have conducted classes in religious education, of whom the majority is men (the exact number is impossible to establish because teachers are contracted by a special agreement for a limited time—for the most part they do not have full time jobs in schools, but rather they work in several schools so that they can fulfill their weekly class load as outlined by the Law).

DATA ABOUT THE RELIGIOUS EDUCATION CURRICULUM: GENDER AND INTERRELIGIOUS PERSPECTIVE

I have analyzed texts in the Book of Regulations for the curriculum of the religious education for elementary schools[6] which was written by the Ministry of Education in Serbia, and as a comparative material I have used the same document for high schools[7] for Orthodox (in Serbian and Roma), Catholic (in Croatian), and Islamic (in Bosnian) teaching which is conducted in a multicultural and multi-ethnic Vojvodina. In the curriculum, I have looked for elements of (discouragement)/encouragement for interreligious dialog and for (un)recognition of gender equality.

The number of credits is the same for all denominations for religious education: 1 *h* a week, which totals 36 h annually. At the beginning of every school year students select their elective which can be religious education or civil education (knowledge about themselves and others). The success of students in religious education is evaluated by instructors in a descriptive manner (good and satisfactory). The grade does not affect general success of a student (other relevant information can be found in the book by Zorica Kuburić and Slobodanka Dačić.[8]

However, there are differences in the description of individual curriculum, from the perspective of general intent, which can be exemplified by comparing goals of religious education in the first grade for Orthodox, Catholic and Islamic teaching of religious education.

The goal of teaching of *orthodox* catechism for the first grade of elementary schools is "an acceptance that existence is an expression of the wholeness of an individual, and that an individual exists only in a community of freedom with other people." In order to avoid the danger of interpreting every kind of community to potentially be the basis of true existence, it is necessary to have in mind and emphasize "*the liturgical community as the only true one*" because within it the communion with God and Christ is realized[9] (italic S.S.). And in a liturgical community are those that belong to an Orthodox religion.

Furthermore, under general remarks for the first grade it is stated: "When it comes to holy holidays, special attention should be paid to the holy Serbs: St. Sava, St. Simeon, during the holy holiday, St. Vitus, etc."[10] Creators of the curriculum for teaching religious education for orthodox catechism (the majority of Serbian people) teach students about their national identity and their own community. However, teaching students about the connection between religious and national interests is missing from their religious education class in the curriculum of other religious groups because their members belong to different national communities in Vojvodina (for example, students of Croatian, Hungarian and Slovakian nationality choose Catholic religious education, and the students from Protestant churches are of very different national identities in the same religious group). Therefore, some religious groups are nationally homogenous, while others are heterogeneous.

The goals of teaching Islamic religious education in the first grade of elementary schools are: "recognition of the basic teachings of their religion; getting to know the most important dates with Muslim people; getting to know the importance of everyday teaching of Koran."[11] The holy book is the basis of teaching of religious education from the very beginning, written in Arabic (and in a mosque prayers are conducted in that language) so the students need to, from the very beginning, through their religion, learn Arabic, too, which binds all pious people of Islam regardless of their national identity. It appears as if the textbook in this teaching had less importance than the person conducting the class. In fact, in the curriculum there are estimates that religious education is a joint effort between the teacher and the student, and for its teaching it is recommended in the textbook, *Religious Education Textbook for the Second Grade* by Hazema Nistović that "the starting point be the reality...the material studied...has to find its application in the life of a student."[12]

"The goal of *Catholic* religious education in the first grade is to familiarize students with God, Father, His Love, to have them understand that *the parent* and this beautiful world are God's gifts, then to get to know Jesus Christ, who was sent to us by Father as a token of greatest love... Our goal is to instill in a student joy and to make him/her give back Father's love with joy."[13] (italics S.S.). In this instance, parents are introduced as a component of religious education teaching, which is missing in the goals of other above-mentioned groups.

We can conclude that what those three teachings of religious education in the first grade of elementary schools have in common is the fact that interreligious communication in the curriculum is missing, which is otherwise explicitly present in the curriculum for the first grade of elementary schools of the two Protestant churches: (in Slovakian) for Evangelican-Luteran religious education of the Slovak evangelical church A.D. and (in Hungarian) for the Reformation-Christian church. For the former it is stated: "The goal of the religious education in the first grade is to share with children happy news of the God's words and God's truth as well as *development of positive attitudes towards the members of other religious doctrines and their* Tradition *and culture*"[14] (italic S.S.). And for the latter: "The goal of religious education is to share with children happy news of God's words and God's truth" as well as to *develop positive attitudes towards the members of other religious doctrines,* their tradition and culture (italic S.S.).

In the holistic attitude in the teaching of religious education as directed toward its own doctrine during the development of spirituality, above-mentioned examples for the initial shaping of spirituality in the first grade of elementary schools serve as evidence for an orientation toward national religious identity with the majority of people, the influence of parents, referral to the holy book of all (Muslims) as well as toward an inherent component of a child's spirituality, but not toward interreligious connections. Only the examples of Protestant churches (in minority), already in the first grade of elementary schools direct their teaching of religious education toward other religious communities and cultures and thus they interlink spirituality "with others" from the very beginning of their education of a child's individuality (what remains is to explore to what degree this kind of approach contribute to interreligious dialog in later years of their education).

Efforts for consistent gender perspective are missing from the curriculum and; they imply misogynistic relationship toward woman, which can then be explicitly found in the texts and photos of individual lessons in the textbooks for religious education.

RESULTS OF ANALYSIS OF TEXTBOOKS FOR RELIGIOUS EDUCATION FOR THE FIRST GRADE OF ELEMENTARY SCHOOLS OF ORTHODOX RELIGION IN THE SERBIAN LANGUAGE

I have analyzed the first text of the orthodox catechism for the first grade of elementary schools. The text of the whole textbook is in Serbian written in Cyrillic alphabet, unlike the Catholic textbook for religious education where already in the first grade quotes from the holy script are introduced, which is, in Islamic religious education from Koran and thus make students pay attention to the differences between the texts of the textbook authors and the texts from holy scripts. The author gives titles of the lessons in accordance with the proposal from the Curriculum for the first grade. After the main text, there follows a didactic section divided into three basic units: message about religion, questions, suggestions for activities (drawings, conversations, etc.).

The main text of the first lesson, "Love," I divided into three basic units (here they are separated by dashes): child's joy about the bird, the loss of the bird, message about love. Then I divided the whole text into sentences—37 sentences total. Before every sentence I have provided the total number of words in it; then I added up the number of words in all sentences and got a median length of a sentence for the first session—17.2 words on average.

(the number of words in a sentence is given at the beginning)

"Love"
(the first unit: a child's joy for the bird)
8 The mother gave little Bogoljub a little bird for Easter.
5 Bogoljub was very happy about the gift.
8 He for his part could not tell why he was so happy.
18 Bogoljub had many toys and all of them were dear to him, but he showed special love for this little bird.
17 In the end he understood: the little bird was especially dear to him because his mother gave it to him.
5 And he loves his mom very much.
11 With the little bird that he called Kica, Bogoljub developed a special relationship.
15 He fed it and took care of it—to be clean, that it does not get cold during winter...
9 Or that by any chance, a cat does not grab it...
7 And the little bird specially loved little Bogoljub.
13 When Bogoljub returns home from school, it will merrily chirp.
27 It would land on his shoulder, put its beak into his ear and would gently murmur as if it were saying something to him, something it did not want others to hear.[15]

SECOND UNIT:
(second unit: the loss of bird)
8 One day Bogoljub returns home from school.
9 He enters the house, but he does not hear his friend Kica.
6 He enters the room, but there is no Kica.
11 He realizes: the cage open, the window open, and there is no bird in the room.
6 He searched for his Kica for a long time.
5 Since he could not find it, he began to cry.
17 Little later the mother and father come home and find little Bogoljub in tears over lost Kica.
20 They comforted him and promised that already tomorrow they would buy him another little bird, more beautiful than Kica.
6 But little Bogoljub did not want the other.

15 He mourned for his Kica and wanted it back, only that bird.

19 Mom and dad were telling him that it was not possible and they could only get him a new bird.

7 Little Kica is probably now with its friends.

20 It is also having a hard time without you, but it is still a bird and it should be where other birds are.

17 However, it will not forget you, and you will not forget it—**dad and mom** were saying to little Bogoljub.

14 When this other little bird you fall in love to—they were telling him—it will then be your most precious Kica.[16]

THIRD UNIT:

(third unit: message about love)

4 Love brings us happiness.

12 It makes people and nature unique and original.

33 This last one little Bogoljub understood, because with his love he made all his toys come alive, but he could not understand why Kica cannot be replaced by any other bird.

12 It is probably because he loved his Kica very much.

4 And Kica loved him, too.

29 Little Bogoljub was in the end comforted when his dad and mom told him that Kica was certainly alive and it is for sure happy because it is with its friends.

22 Because of this Bogoljub, whenever other birds came into their garden in front of the house, he saw his Kica among them.

6 Or it only appeared that way to him?

2 He does not know.

16 However, from then on, Bogoljub loved and took care of all the birds, because they all became his.[17]

I have concluded that this text is way too long and very complex for a child that is just starting the process of literacy at the beginning of the school of the first grade. The length of a sentence does not work for the initial process of literacy for children. The number of words and the length of sentences in this lesson are bigger than is the linguistic knowledge of the first graders as related to the reading of a text, but also in terms of their spontaneous production in a conversation with grown-ups and their peers; for reading purposes those sentences are not adjusted to their age group and their cognitive faculties (fine print, complex orthography rules) in order for them to capture the meaning of love from those sentences and then to translate it into their own linguistic and religious experience—to further explore the results intended by the text—acquiring spirituality.

Message about the religion is a didactic part of the lesson. The total number of sentences (6) I have divided by the number of words (73) and have concluded that the average length of a sentence is too long for this age group—12,1 words. According to established standards for students in the age group 6–7, the length of a sentence should not be longer than 6–8 words.[18] The next step was to analyze the content in the message about the religion. Is there a message and if so, how is it related to the main text? We found out that those two parts of the lesson did not have an immediate connection, and in the text about this message the content is provided which students should know as a dogmatic truth about their own religion:

12 With *love* we can find out things which we cannot find using *reason* and other senses.

20 Nature that surrounds us, and specially people, we know best when we fall in love with them, that is, when we become part of that community based on love.

13 However, *God* we cannot discover by any means, not with reason, not by vision—only with love.

7 Because nobody has ever seen God.

12 *God's Son* who became man, Jesus Christ, discovered God to people.

9 When we fall in love with another man, then we discover God in him.

I have marked the words here which I believe children in 6–7 age group at the beginning of their schooling in the first grade do not know the meaning of: *God, reason, community of love, God's Son*. I have estimated that it is difficult for them to understand the meaning of the following sentence: *When we fall in love with another man, then we discover God in him*. A child can only rely on adults (parents) to read him/her the text and by repeating it several times to memorize it which is the message about religion by imitation, so that he/she can use the memorized sentence in a context.

Questions are the second part of a didactic apparatus. In the end, in the same way I have calculated the length of questions: the number of words in a sentence and evaluate the relationship between questions and the main text.

3 What is love?
7 How does the nature look when we love it?
12 Can we love nature and not love a single man?
19 How do you feel when you are alone, and how, when you are together with those you love and those they love you?[19]

The questions refer to the main text, however, for a child in the age group 6–7 it is not easy to answer them. The last question consists of two questions which methodologically is not appropriate for this age group.

1. How do you feel when you are alone?
2. How do you feel when you are together with those you love?

The size of characters can also be included in the linguistic analysis and thus we can claim that they are too small for students of this age group to recognize as letters inside a word. Furthermore, we can include the application of orthography in this analysis (the use of capital letters in a manner established in religious print, but not in textbooks, that is, capital letters for pronouns when they mean God, Son, Holy Spirit—He, Him); additionally, the use of punctuation in the text (period, coma, dash, colon—all of which children learn in later grades). If we look at types of sentences we can see they are complex and they are dependent complex (as it is the case with relative and conditional sentences which students learn in later grades), then inserted sentences etc. I have here concluded that the verbal part is not appropriate for this age group.

I have then analyzed images that accompany text and concluded that questions have no connection to the visuals. Images do not even have a function for the text because the author does not refer to them, but rather, in the end he provides instructions for a free selection of activities (draw what you like most).

Additionally, there are words in the text that we believe children of this age group do not quite know the meaning of. The most frequent words in the textbook for the first grade of Orthodox religion (but also for the second and the third grade) are those which support authority of religion, which is expected (*Jesus, God*) but also authorities in the church as an institutions (*priest, episcope*), which is less expected.

In short, at all three levels of linguistic analysis (text, sentence, word) of the authored text we have concluded that parts of the lesson are not functionally linked in order to support knowledge of students through incremental guidance from the text to the questions about the text and linking the text with the non-verbal material.

These few pieces of data indicate that the text in the textbooks for religious education written by a church authority (episcope) does not develop critical thinking of students; this kind of didactic design of individual lessons in textbooks does not contribute to the overall goal of education, as well as to the goal of a good textbook.

EXAMPLES FOR DEEPENING INTERRELIGIOUS SIMILARITIES AND DIFFERENCES

One of the tasks of religious teaching is to develop love toward others, as the foundation of both Christian and Islamic religion, and those others could be people of a different religion. In the lesson for the senior level in high school titled "Some differences between Roman Catholic and Orthodox organization of Church the text ends with the sentence: "It is necessary that the whole structure of Roman Catholic church aligns with that which was in existence before schism, and which is still preserved by Orthodox church."[20] This sentence suggests that those others should change in the direction of the Orthodox organization of Church, which sounds more like a call to non-cooperation than love. For now, we can conclude that textbooks for religious education for the most part do not contribute to the development of critical thinking when it comes to interreligious dialog.

There are numerous opportunities for teachers of religious education to introduce a dimension of interreligious sensitivity using the material itself adopted by religious communities. For instance, religious texts from two sister churches (which pious people recite every time they go to the service) can be introduced, but in such a way to show *similarities* in that basic prayer among the three Christian confessions. Students alone can come up with conclusions about the differences, after they see similarities.

Examples for Deepening Gender Sensitive Communication in Orthodox Textbooks for Religious Education

Almost all research on the textbooks for elementary schools for various subjects (native language, social sciences, history, civil education, etc.) show that gender perspective is for the most part missing, so it is not unexpected that we will not find it in the textbooks for religious education in Serbia, but it is, if compared to the situation with textbooks in other countries in Europe.[21] In the analyzed, textbooks for Orthodox religion the basic approach of the author is to exclude woman from God's creation. That basic idea is realized in various verbal and non-verbal ways consistently in different lessons.

In the second grade there is a text titled "God we believe in, is Father." The author consistently uses the verb *give birth (roditi)* for man, though this verb is always associated with woman in the Serbian language; the author "deprives" woman of her gender-specific characteristic and assigns it to man. In the following text the father explains to the son:

> God didn't give birth to us in order to be our Father;
>
> You are the father to only Milica and myself because you gave birth to us.
>
> We call God Father because He is the Father of Jesus Christ, who he gave birth to.
>
> We do not call our parents fathers only because they gave birth to us but primarily because we love them.
>
> Here is an example: your friend Goran was adopted by my friend Bogoljub, which means he didn't give birth to him.

The author continues to explain why it is important to know who gave birth to you because "this signifies a relationship of love that the two of us share," as the author states. Mother, woman is therefore excluded from parent love as she is excluded from God's creation, too. She is only implicitly present in the explanation about love. The author further excludes mother from a much more important space, and that is liturgy. The author further states:

> This means we live in a community in which God is our Father, and we,
> his *sons*. This community with God we create during Liturgy.

In this lesson (and consistently in those given in the form of discussions
with children) a basic patriarchal model of communication only with the
same sex partners is mirrored: female–female and male–male, when experience and knowledge are transferred from the adults to the young. So,
in the first lesson the grandmother talks with the grandson, and in the
second, father talks with son.

Additionally, the words, *girl or female student* are not used in the text,
among family members *son and father* dominate; for a female person we
can rather say that she is absent than present in the text of these textbooks (there is no mention of *daughter or mother* in the explanation of
God's love, either).

**Examples of deepening the gender sensitive communication in
the textbooks for Islamic religion** Zilka Spahić Šiljak has concluded
that the textbooks for Islamic religious education mirror patriarchal values and roles of man and woman in the society in this form of religious
teaching in schools.[22] In the lesson, "Obligations toward a family" in the
textbook for the first grade students read the following:

> Family members assembled: mom, dad, grandma, grandpa, younger
> brother. Older boy, older brother and older sister. Everybody does their
> own thing. Grandma lulls a child to sleep. Dad learns Koran, grandpa and
> older brother bow, mom and Suada wash dishes, older sister reads a book.
> Suada's home is full of love and work.

Men are in charge of prayer in the family and in the mosque, and mother
and Suada wash dishes.

The author has concluded that women's activities are shown as they
have an inferior status in the society, for the most part service sectors where the life of the community as a whole is ensured, or its male
members. She also came up with a conclusion that there is a stereotypical presentation of woman in the main text and in a didactic apparatus.
The author did not pay a special attention to the possibilities of interreligious dialog, so I can only add here that in these textbooks there are
explicit teachings that we have to deprive ourselves from everything in
the service of others, and this implies that those others are from another

religion. As for the language, texts in the textbooks for religious education for Muslim children are for the most part adjusted to the age group of students in such a way that texts are short and written in a simplified way, as in the first reader in the first grade of elementary schools.

The type of the text formation conforms to what students learn in their native language classes of this age group. However, methodological questions remain open when we consider alphabet used in these texts in the second grade: Cyrillic alphabet (initial alphabet for students of the first grade in the Republic of Serbia), but the words are from Arabic inventory, which can create a problem for students, above all because some sayings are also written in the original Arabic alphabet.

When it comes to gender perspective in those textbooks we can conclude that stereotypes associated with girls and boys have been repeated. Girls are dressed in alignment with their religious requirements: covered heads, long sleeves, long skirts.

THE TEXTBOOK FOR ORTHODOX RELIGIOUS EDUCATION FOR THE FIRST GRADE OF ELEMENTARY SCHOOLS IN THE ROMA LANGUAGE

In 2002, the textbook for religious education in Gurbeti dialect of Roma language was printed, for the first grade of elementary schools, which was a translation of the textbook for Orthodox religion for that grade which means it was intended to mainly Roma children in Vojvodina and north Serbia (because in other parts of Serbia other Roma dialects are used, most often Arli).

Synod (who recommends textbooks) and The Institute (that prints textbooks) assume that the majority of Roma children in Serbia practice Orthodox religion, and that the Roma children belonging to other religious communities (Catholic, various Protestant and Islamic) should join those groups during classes for religious education in their own native language.

In practice, there are many different cases, of which we here mention only a few. Roma children already born in Vojvodina of immigrant parents from Kosovo choose Islam for their religion. Those Roma children attend classes in Serbian in elementary schools (subjects such as The Serbian language, mathematics, natural sciences), they have, as elective, the subject, Roma language with elements of culture (in the

Roma language) and Islam religious education as an elective (it is not in the Roma language). The textbook for the first grade for Orthodox and Islam religious education is written in Cyrillic alphabet with Arabic words of religious content, because of the first alphabet in the first grade for all children in Cyrillic. For Catholic children who attend classes in the first grade in Serbian, there are textbooks for the first grade in Latin alphabet. It is well known that students learn Latin alphabet in the second grade according to the current curriculum approved by the Ministry of Education.

I introduce here the example of religious education for the children from Roma national community, which is the largest community in Serbia of all minority communities, to show the complexity of the linguistic-didactic teaching of religious education in the process of the spiritual development in order to justify a stand that the religious education as it is conducted in schools across Serbia is not well organized for students of all religions and different native languages. Such empirical data can reevaluate the hypothesis that native language and spirituality are interconnected in such a way that they condition each other. That is, data can dispel the stereotype that spirituality is linked to a nation and native language, which Orthodox teachers of religious education require.

I did not study in detail the ways teachers of religious education use the analyzed text in the Roma language in practice. 2000 copies were printed total in 2002, and as of today, the edition has not been reprinted yet, which serves as evidence that the textbook has not been distributed to Roma children in schools across Serbia and thus it has not been implemented in classes. I have concluded that printing of this textbook has had a political background—something important has been accomplished for Roma children from the perspective of taking care of their spiritual development in their native language.

Conclusion

The main goal of this research is to establish to which degree interreligious and gender perspectives are embedded into the goals and realization of published textbooks for religious education in Serbia.

The hypothesis stated that textbooks mirrored the Curriculum approved by the Ministry of Education, therefore what appears in the authored textbooks is not a desire of individuals but rather an approach approved by the state of Serbia.

I have analyzed approved curricula by the Ministry of Education from the perspective of their main goal, team members who reviewed the material, selection of textbooks authors, main and didactic parts of textbooks lessons, in order to show the complexity of this issue in Serbia which is a multireligious, multilingual, and multicultural state community, with two selected dimensions—interreligious and gender based.

The results of analysis show that the approval of the textbooks for religious education in Serbia is a tightly controlled process on the part of religious authorities who are involved in the design of the curriculum, selection of the textbook authors, the selection of the reviewing team and the selection of teachers (they give blessing) to work with students in elementary and high schools.

A detailed analysis of the main didactic text of the lessons shows that textbooks authors (high ranking men in the hierarchy of a religious community—episcopes and bishops) lack didactic knowledge.

The general conclusion is that the textbooks for religious education for all three religious communities in three languages (Serbian, Croatian and Bosnian) reflect and support gender stereotypes and gender roles of patriarchal man and woman. The data aligns with the research of other female authors in Serbia and the region. Though there are some implicit instructions in the lessons that others must be loved (as the text of holy scripts commands its pious people), there are no explicit instructions in the analyzed textbooks that others should be loved that are of other religions.

It is recommended that The Ministry of Education allow the use of textbooks for religious education which connects the two ideologies: the ideology of human rights applied in the elective, Civil Education, and Christian and Islam ideology of religion as it relates to the development of spirituality visible in an interreligious and gender practice.

Notes

1. (Official Herald of the Republic of Serbia, 2001, 7, italic S.S.)
2. Svenka Savić, i s. Rebeka Jadranka Anić (2009), *Rodna perspektiva u međureligijskom dijalogu u XXI veku*, Futura publikacije i Ženske studije i istraživanja, Novi Sad.
3. Janja Baćevic, (2004) *Rodni stereotipi i politika obrazovanja: primer srpsko-pravoslavnih verskih udžbenika*, Angela Peseka ur. Gender perspektiva u nastavi—mogućnosti i poticaji, Fondacija Heinrich Boll, Kultura Kontakt Austria, Sarajevo, p. 69–79.

4. Zorica Kuburić, Zorica i Snežana Dakić (2004), *Metodika verske nastave*, CEIR, Novi Sad.
5. *Lidija Radulovic* Religija i rod: kritički osvrt na pristupe istraživanju, Originalni naučni rad UDC 305-055.2:2, Antropoligija 1 2006.
6. Official Herald—Educational Herald, number 10, August 12, 2004.
7. Official Herald—Educational Herald, number 11, October 10, 2003.
8. Zorica Kuburić & Snežana Dakić (2004), *Metodika verske nastave*, CEIR, Novi Sad, p. 72–75.
9. Ignjatije Midić, (2006) *Pravoslavni katihizis za prvi razred osnovne škole*, Zavod za udžbenike i nastavna sredstva, p. 73.
10. Ignjatije Midić, (2006) *Pravoslavni katihizis za prvi razred osnovne škole*, Zavod za udžbenike i nastavna sredstva, p. 72.
11. Ignjatije Midić, (2006) *Pravoslavni katihizis za prvi razred osnovne škole*, Zavod za udžbenike i nastavna sredstva, p. 74.
12. Hazema Ništović, (2003), *Vjeronauk za drugi razred*, Sarajevo, El-Kalem, p.75–76.
13. Ignjatije Midić, (2006) *Pravoslavni katihizis za prvi razred osnovne škole*, Zavod za udžbenike i nastavna sredstva, p. 79.
14. Ignjatije Midić, (2006) *Pravoslavni katihizis za prvi razred osnovne škole*, Zavod za udžbenike i nastavna sredstva, p. 78.
15. ORIGINAL:
   8 Mama je malom Bogoljubu za Vaskrs poklonila ptičicu.
   5 Bogoljub se mnogo obradovao daru.
   8 Ni sam nije znao zašto se toliko raduje.
   18 Imao je Bogoljub mnogo igračaka i sve su mu one bile drage, ali je ovu ptičicu posebno zavoleo.
   8 Biće da je to stoga što je živa.
   18 Doduše, kad god bi se igrao sa drugovima, on je i igračke nekako gledao kao da su žive.
   17 Na kraju je razumeo: ptičica mu je bila posebno draga zato što mu je nju poklonila mama.
   5 A on mamu mnogo voli.
   11 Bogoljub je sa ptičicom, koju je nazvao Kića, ostvario pravu zajednicu.
   15 Hranio je i brinuo se o njoj - da bude čista, da se zimi ne prehladi...
   9 Ili da je ne bi, kojim slučajem, dohvatila maca...
   7 I ptičica je posebno volela malog Bogoljuba.
   13 Kad bi se Bogoljub vratio kući iz škole, ona bi tako veselo čavrljala.
   27 Sletela bi mu na rame, stavila mu svoj kljunić u uho i milo mrmorila kao da mu priča nešto posebno, nešto što nije želela da drugi čuju.
16. **8** Jednog dana mali Bogoljub se vrati iz škole.
   9 Uđe u kuću, ali ne ču svog prijatelja Kiću.
   6 Uđe u sobu, ali Kiće nema.

11 Vidi on: kavez otvoren, prozor otvoren, a ptičice nema u sobi.

6 Dugo je Bogoljub tražio svog Kiću.

5 Pošto ga ne nađe, zaplaka.

17 Malo kasnije otac i majka se vratiše kući i zatekoše malog Bogoljuba kako plače za nestalim Kićom.

20 Tešili su ga i obećavali mu da će mu već sutradan kupiti drugu ptičicu, lepšu nego što je bio Kića.

6 Ali, mali Bogoljub nije hteo drugu.

15 Tugovao je on za svojim Kićom i hteo je da mu vrate njega, samo njega.

19 Mama i tata su mu govorili da to nije moguće i da jedino mogu da mu nabave drugu ptičicu.

7 Mali Kića je sada sigurno sa drugovima.

20 I njemu je teško bez tebe, ali on je ipak ptičica i treba da bude tamo gde su ostale ptice.

17 No, on tebe neće zaboraviti, a nećeš ni ti njega - govorili su **tata i mama** malom Bogoljubu.

14 Kada tu drugu ptičicu zavoliš - govorili su - i ona će biti tvoj najmiliji Kića.

17. **4** Ljubav nam donosi radost.

12 Ona čini da ljudi i priroda oko nas budu jedinstveni i neponovljivi.

33 Ovo poslednje je mali Bogoljub razumeo, jer je on svojom ljubavlju činio da sve njegove igračke budu žive, ali nije mogao da razume zašto Kiću ne može da zameni ni jedna druga ptičica.

12 Biće da je zbog toga što je on svoga Kiću mnogo voleo.

4 A i Kića njega.

29 Mali Bogoljub se na kraju ipak utešio kad su mu tata i mama kazali da je Kića svakako živ i da je sigurno srećan jer je sa svojim drugovima.

22 Zbog toga je Bogoljub kad god su dolazile druge ptičice u njihovu baštu ispred kuće, tu među njima video i svog Kiću.

6 Ili mu se bar tako činilo?

2 Ne zna.

16 No, od tada je Bogoljub voleo i pazio sve ptičice, jer su sve one postale njegove.

18. Ivan Ivić, et al. (2008), *Vodič za dobar udžbenik: opšti standardi kvaliteta udžbenika*, Platoneum, Novi Sad.

19. **3** Šta je ljubav?

7 Kako nam izgleda priroda kad je volimo?

12 Da li možemo da volimo prirodu, a da ne volimo nijednog čoveka?

19 Kako se osećaš kad si sam, a kako kad si zajedno sa onima koje voliš i koji tebe vole?

20. Ignjatije Midić, (2006) *Pravoslavni katihizis za prvi razred osnovne škole*, Zavod za udžbenike i nastavna sredstva, p. 97–98.
21. Janja Baćević, (2004), Rodni stereotipi i politika obrazovanja: primer srpsko-pravoslavnih verskih udžbenika, Angela Peseka ur. Gender perspektiva u nastavi—mogućnosti i poticaji, Fondacija Heinrich Boll, Kultura Kontakt Austria, Sarajevo, 69–79; Spahić-Šiljak, Zilka (2008), The Analysis on Image of Women in the School: Religious Textbooks in Bosnia and Herzegovina, Moravcikova, Michaela, Greskova, Lucia (eds.) Zeny a Nabozenstva (Women and Religions) 2. Bratislava: Ustav pre vztahy statu a cirkvi.
22. Spahić-Šiljak, Zilka (2008), The Analysis on Image of Women in the School: Religious Textbooks in Bosnia and Herzegovina, Moravcikova, Michaela, Greskova, Lucia (eds.) Zeny a Nabozenstva (Women and Religions) 2. Bratislava: Ustav pre vztahy statu a cirkvi.

APPENDIX: THE GOD WE BELIEVE IN IS THE FATHER

Radomir, Milica's brother, is older than Milica. He, too, attended Liturgy on Sunday with his mom and dad. However, not for the first time as Milica, but he, too, has a lot to ask about Liturgy. He is standing in the garden beside his father who is weeding flowers and apple trees and asks him: "Dad, why does the bishop say to the God: 'Father', when we all pray to God in the Church? Is the God really a Father to the bishop and us?"

Father raised his head and said: "Yes, the God is the Father to all of us in the Church." "But how?"—Radomir asks—"we were not born by him so that he could be our Father."

"You are right, my son"—the father said. "But, the God also has a Son, Jesus Christ, so he, too is the Father. We call the God our Father because He is the Father of Jesus Christ, born by him, which was revealed to us by Jesus Christ himself. However, the fact we call the God, the Father is not only because He has a Son, but also because we love Him, too, and wish to have Him as our Father, too. Jesus Christ also calls God the Father not only because He is his Father but also because he loves him the most."

"You see"—the father continues—"we do not call our parents—fathers—only because they brought us to the world, but above all, because we love them. For instance, your friend Goran was adopted by my friend, Bogoljub, so, he was not born by him. However, he calls

Goran his son and he is indeed his son because he loves him. And Goran loves him, too, and that is why he calls him his father. So, the fact that I call you my son is not only by nature. This signifies the relationship of love that we both share.

Similarly, we in the Church call the God, the Father, because we love Him and we want Him to be our Father. This means we live in a community where the God is our Father, and we, His sons. This relationship with the God we exercise at Liturgy. Jesus Christ made it possible for us. When on Sunday we all rush to the Church, we show our love for the God that way, and the desire to meet him and see him, as we do with our dearest friend who we have not seen for a long time and with whom we made the appointment at a specific place, at specific time. That is why we try not to be late for Liturgy, which is our meeting with the God, the Father, because otherwise it would mean that we did not really care that much for him."

CHAPTER 13

The Analysis of the Textbooks for Orthodox Religious Education in Serbia

Zorica Kuburić

INTRODUCTION

After the breakup of Yugoslavia, a trend of ethnic and religious homogenization has become noticeable and the introduction of confessional religious education in public schools, starting with Croatia in 1991 and then Serbia in 2001, contributed to political trends of formation of small national states that desire to have an independent religious and national identity.

The reform of the system of education in Serbia started at the same time with traditionalization and modernization of the society, by returning to the traditional values and introducing civic education. This was a result of wider social changes that occurred after the nineties, such as the breakup of the country that had previously integrated differences by means of atheization of the society. The need for this kind of reform was established by an increase in religiosity of the citizens, on the one hand, and the need for a stable value system that would integrate the society, on the other.

Z. Kuburić (✉)
Philosophy, University of Novi Sad, Novi Sad, Serbia

G. Ognjenović and J. Jozelić (eds.), *Education in Post-Conflict Transition*, Palgrave Studies in Religion, Politics, and Policy, https://doi.org/10.1007/978-3-319-56605-4_13

Nikola Knežević, starting from the position of well-known political theologian Metz[1] that privatized religion, and thus apolitical religion, is socially irrelevant and purposeless, says that one of the greatest myths is the one that represents religion as an apolitical phenomenon. Even if we tried to place religion entirely in the domain of personal experience, it would still be a part of the collective, depending on the importance that it has for the worldview of an individual. Modalities through which interaction potentials of Religion and Politics come to expression in the contemporary sociological thought are defined as politicization of religion or religionization of politics.[2] Politicization of religion can be regarded as a political and ideological interpolation of a religious discourse, in other words, it is a moment when this discourse is in service of a certain ideological or political construct. In the Balkans, it appears that the *ideological* element is the most expressed of all three constitutive elements of religion, which can be observed in *rationalization of a group interest*, which in this case means preservation of the national consciousness and its historical, social and political interests.[3]

Religious education in the public schools has its devoted proponents, but there are also those who constantly oppose it. The principal objection is that children are divided according to their religious affiliation. Besides, as an elective course, which is not graded and with teachers whose employment status is not regulated, it has a potential either to become equal to other courses and to be transformed into a general education course without a confessional character or to be canceled again in public schools. This is the seesaw that preserves the dynamics of cooperation of the state and the Church.

The analysis of the contents of textbooks of Orthodox catechesis clearly indicates the effort to preserve the national identity of Orthodox believers, and this is a political reason for confessional religious education instead of an integrative approach to studying religion as a phenomenon either in the form of religious culture, sociology of religion or the history of religion. In this way, religion is used for political purposes. The textbooks that have been used in Serbia for 15 years pointed to the liturgical community and the importance of religious identity of the community in the context of ontological catechesis.

CONFESSIONAL RELIGIOUS EDUCATION

Confessional religious education was introduced in the Serbian public school system as a multi-denominational and optional subject with the alternative choice of either Civic Education. In 2001, Serbia opted for a

confessional, segregated, multi-denominational model of religious education that may be conducted in public schools by seven "traditional" or "historical" religious communities: the Serbian Orthodox Church (SOC), the
Roman Catholic Church, the Islamic Community, the Jewish Community,
the Slovak Evangelical Church, the Christian Reformed Church and the
Evangelical Christian Church in Serbia—Vojvodina. Since 2005/2006 this
opportunity has been given to the Romanian Orthodox Church as well.[4]

In the autumn of 2001, Religious Education was introduced into
our schools for the first time in almost half a century. Civic Education
was introduced, for the first time, as an alternative subject to Religious
Education. The programme of Religious Education for the schools in
Serbia is designed for one hour of classes per week, or 36 h annually.
Curricula and textbooks are proposed by the seven "traditional" religious communities. The tasks and contents of Religious Education are
defined for each of these seven churches and religious communities.[5]

The reform of the educational system in Serbia started with the introduction of religious and civic education. This was the result of a broader
social change. The return to religion and rise of religiosity were some of
the most important reasons for introducing religious education.[6]

The aim of the Religious Education subject is to promote confessional
religious beliefs, provide information on the students' own religion, and
to encourage and train students to perceive and to practice the Liturgy.
While the specific contents of the subject are confessionally defined for
each of the traditional churches and religious communities, the stated
aims are largely the same for all.

The goals of Religious Education, aims and tasks were identically
formulated for the elementary and high schools.[7] The general goals of
Religious Education in Serbia are to acquaint the students with the faith
and spiritual experiences of their own church or religious community, to
enable them to get an integrated religious view of the world and life, and
to enable them to acquire the spiritual values of their church or religious
community, as well as to preserve and cultivate their own religious and
cultural identities. One might say that the goal of religious education is
to develop a theistic world view, faith in God, and the capacity to practice religion in everyday life. The goal of Orthodox catechism in the first
grade of high school is to develop trust, love and unity with classmates
and fellow students, and to cultivate solidarity and mutual assistance, and
care for nature and the world. Another goal is to point out the basics of
the faith and experience of the Church as a source and inspiration for
personal and community development.[8]

Talking about religious education in high schools, Orthodox bishop and textbook author Ignjatije Midić says that adolescence is actually the best period for making live contact with God and attending church. However, Midić thinks that religiosity is not established by the simple presentation of a certain worldview, or by teaching a certain number of concepts and aspects of theology, thus enforcing ethical norms and rules of conduct. Religiosity represents an ethos of freedom and love. This is why the goal of the classes for the first high-school grade is to develop the awareness of students that Christianity is a church, a liturgical community, and to draw the attention of students to the notion of character as a basic Christian concept. Without an adequate understanding of the concept of character, it is impossible to understand that the Christian belief in God is a way of life, and not an academic doctrine or ideology.[9]

Orthodox Catechism in the Educational System of Serbia

The curricula and textbooks are proposed by the religious communities. The textbooks are written by authors from within the religious communities. All books must be revised by the Commission of the Ministry of Religious Affairs which controls and approves the textbooks. This Commission, which meets several times a year, includes seven representatives from the seven traditional religions and three representatives each from the Ministries of Education and Religious Affairs (since December 2004) plus the Chair of the Commission, 14 members altogether. A Serbian Orthodox priest or bishop heads the Commission. All textbooks are published by the monopoly publisher, the Institute for Textbooks and Teaching Supplies (Zavod za udžbenike i nastavna sredstva). Orthodox textbooks *The analysis of the textbooks for Orthodox Religious Education* clearly reveals their confessional character. The only author of all textbooks for both—teachers and students—is Ignjatije Midić, a Serbian Orthodox bishop and professor of Dogmatic.[10]

The textbooks for students have a typically Orthodox visual focus on icons and pictures. The book *Crkveni slovar* (Church Grammar) for the first grade of the elementary school has 11 lessons.[11] Each one is accompanied by an "Instruction in Faith" and questions about the lesson. The illustrations are very traditional and diverse. Each lesson is written as a story with key concepts such as love, church, selfishness, generosity, baptism, liturgy and the Eucharist.

Several studies have looked at attitudes towards religious education prior to its introduction to the Serbian educational system.[12]

The option to select those subjects was cancelled, so that Religious Education and Civic Education became the alternative subjects. More than 50% of elementary school children, and half as many in high schools, applied for Religious Education.[13]

The Ministry of Education, Science and Technological Development has entrusted the Institute for Education Quality and Evaluation with an evaluative research which has a goal to examine the quality of teaching programmes and competencies of teachers of religious education.[14] This report presents and comments on the results of the evaluation of the Orthodox Catechism. The sample of the research was comprised of 192 teachers of the Orthodox Catechism from six cities in Serbia: Belgrade, Kruševac, Šabac, Niš, Leskovac and Čačak. This sample included twice as many males than females, which is in accordance with a ration of theology student at the Faculty of Theology in Belgrade.[15]

According to the results of the study, almost two thirds of the religious teachers is unsatisfied with religious education textbooks used by students, while one third finds them good. Only 27.6% of religious teachers believe that the textbooks and handbooks are good, while only 6.8% of them completely agree with this claim. On the other hand, 35.4% of religious teachers completely disagree with the claim that the textbooks and handbooks for religious studies are good. Given by grades of elementary school, the worst score was given to the teaching topics of textbook for the first year of elementary school (1.75), while the best scored for the third grade (3.55). In total, scores for the teaching topics by years are as follows: for the first year 1.75; for the second year 2.75; for the third year 3.55; for the fourth year 3.54; for the fifth year 3.19; for the sixth year 3.51; for the seventh year 2.67 and for the eighth year 3.13.

When it was assessed whether the teaching topics were age-appropriate, interesting for school children, and relevant for achieving the expected goals of the subject, the best grades (4.00) were given to the following topics: God created a unique world as well as many distinct species out of nothing (the cause of the creation of the world is God's freedom); Christ's Calvary and Resurrection; The refusal of the first man, Adam to combine the created nature with God, i.e. to cooperate to realize God's plan for the world (the fall of man and its consequences—the original sin); The structure of the Liturgy (a bishop, priests, deacon and people).

It can be concluded that religious education teachers are seriously critical about the quality of the programme for the first year. Only one of six topics (Man as a being of a community) was assessed as age-appropriate, interesting, adequate in contents and important for achieving the expected outcome of the subject (3.50). The other five topics obtained very low scores on all four criteria. Because of that, the total score of the programme is 1.75. Respondents believe that topics that scored low should be shifted to some of the older school years, because students do not understand them and inapplicable to life. It is especially emphasized that the topic—Jesus Christ is a mediator between God and created nature—is incomprehensible to 7-year-olds, and that the topic—the Church is a communion of all people and the entire nature with God though Christ—is interesting but age-inappropriate.

Religious education teachers believe that the greatest advantage of the subject is in moral guidance which students receive. Approximately 75% of respondents think that the advantage of the subject is in the goals related to the development of a complete view of life, an encouragement to personality development and providing a foundation for a responsible and proactive life in a contemporary society. Only 9% of the respondents see the advantage of the subject in its contents, and less than 3% in the methodology.

Teaching contents presented in the textbooks of the religious education of the Orthodox Catechism can be observed and analyzed in different ways. In this paper, I will attempt to present the topics though content analysis all book for elementary schools.

ONTOLOGY-BASED CATECHISM

According to the Curricula of the Orthodox Catechism, whose author is the Bishop of Braničevo Dr. Ignjatije Midić,[16] the goal of the course is to provide a complete Orthodox view of life and the world, taking into account two dimensions: historical life of Christians (historical reality of the Church) and the eschatological (future) life (the dimension of the ideal). This means that students are systematically introduced to the Orthodox faith and its doctrinal, liturgical, social and missionary dimension, whereby it is sought to present that the Christian view includes all positive experiences of people, regardless of their nationality and religious education. Such a formulation indicates that this is a confessional religious education which is directed to itself and to the formation of its own identity, which, in broader sense, represents a foundation for a religious dialogue, because one cannot discuss what one does not know.

In a teacher's book, written by the author of all textbooks for the Orthodox Catechism, Dr. Ignjatije Midić, we can read that the programme of the Orthodox Catechism is different in content and in structure both from classical catechism programmes in public school in the period before the Second World War and from those which are realized in church schools today, and thus it is different in the goal which it is to achieve. The author makes a distance from classical catechism programmes, because they are taken from the West, just as the very form of contemporary school education. Their essential characteristic lies in the fact that they assume that the being, existence, is based on the nature and its laws, not on the personality. Therefore, freedom, both of God and of man, is not a foundation and the cause of the existence of nature, but merely a superstructure of and an addition to the already existing nature, and a personality is identified with an individual, stresses Midić in his instructions for catechists.

Midić believes that individualism is a threat to the Church, because it defines a person as an individual independent from another being in this existence. Man is an individual only if he is independent in his existence from another man or God. Moreover, the other is a hindrance to our realization as an absolute being. Such understanding leads to destruction of the Church as a concrete community and its liturgical structure and to multiplication of animosity among people. A criticism which he makes and which motivates him to write textbooks in a completely different manner is related to subjectivism which identifies a personality of a man with his inner world (emotions, thoughts, conclusions) and puts his external activities and the visible world in opposition to this internal spiritual world. In the experience of the Church, this means the development of pietism as spirituality at the expense of ecclesiastical liturgical order. Individualism, coupled with subjectivism, equates a human experience of the world and God with his emotions and individual experience, which diminishes the importance or even completely eliminates the experience of the Church as a concrete liturgical community.

Elevating a rational element in man to a crucial element for determining the truth and the existence creates a man and his mind a measure of the truth which questions everything that cannot be logically confirmed. This leads to rejecting everything that is supernatural, such as, first and foremost the existence of God and the faith in God. Freedom of personality, on the other hand, coupled with individualism and subjectivism, leads to rejection of any authority and the creation of consumerism in man's relation with the nature that surrounds it.

An ontological approach to teaching catechism, in contrast to some pre-war religious education programmes or to a new programme in the Republic of Srpska, which explain the Salvation as a fulfillment of a moral code though obeying the Ten Commandments or the natural law, which is applied to all people, the Salvation is put here in the context of participation in a concrete liturgical community. In other words, it is based on a belief that man does not save himself by being moral, because there are many moral people outside the Church, but he saves himself by being in communion with God. Morality is, therefore, not dismissed, but it is based on a completely different foundations. Furthermore, the Ten Commandments are also not dismissed, but it is insisted that the Commandments serve to bring man into and to keep him in the community; thus they are means, not a goal on their own. The goal is a union with God and other people in the Liturgy—a union of concrete persons with the concrete Person.

Miloš Jelić, a religious education teacher and a PhD student at the Faculty of Theology in Belgrade, offers an example: "How can it be possible to love my enemies, when it is in the very nature of things that enemies are those who threaten me and it is natural to hate them and fight against them in order to protect myself? But, if I see an enemy as someone who can repent and stop being my enemy, in other words, as someone who can become a saint and a member of the future Kingdom of God, then my relationship with that person is radically different. In that case, my ethics is not based on the nature, but on love towards any person as an icon of God—may they be Muslims or Jews or atheists, antitheists, and so on. There's a foundation for an interreligious dialogue!"[17]

In order to better understand the differences between these two approaches in making programmes and textbooks of the Orthodox Catechism, even within the same Serbian Orthodox Church, I will mention the programme that is realized in the Republic of Srpska,[18] where during the nine years of elementary schools, only few classes are dedicated to the Liturgy, but almost each year it is insisted on morality and rule of conduct. The teaching plan and programme for the Orthodox Christianity religious education was published in Banja Luka in 2015. It contains a list of outcomes of the course. I will quote the outcome of the course in the fourth grade of elementary schools as an example: "list the

Ten Commandments; compare what is regulated by the Commandments on the first and on the second stone tablet; understand the significance of fulfilling the Ten Commandments; understand the existence of only one God; define the concept of an idol and other gods; understand what it means to take the Lord's name in vain; understand what it means to remember the Sabbath day—the day of the Lord; understand with it means to honour your parents; explain the sins: murder, adultery, stealing, bearing false witness and coveting".

According to Miloš Jelić, the teaching plan and programme of the Bishop Ignjatije Midić in Serbia is based on the model of the Early Church. "The Early Church was comprised of those who were preparing for baptism—they were called catechumens or—they used to go through a certain period of preparation which lasted 6 months, a year or even longer, and during that period they were taught about the faith (hence preserved Catecheses—instructions about the faith by Church Fathers—bishops who delivered sermons, just like bishops do today, in which they taught, i.e. interpreted the Holy Bible and taught about the faith in general). Before their baptism, catechumens participated in liturgical gatherings, listened to readings from the Holy Bible, listened to interpretation of the read, and were taught about the faith. This was, in fact, religious education in the Church, which had a goal to prepare them to become members of the Church. This catechism that we have today is designed in this way in order to compensate for the fact that there are no more catechumens in the Church today and that it is expected from religious education at schools to prepare students to join the Church and actively participate in the Liturgy. I believe this is the cause of a certain distance that Bishop Ignjatije makes in relation to the context in which religious education is held, because the natural place of Catechism is the church and liturgy (that is why it is called liturgical catechism), and only then in a scholastic-school system".[19]

Rastko Jović, an assistant professor at the Orthodox Faculty of Theology in Belgrade, which is also engages in giving seminars to religious education teachers in the Republic of Srpska (22 August 2016) believes that "the textbooks of Ignjatije Midić are based on his dogmatic belief, which is in turn based entirely on John Zizioulas. Insisting on the Liturgy comes from the fact that it is clear today that the first Christians did not have the Holy Bible at the beginning, but the liturgical community created the Script, which means that the liturgy precedes the Bible. The theology of Zizoulas is the latest thing which the Orthodox has, and this is commendable about the textbooks".[20]

In the Republic of Srpska, based on Article 34 of the Law on Publishing[21] and the Textbooks Plan for the school year of 2016/2017, a new Teaching Plan and Programme was introduced and a competition for new textbooks was announced by the Catechesis Committee of the Serbian Orthodox Church in the Republic of Srpska and the Federation of Bosnia and Herzegovina in Banja Luka. According to the information found on the website of the Catechesis Committee,[22] all textbooks are obtained, with an exception of the textbook for the ninth grade, for which a new competition is announced in accordance with the Textbooks Plan of the Catechesis Committee for the school year 2016/17.

Content Analysis of Elementary School Textbooks for the Orthodox Catechism

The content of the course in the Orthodox Catechism is arranged according to a linear-concentric (symbiotic, spiral) principle. Certain contents were chosen for each school year, and then, previously acquired knowledge and formed skills are activated within each of the topics that successively follow one after another. New topics are introduced in each school grade, which acts as a foundation for further knowledge in following grades. The sequence of the topics in lower grades is directed downward, which means that it is based on presenting the material in accordance with psychological accessibility, while in higher grades, it is directed upwards, i.e. it is based on the principles of theological scientific systematic.

The First Grade

Topics: Man is an icon of God. God is a union of the persons of the Father, and the Son and the Holy Spirit. Man as a being of a community. God created the world out of love together with the Son and the Holy Spirit. Jesus Christ is a mediator between God and the created nature. The Church is a communion of all people and the entire nature with God through Christ. The Orthodox iconography represents the world and man in the communion with God.

Key sentences which describe the communion and love in the textbook for the first year of elementary schools point to the relationship with the nature, another person and God, emphasizing that this world belongs both to the innocent nature and responsible humans. "If we destroy nature, we cause pain both to those who love us and to those we love, but also to ourselves". "When we love another person, we discover God in them".

God is in the textbooks presented as a love that is expressed in human relations. "Love is a union with another person, i.e. with God who makes plants and animals and people alive—all of them who are with us and everything that exists". "We know people best when we love them, i.e. when we make a union of love with them".

Like the entire concept of religious education, the content of the textbook for the first grade indirectly points to an internal relationship policy, to "a union with friends", it indicates that children are directed to their faith which assumes a relationship with "Christ and God the Father and with other people who are members of the Church".

The Second Grade

> Topics: God is a union of the persons of the Father, and the Son and the Holy Spirit. The Liturgy as an icon of the future era, the Kingdom of God. The Liturgy – discovering God. The structure of the Liturgy and the Church (bishop, priests, deacons and people). The Liturgy is both the presence of Jesus and expecting his return. The Orthodox iconography represents the state of the world and man in the future era.

The textbook for the second grade also emphasizes the importance of the community and its hierarchical structure, in which the union with God is the most important and it has its form in the liturgy: "The liturgy is a communion of all people with God through Christ. There are men and women, the young and the old. In order for the liturgy to be genuine and truthful, everyone needs to participate, regardless of their sex, age or nationality".

The crucial message, in which we recognize the mankind as a communion of all people governed by peace and prosperity, is expressed in the textbook in the following way: "We prayed God to give us peace, and that there is no war, and to live with each other in peace and harmony, all people in the world to be together, and the ill to get well, and the weather to be nice and fruits, wheat and corn to yield, and birds to be cheerful, and animals tame and all in this manner".

The community within the Church has its ecclesiastical hierarchy in its structure, without which there is no salvation: "The most important ministers without whom there is no liturgy are: a bishop, priests, deacons and people". The ministry of a bishop "is a ministry through which Christ is present in the Church as its head... The priestly ministry indicates the presence of the apostles in the Church... The word deacon means servant. Deacons assist bishops during the liturgy and in other church businesses, and they also assist priests. They make a connection with people". "The people of God become all those who are christened". "And for that reason Christ remained present on the Earth in the form of common people who gather at the liturgy, first and foremost he is present though a bishop". "That is the reason why we go to the liturgy in order to meet with God the Father and to talk with Him, because only there is Christ present in the person of a bishops'—finished the teacher". "Gathering around a bishop at the Liturgy, who is the first among us, is like gathering around Christ and we make a union of freedom with God the Father".

The importance of the Church, the faith and the identity is strictly defined. Although the key word in all textbooks for all grades is "freedom", it is a theological concept which means the freedom to decide to be for God or against him, but it does not imply freedom of variations within religious movements.

Miloš Jelić explains that in the following words: "The Church in her nature absolutely affirms freedom of an individual, albeit this freedom is always freedom in communion with another, and it is never freedom from another person, which is individualism. One cannot be an individualist in the Church, although individualism is not excluded".

The quote which describes the relationship with the Church as a community carries a message that this relationship is unbreakable and "for all time": "The Church is a communion that gives us existence and defines who we are for all time". By emphasizing the identity in a communion, individualism is indirectly negated here: "I think this is because we are who we are and that we know who we are when we are in communion with someone. We cannot even imagine ourselves outside communion with someone else. It is as if man on his own does not exist. That is why it is important to belong to some communion in order to be able to say who we are".

Man and God are two parallel worlds, one that is ideal and the other that needs to approach the former in its kindness and love, while hatred against another man is equal to hatred against God: "Hatred against another man is hatred against God" and "Love needs to constantly confirm itself".

The Third Grade

Topics: God created a unique world and many different species out of nothing. Consequences of createdness on the nature and its existence. Creation of man at the end of all creation "in the image and likeness of God" (difference between the nature and the personality of man). The Eucharist as the world in miniature. The creation of the world and man in the Orthodox iconography.

The textbook for the third grade discusses the creation of the world that is based on man's freedom in contrast to the nature, with a message that life is beautiful, the nature is beautiful and death is the only enemy and it will be conquered in the Kingdom of God. The relationship with another man is based on freedom. An invitation is sent to children that say that if they want to become sons of God, they need to become participants in the Liturgy.

"Life is beautiful, regardless of how difficult it is, and the nature is beautiful. It will be shown at the end of history, when death will be cancelled". "When we love one man and he loves us, than the whole world appears beautiful". "This means that the person whom we love gives the world its existence, beauty and importance for us". "You cannot be in communion with someone if he does not want it".

The Fourth Grade

Topics: The goal because of which God created the world. The church is a concrete liturgical community. Liturgy is a communion of many people and the nature with God the Father though one man – Christ. The structure of the Liturgy. The Church as an icon of the future Kingdom. The rejection of the first man, Adam, to unite the created nature with God. The Church in Christians architecture.

The message of the textbook for the fourth grade is a renouncement of an attempt to seek salvation and immortality in the nature and reality, because immortality is realized only by becoming a member of the Church: "Believing in God's promise and expecting the Kingdom of God to be fulfilled in earth, Christians lives in accordance with this faith.

They were always kind to others and invited them to join the communion with Christ, in other words to become members of the Church so as to realize what all people want, which is immortality".

Textbook is made a clear distinction between theism and pantheism where it is emphasized that God is different from the existing world: "By its nature, the world is something else than God and it is separated from God. God is uncreated, while everything else that exists is created". "The createdness of the world means that it has its beginning, i.e. it exists in time and space". "God exists out of time and space, because He is uncreated, eternal, does not have the beginning and the end". "At the end of the creation, God created man from the dust of the earth, i.e. from the nature that all other creatures are made of, and He gave him freedom, i.e. His divine image. Because God is also a free person, not an impersonal nature".

The fall of man is explained by man's attempt to seek immortality in the nature, by eating a fruit from the forbidden tree, which made him lose his union with God: "At the beginning, He gave him an easy task, not to eat fruits from only one tree, because he wanted man not to seek the source of immortality in the mortal nature, but in Him—God". "The sin of the first man, Adam, was, therefore, that he sought immortality in the created nature, not in communion with God, and that is why he remained mortal. Instead of seeking immortality in the union with God, he sought it the created nature. This mistake has been repeated by many people ever since".

The most important issue that theology deals with the problem of death: "Similarly to people who can act against the laws of nature: to fast when they are hungry, to love other people, although they are sinful, ugly and belong to another nation etc. Although man's freedom in relation to the laws of nature is limited, it still demonstrates that man is created to exist freely, in communion of love with another man, i.e. to overcome the natural laws, i.e. death". "Man is also conscious of immortality cannot be found in the created nature, and that is why he seeks in the context of realization of a communion with the only being that is out of nature, i.e. with God".

The textbook for the fourth grade introduces Mother of God into the hierarchical system, and her place is just after Christ: "The fist in the Church is Jesus Christ, because he is the Son of God who became a man so as to others could connect the God the Father through him. The first after Christ is Virgin Mary, Mother of Christ, and then come the Apostles as his first friends and all the other who join the communion with Christ. Every member of the Church is a person and is different from others in the way he expresses love to Christ and depending on when they showed love. The Mother of God comes right after Christ, because she gave birth to him and she loves him most. Without the Mother of God there would be no Christ. The Apostles come after the Mother of God".

The freedom given to man is the highest value: "You can treat animals and things in any way you like, because they have no freedom, but you cannot do that to humans without their willing consent. Otherwise, you reduce people to animals and things".

The Fifth Grade

> Topics: The preparation for the arrival of the Son of God to the world. The choice of Abraham and his descendants as the beginning of the Church. Abraham and Jewish people as a pre-image of Christ and the Church. The Ten Commandments. Human effort to find salvation from death (different religions, mythologies, philosophy, science). Motifs from the Old Testament in the Orthodox iconography.

The textbook for the fifth grade instruct students to love other people and we find again the idea of identification of man with God, because God loves by showing love to man. Since man is sinful by his very nature, love that is mention here is unconditional love, and He treats a sinful man "as if he is without sins", and man makes himself "though an experience of love toward another person". "Because, when we love another person, we see God in them". "In liturgical experience, to love God means to love people... other people, who are still not participants of the liturgy, as well".

However, we can identify here an indirect exclusion of the others, because the message which is emphasized is: "No one can make a communion with God without Christ. Who does not make a communion with God cannot live eternally". "With freedom there is also a belief of man that a communion with God is realizes in the Church, and thus the eternal life".

In addition to the false gods of pagan world in the textbook points to another danger of giving too much importance leaders: "Coming in contact with other peoples who were pagans". "There was a threat for Israelites to proclaim their leaders gods".

Therefore, the relationship towards the others has some layers of dissociations. The communion of love towards one's own kind assumes separation from pantheistic view of the world, from idolatry that worships nature and from worshiping man and his powers.

The Sixth Grade

> Topics: The secret of Christ – unity of God and Man. The birth of Christ "from the Holy Spirit and Virgin Mary". Christ is a Son of God who became Man, new Adam, in order to unite his created nature with God. The role of God in Salvation. The role of man in Salvation. Christ's suffering and resurrection. Christ's life in the Orthodox iconography.

Topics in the textbook for the sixth grade are Christian understanding of history and the importance of understanding God who is completely different from the nature, i.e. the created world, transcendental God and God who is a Personality. It is emphasized that God became man, i.e. the Son of God became Christ, God-man. If God remains exclusively in his transcendence, we could not have a communion with Him, and therefore, there would be any salvation from death. The second division that is important is the division of history to before and after Christ. However, this division is of an integrative nature, since the Jewish people was chosen to mediate the salvation of the world: "by preparing the human kind through the Jewish people and demonstrating that the Son of God will become man and that he will die in order to save people and all the nature from death".

The distinction between good and evils also significantly emphasized: "This cosmic historical event, which divided the history of the mankind into one before and one after Christ, is of a great importance for all people and all the creation. On that night, the Son of God was born in Bethlehem and he became man like other people—he who created people and all things visible and invisible. The Son of God became man to unite in himself and to make peace between the Creator and the created". "God, who is the Holy Trinity, revealed Himself at the baptism of Jesus: The son who was being baptized, the Spirit in the form of a dove and God the Father as a voice from heaven. The will of God was revealed on that occasion, i.e. the will of God the Father concerning the world and its salvation through Christ".

Hostility that exists in the world is also personified: "Devils are, as we have already said, free beings that rejected the God's plan of salvation through the communion with God. The temptation of Christ by those who are against God and God's plan about the created consisted of an offer to Jesus Christ to disobey God because of bread, power of his egotism, i.e. to proclaim himself a god without the union with God the Father, and thus, the plan of God for His Kingdom on earth to fail". "In contrast to the first people, who repented for their falsely used freedom against God, devils are those who remain insistent in their opposition to fulfillment of the Kingdom of God on Earth".

Freedom of choice between good and evil is man's privilege but also a responsibility. "Evil and death are not punishments of God directed to people, they are wrongly used freedoms by free beings in the created world. Instead of expressing their freedom as the love of God and His creatures, people wanted to become independent from God in their existence. That causes death in the nature, since the created beings are not immortal by their nature". "Because guilt exists only among those beings who have freedom to choose if they want the union with God or not, and these are people".

The relation between legalism and mercy is explained by placing blind obedience to the law in direct opposition to man: "Christ angered many Pharisees and teachers of law, who blindly held to the letter of the law, because Christ, who was doing good to people, did not carry much for the law. People and their salvation were more important to him than blind fulfillment of the law".

It is important to mention that students are encouraged to take freedom without fear: "Because fear and coercion annihilate freedom in man, and man without freedom stops being man.""As Christ died and rose again, so will those who are with Christ—they will rise on the last day, i.e. those who make a communion with Christ, even if they die, they will rise when he returns. Then all the creatures that willingly united with the Son of God, Jesus Christ, will become immortal in the Church, and those who died will rise from the dead and everyone will live eternally".

"The Kingdom of God will be a congregation of all willing peoples around the Lord Jesus Christ, who will bring them into the communion with God the Father". "All of those who are baptized in the name of Jesus Christ are baptized with the hope that Christ will come soon and that he will finally abolish death and establish the Kingdom of God on the Earth. From that day on, the Church of Christ will grow until the entire universe becomes the Church of Christ".

An important part of the teaching is related to the theology of man, i.e. to understanding of the human nature. The importance of the body, the salvation of the body is emphasized in this part; there is not a single word about heaven and hell, no spirit in life outside a body, because resurrection is the most important reaching in Christianity:

"This is important for our salvation, because it indicates that the eternal life is a resurrection and life in the body. Without the resurrection of the body we cannot speak about the salvation, i.e. about the eternal life of people. More so if we understand that salvation is a salvation from death, which is the essence of the Christian faith, because death is first and foremost death of the body. Abolishing death means an eternal life of the body, and therefore an eternal life of the nature. Because our body is an integral part of the nature. If it lives, the nature also lives".

"Resurrected Christ is an image with the body with visible marks of his suffering, wounds from the nails on hands and feet and ribs pierced by the lance".

"This was in order to show that Christ's resurrection was not an illusion or an appearance of Christ as a ghost, but he resurrected in body and it was the same body he had had before death".

"God wanted the created world to exist forever in communion with His Son, but he did not want that without the willing consent of created beings. He did not want to realize his wish by force, without freedom and the consent of the world. Therefore, he gave freedom to the created beings to decide on their own if they wanted communion with God and thus the eternal life, or not".

The difference between man and God is explained by differentiating between two types of freedom: the freedom of God and the freedom of man, and man is related to God as a child with his parents. God is uncreated, while man is created and therefore he could not have been asked about his existence before his birth. For that reason, man has an opportunity to freely choose an eternal life and be reborn by his freedom. In this way the textbook emphasized the message of religious freedom as an individual act and salvation as a collective one.

"In contrast to God, man is given everything, i.e. everything is imposed on him: both his existence and the existence of everything else. However, since he is an icon of God, man wants to exist freely as

God does. Hence, when man grows up, he comes into conflict first with his parents, asking them why they gave birth to him, when he did not ask him. In that way man expresses his wish to exist only if he himself wants to, i.e. to exist freely, like God, and not to be given a life without permission".

"However, parents did not ask him before they gave birth to him, because he did not exist before they gave birth to him. Therefore, they could not have asked him. It is the same with God who created us without asking us if we wanted to exist. Because we did not exist before God created us and he could not have asked us if we wanted to. God asked us that question later, after the creation". "He comes into conflict with his parents because they gave birth to him without asking and by doing that they denied him freedom; but he loves friends because he chose them himself".

Conflicts with other people are also explained in terms of the need of freedom, a need to be asked about one's own life: "Simultaneously, man comes into conflict both with other people and with the rest of the nature. Because they also exist against his will, while he would want them to exist as a product of his freedom. In his aspiration to be like God, i.e. to be free and everything to depend on his freedom, man comes into temptation to express his freedom by negating the existence of himself and the others, in order to create his own world, different from the existing one, created by God".

"Because man contains both spiritual and material nature... that is why he is a key being in the existence of the world, beside the Son of God. Without him and his free consent, a union of all created beings with the Son of God could not have happened. Any forced union between the nature and the Son of God, without the participation of man, i.e. without free consent of the creation, would be a torture for the creation and its destruction. Man is the only one who has freedom and he is the only one who could mediate the union between the created nature and God. In order for the created nature to exist eternally, the Son of God and man need to unite freely. More precisely, it is needed for the Son of God to become man, with a free permission of man, and that the Son of God becomes the head of the entire creation instead of man, so that man could become the Son of god and the entire creation the Body of the Son".

Hatred was presented in the textbook as the final expression of freedom: "Those who hated Christ will continue to hate him and that hatred will be their greatest torture, because they will not be able to change anything". "Man may express his freedom in the form of hatred against others". "However, if man expresses his freedom so that he hates, i.e. denies God, another man and nature, he does not become free. On the contrary, he becomes impersonal, i.e. he becomes no one and nothing and finishes in death. Because only the union with God, with another man and nature gives man the unique and eternal existence".

The Seventh Grade

> Topics: God in whom Christians believe is the Holy Trinity: the Father, the Son and the Holy Spirit. The Father, the Son and the Holy Spirit are three eternal, concrete persons. The Holy Trinity is one God. The cause of God's existence is the Father. God the Father expresses his free existence as love for the other persons – for the Son and the Holy Spirit. The Christian ontology (the being as a communion of freedom). Anthropological consequences of the belief in the Holy Trinity. The Holy Trinity appears through the Liturgy (the Father accepts liturgical offering, the Son, Jesus Christ, offers, and the Holy Spirit gathers all around Christ and unites all with Him). Baptizing and Liturgy as a practical manifestation of faith in God who is the Holy Trinity. The Holy Trinity in the Orthodox iconography.

The ontological character of the Orthodox catechism is recognized by placing not only the law in the background, but also the idea, i.e. teaching and ideology, because they become dangerous for the existence: "Love that loves idea, and forgets the living man is also dangerous for the existence. For that reason people were killed in communist societies but also in other ideological societies dominated by an idea, just in order to maintain that idea. That means that ideas are more important for these communities than living people as persons, regardless whether these ideas are good or bad".

"This assumes that the ecclesiastical community is neither natural, like a family, not ideological, like different ideological communities; it is also not a class or ethnical communities, such as states".

"A natural community is a necessary community. However, what is crucial in our relationships with other, i.e. with God is freedom and love. What we freely love is the most important thing for us. That becomes our source of life, becomes God for us. Natural communities are for us people also important, but they are not an expression of our freedom and they cancel our freedom. A community with parents, brothers and sisters as well as with the nature of a concrete area where he is born is a forced community".

"The Church, connected with the liturgy. And the liturgy does not exist alone as an institution without a union of believers".

"Baptism is, according to teaching of the holy fathers of the Church, a 'second birth'. Baptism is a birth of water and the Holy Spirit". "Baptism is, as we have already emphasized, an entry of man into the liturgical communion. A new birth, which is a birth for the eternal life, assumes a new way of life. That new way of life appears as the Liturgy".

The Eighth Grade

> Topics: Teaching of personality based on the Orthodox triadology. Difference between the nature and the person in God. Ontological consequences of the Orthodox triadology on man and the created world. Man as a person. Union of the material and immaterial nature in the single person of Christ. Worshiping of the created nature in the person of Christ. The Church as the Body of Christ. The future Kingdom of God as the cause of the Church (the final event of the Kingdom of God gives the truthfulness to historical events). Holiness and the Kingdom of God in the Orthodox iconography.

The textbook for the eighth grade presents the theology of God. Understanding of God within Greek philosophy is different from Judaism and Christianity, in which God is a Person, not a part of an impersonal nature. The difference between Judaism and Christianity is that Jesus Christ said that he was the Son of God, and the theological difference lies in the understanding of the Trinity and that the Son and the Holy Spirit come out of God.

"For old Greek philosophers, everything that existed, existed by the necessity of the nature, that was unchangeable. People are born from one impersonal nature and die, i.e. disappear in the same impersonal nature because this is required by natural unchangeable and eternal laws. Everything that is concrete passes away, disappears, only the impersonal nature remains... impersonal and not free?"

"Jesus Christ, however, brought something new in contrast to the Jewish understanding of God. This novelty consists of him saying that he is the Son of God".

"The Jews as the chosen people of God are One".

"Christians too, like Jews, believed in One God, which is testified in the Holy Bible, the Old Testament. For them, too, God does not depend on the world, and he is the almighty creator of the heaven and the earth, everything visible and invisible".

CONCLUSION

Religious education in Serbia is a compulsory subject which can be chosen each year with an alternative of Civics education. Since 2001, it has been gradually introduced so that Religious education is realized in all grades of elementary and secondary schools with one class per week. The teaching plan and programme, as well as all textbooks, was written by the Bishop of Braničevo, Dr. Ignjatije Midić.

An attitude of political authorities towards the religious education is not uniform and there is some insecurity both in teachers and students concerning the future of the subject. On one hand, there are some propositions to increase the number of classes and to introduce the possibility of numerical grading, not only descriptive, as it is the case now, and to equalize catechism teachers with other teaches so that do not work with 1-year contracts. However, the Ministry of Education suggests the cancellation of the subject, reduction of the number of years in which this subject is taught or introduction of a new subject—Religion, which would have general educational and not confessional character.

In such context, religious education has had its proponents and opponents, and it appears that all reforms were aimed at regulating the relation towards religion, since the return to traditional values is already present in the Serbian society. Many questions have been asked about the effects of the religious education on students, about its contribution to the quality of social relationships and morality, and when it is criticized it is usually in reference to its effects both on individuals and the society.

The understanding of the catechism, as designed by Bishop Ignjatije Midić, assumes the same understating of the faith by a teacher. However, in practice, but also in the Orthodox theology itself, and in Christianity in general, there are two types of faith—legalistic and ontological, such as presented in this paper. Religious education textbooks used in Serbia thus far present the ontologically based Orthodox catechism; therefore, this type is far from any kind of traditionalism, because it requires a new approach. The textbook is furnished with illustrations adequate to children's age, which are given as stories from everyday life that can explain abstract theological concepts.

The essence of theology is presented in the context of a communion between man and God, and man and another man and nature. This relationship is dominated by an unconditional love which is not based on the reality but on the expected future time that will bring changes. Responsibility is expected from man since the freedom is the essence of the existence of personality. Other aspects of life come out that freedom.

Teachers are of greater importance than the textbooks, since they, with their interpretations and their personality, realize the theology in the practice, building good and bad interpersonal relationships. Moreover, since the process of maturation in faith is not finished either in teachers or in believers, everyone interprets religious teachings on their own level, and thus the effect of religious educations are different.

We may conclude that the textbooks for Orthodox religious education are confessional and catechetical in character. They try to explain the Orthodox understanding of Christianity. Key words of the textbooks of the Orthodox catechism presented here are communion, the Liturgy, love and freedom and they come from the understanding of God which is presented as the Holy Trinity, God the Father, the Son and the Holy Spirit, in which the hierarchy of relationships is not linear and individual, but it is presented as an unbreakable union which comes out of God the Father who is One.

NOTES

1. Johann Baptist Metz, *Politička teologija* (Zagreb: Kršćanska Sadašnjost, 2004).
2. Srđan Vrcan, "O suverenim religijskim promjenama u optici političke sociologije religije", *Politička misao*, Vol XXXIII, 4 (Zagreb: Fakultet političkih znanosti Sveučilišta, 1996), p. 190.
3. Nikola Knežević, "Kultura sećanja, problem selektivizacije i politizacije religije u verskom medijskom kontekstu", u Nedeljković, Sremac i Gruhonjić, *Uloga medija u normalicaciji odnosa na Zapadnom Balkanu* (Novi Sad: Filozofski fakultet i Centar za istraživanje religije, politike i društva, 2014), pp 271–289.
4. Zorica Kuburić and Milan Vukomanović, "Religious education: The Case of Serbia", in Zorica Kuburić and Cristian Moe (eds.), *Religion and Pluralism in Education*, Comparative Approaches in the Western Balkans (Novi Sad: CEIR in cooperation with the Kotor Network, 2006), pp. 107–138;

Zorica Kuburić i Slađana Zuković, *Verska nastava u školi* (Novi Sad: Centar za empirijska istraživanja religije i Savez pedagoških društava Vojvodine, 2010).

5. Zorica Kuburić and Cristian Moe (eds.), *Religion and Pluralism in Education*, Comparative Approaches in the Western Balkans (Novi Sad: CEIR in cooperation with the Kotor Network, 2006).

6. Mirko Blagojević, "Verska nastava u državnim školama kao indikator de(kontra)ateizacije društva", u Zorica Kuburić (prir.), *Religija, veronauka, tolerancija* (Novi Sad: CEIR, 2002), pp. 45–50;
Dragana Radisavljević—Ćiparizović, "Religija i svakodnevni život: vezanost ljudi za religiju i crkvu u Srbiji krajem devedesetih", u Silvano Bolčić i Anđelka Milić (prir.), *Srbija krajem milenijuma: Razaranje društva, promene i svakodnevni život* (Beograd: Institut za sociološka istraživanja Filozofskog fakulteta u Beogradu, 2002);
Zorica Kuburić, "Religious Education in Serbia and Montenegro", in Elza Kuyk, Roger Jensen, David Lankshear, Elisabeth Loh Manna and Peter Schreiner (eds.), *Religious Education in Europe. Situation and current trends in schools* (Oslo: IKO Publishing House, 2007b);
Zorica Kuburić and Marija Kuburić—Borović, "Revitalization of Religion in the Balkans", in Danijela Gavrilović (ed.), *Revitalization of Religion – Theoretical and comparative approaches* (Niš: YSSSR, 2009), pp. 45–56;
Zorica Kuburić, "Serbia", in *Encyclopedia of religious practices*, second edition, Vol. 1, Religious and Denominations (USA: Gale, 2004), pp. 131–140.

7. *Službeni glasnik RS – Prosvetni glasnik* (5/2001, 4/2003, 6/2003).

8. Ignjatije Midić, *Crkveni slovar, Pravoslavni katihizis za prvi razred osnovne škole* (Beograd: Zavod za udžbenike i nastavna sredstva, 2001).

9. Ignjatije Midić, *Pravoslavni katihizis Priručnik za nastavnike osnovnih i srednjih škole* (Beograd: Zavod za udžbenike i nastavna sredstva, 2003), p. 63.

10. Zorica Kuburić, "Veronauka u Srbiji – rezultati istraživanja", u Milan Sitarski, Marinko Vučinić (prir.), *Vera-znanje-mir* (Beograd: Beogradska otvorena škola, 2005), pp. 345–352;
Zorica Kuburić and Cristian Moe (eds.), *Religion and Pluralism in Education*, Comparative Approaches in the Western Balkans (Novi Sad: CEIR in cooperation with the Kotor Network, 2006).

11. Ignjatije Midić, *Crkveni slovar, Pravoslavni katihizis za prvi razred osnovne škole* (Beograd: Zavod za udžbenike i nastavna sredstva, 2001).

12. Zorica Kuburić, "Stavovi studenata prema uvođenju veronauke", u *Godišnjak Filozofskog fakulteta u Novom Sadu*, Vol. XXV (Novi Sad: Filozofski fakultet, 1997), pp. 405–425;
Zorica Kuburić, *Vera i sloboda, Verske zajednice u Jugoslaviji* (Niš: JUNIR, 1999);

Zorica Kuburić, "Teologija u funkciji mentalnog zdravlja i/ili bolesti", u *Habitus*, br. 3–4 (Novi Sad: Centar za multikulturalnost); Zorica Kuburić (prir.), *Religija, veronauka, tolerancija* (Novi Sad: CEIR, 2002); Zorica Kuburić, "Orthodox Episcopal Deanery in Kruševac from 2000 to 2010", in Mirko Blagojević and Dragan Todorović (eds.), *Orthodoxy from an Empirical Perspective* (Belgrade: Institute for Philosophy and Social Theory, and Nis: Yugoslav Society for the Scientific Study of Religion, 2011), pp. 189–205; Zorica Kuburić, "Realizacija verske nastave u osnovnoj i srednjoj školi", u Snežana Joksimović (prir.), *Verska nastava i građansko vaspitanje u školama u Srbiji* (Beograd: Institut za pedagoška istraživanja, 2003), pp. 96–124; Zorica Kuburić, *Vera i sloboda. Verske zajednice u Jugoslaviji* (Novi Sad: CEIR, 2002); Dragoljub Đorđević i Dragan Todorović, *Mladi, religija, veronauka* (Beograd: Agena, 2002).

13. Snežana Joksimović (prir.), *Verska nastava i građansko vaspitanje u školama u Srbiji* (Beograd: Institut za pedagoška istraživanja, 2003).
14. See http://www.mpn.gov.rs/wp-content/uploads/2015/08/EVALUACIJA_IZBORNOG_PREDMETA_PRAVOSLAVNI_KATIHIZIS.pdf, accessed on June 2, 2016.
15. Zorica Kuburić, "Theological Faculties and Religious Education in Serbia", in *Religija i tolerancija*, Vol. VI, No. 9 (Novi Sad, 2008), pp. 23–36.
16. See http://veronauka.sabornost.org/files/Uputstvo_za_katihete.pdf. Accessed on June 2, 2016.
17. An interview with Miloš Jelić about the religious education textbooks was conducted in Novi Sad on May 16, 2016.
18. See http://www.vjeronauka.net/uploads/5/9/1/8/5918968/npp.pdf. Accessed on June 2, 2016.
19. Miloš Jelić, e-mail correspondence form August 16, 2016.
20. Rastko Jović, e-mail correspondence from August 17, 2016.
21. *Official Gazette of the Republic of Srpska*, No. 46/04 (2004).
22. See http://www.katihetskiodbor.organdhttp://www.vjeronauka.net/. Accessed on June 2, 2016.

CHAPTER 14

Afterword: Religion at School: To Teach or not to Teach? The Case of Kosovo

Gjylbehare Bella Murati and Vedat Sahiti

The revival of religion in postwar Kosovo has brought a new set of issues that deserve thorough analysis. Following the long sleep caused by the communist regime and the subsequent war, religion found a way to make itself visible in the newly emerging social context.

Through the decades, the Albanian community invested heavily in strengthening national identity, broadening access to schools and universities. Yet in an aftermath of armed conflict, the revival of religious convictions has occurred among the younger generation. In contrast to Albanian community the revival of religion among other communities living in Kosovo, namely, Serbian, Turkish, and Bosnians occurred much earlier, after the fall of communism, in 1989. For them, religion became a powerful base of personal identification and collective association. Out of sudden, the Eastern Orthodox Church became a powerful generator for the strengthening of the national identity, in collaboration with the political elite[1].

G.B. Murati (✉) · V.Sahiti
European School of Law and Governance, Pristina, Kosovo

© The Author(s) 2018
G. Ognjenović and J. Jozelić (eds.), *Education in Post-Conflict Transition*, Palgrave Studies in Religion, Politics, and Policy,
https://doi.org/10.1007/978-3-319-56605-4_14

Nevertheless, the state-building actors (both international and national) in Kosovo opted for a democratic state, with a strong civil society that balances state authority. The aim was to establish rule of law and promote a culture of respect for human rights within a worn-torn society. In light of the above, for some years, the discussion about freedom of religion has been strongly linked with the debate on religious education in public schools. The very idea has been strongly opposed by the so-called secular elite.

This contribution sheds light on the current debate regarding religious education in public schools. It provides an overview of the clashes that occur between an aggressive form of secularism to close the door to religious education in public schools and the views that favor the introduction of religious education in public schools.

The aim is to assess whether and how can Kosovo state combine its responsibilities to safeguard the religious rights of all citizens with its interest in preserving its secular identity.

FREEDOM OF RELIGION AND BELIEF IN KOSOVO

Nowadays, there are five religious communities recognized by the Law on Freedom of Religion of Republic of Kosovo, namely, Islamic, Roman Catholic, Orthodox Christians, Protestants Evangelical, and Jewish.[2] The legal framework sets a secular political system in Kosovo.

The majority of the Muslim population belongs to the Hanafi School, although a number follow Sufi traditions. After the war, a new ideology has emerged, so-called Salafist ideology. The majority of the Muslim population neverthelessremains opposed to the rhetoric espoused by Salafistideologists. This has led to a number of internal clashes between clerics, as well as became the subject of wide political and academic debate.

The right to freedom of religion or belief is a fundamental human right recognized in all the major human rights treaties, namely the Universal Declaration of Human Rights (UDHR), the International Covenant on Civil and Political Rights, the European Convention for the Protection of Human Rights and Fundamental Freedoms (ECHR). All three state that this includes freedom to change one's religion or belief and freedom, either alone or in community with others and in public or in private, to manifest one's religion or belief, in worship, teaching, practice, and observance. All these documents are directly applicable in Kosovo. Further, Kosovo has its own Law on Freedom of Religion, which expresses the values of religious freedom, nondiscrimination, and religious neutrality.

WHY RELIGION SHOULD AND SHOULD NOT BE ALLOWED IN PUBLIC SCHOOL?

Much of the war debate about religion in public school has been framed in terms of the combat between two polarized groups: the secularists who insist on neutrality in relation to matters of religious belief, neutrality that excludes religious moral beliefs from the realm of public institutions,[3] and religious community who sees religious education as an important component of freedom of religion. In addition, there is a group which considers that schools should teach children in a neutral, objective way about the different beliefs that different people have about Gods, and leaves it up to parents and churches to teach specific religious beliefs outside of school hours[4]. This appears that the former would be an unacceptable form of indoctrination, while the latter would be an acceptable form of education.

Battles about this issue are often fought at the round tables, newspapers, TV debates, but never in the courtrooms.

The legal framework governing the preuniversity education in Kosovo does not permit public institutions to teach religion in schools. It states: *"Public education institutions shall refrain from teaching religion or other activities that propagate a specific religion"*.[5]

This law has been served as a ground for the Ministry of Education to issue an administrative decision and ban the wearing of headscarves in public schools.[6] The administrative decision has been subjected to a wide criticism by the representatives of Muslim Community. It has been considered as discriminatory as it lacks clarity. It has been argued that the decision (AI 6/2010) that regulates code of conduct lacks clarity as the authorities fail to provide a proper definition of the meaning of the "religious uniform".[7] According to international standards,[8] this can lead to different interpretations which might lead to illegal and proportional restriction on the right to freedom of religion or belief. Namely, limitations to the manifestations of religion or belief must be clear and precise.[9] Following that order, several public schools in different municipalities have prohibited students from entering school premises.

The religious education in schools is not only opposed by the political elite, but also by two other religious communities. For instance, the Protestant Church considers that teaching faith in public schools is not a state priority nor of our society as a whole.[10] It goes further by stating: "*We have also expressed our deepest concerns towards the idea of introducing 'Religion' in the public schooling curriculum. Not only that such action would seriously harm the tolerance in the country but we are concerned it will make our public schools as camps for training Islamic terrorists*".[11]

While according to the Catholic Church in Kosovo, the issue must not have the purpose of some ambitions for political benefits, but common goals to educate the new generations in the spirit of our Renaissance. According to them, "*for the sake of this wealth that we have inherited religious tolerance and peaceful coexistence, we believe that religious education should take place in churches and mosques, while learning about religions, for tolerance and coexistence historic interfaith may be part of public education*".[12]

In contrast to Protestant and Catholic , Kosovo Islamic community considers that religion is a key component for the proper education of new generations, as a tool to fight the negative phenomena such as alcoholism, drugs, violent extremism, etc.[13] Accordingly, the aim of religious education in school is to provide a real picture of religion, to contribute to improvements of student's behaviors, etc. The Kosovo Islamic community is of opinion that introducing the religious education would take time as it would require some preparatory work. For instance, the potential teacher would need adequate training that will equip them with knowledge and teaching skills that can provide relevant guidance to promote religious values.

This is, in turn, will protect young generation from extremist propaganda and practices that continue to hamper the entire society.

Yet, while Albanian religious communities continue to debate whether to introduce religious education in schools, the Serbian Orthodox Church has managed to spread its influence rapidly throughout society. In the last few decades it has gained increased influence over the public institutions.[14] As a result, the Government of the Republic of Serbia has introduced the religious education in 2001 in all Serbian schools, not as mandatory but as an optional subject which is in compliance with international standards.[15] In this context, it has been observed that the number of pupils attending this course is very high.[16]

Reconciling Conflicting Aims of Islamic Community and State

Kosovo's political elite tends to keep religion out of politics, pretending that religion is nothing than a private matter. Those who tend to push religious education in the context of human rights framework would need to get courage and challenge the existing law. However, it is likely that courts will draw on the experience of the *European Court of Human Rights*, which showed on several occasions that the exercise of balancing rights is a complex one, different scenarios in which there are competing rights to be carefully examined in light of all the particular circumstances. In this context, given different national histories and cultures, states have the discretion to adopt freedom of religion in light of the needs and values of their particular societies. The Court refers to this discretion as the states' "margin of appreciation."

Yet, one may only wonder what would Kosovo Courts say if they would ever need to decide whether the existing law violates the freedom of religion of the biggest religious community in Kosovo? Would national identity get primacy over freedom of religion?

Conclusion

Education, as the most important tool for the development of an individual as well as for society, has to be a safe place where all can acquire basic skills, knowledge and values without prejudice of any kind.

The contributions in this book give us an insight into how education can be a tool in the hands of the political elite who deny opportunities to many to achieve the basic skills through education, skills which are essential to their further development as human beings. The overall functioning of the educational system in the Southeast has been compromised by overtly political influence and the politicization of its content. Such politicization of the learning process is jeopardizing the integrity and dignity of the entire educational system.

The main objective of the state in this context should be to prevent abuse and irregularities in the educational system and the protection of the system from all unwanted influence, above all political, and to provide conditions for a politicized education.

Unfortunately, the contributions in this volume show that even the government, which is responsible for the individual's realization of their right to education, actively participates in creating a grotesque form of politicization by allowing the use of questionable textbooks, or thus by supporting the structure, form and system of segregated schools, bringing education closer to the edge of a downfall.

What the contributions in this volume about religious education analyze is how the politicization of religion i.e. religion as instrument of achieving a political goal, in the hands of the political elite seem to be a perfect instrument for retaining the segregation achieved through the war across the Yugoslav successor states. Educational politics, in other words, prolong this ethnic segregation as a 'normal state of affairs' until today. Finally, examples of segregation in schools analyzed here only confirm that in the Southeast the educational system is a system of apartheid: confessional and religious affiliation being the form of existence and a non-affiliation becoming an indicator of abnormality.

NOTES

1. NonkaBogumilova, Religion, Law and Politics in the Balkans in the end of the twentieth and the beginning of the twenty-first century, Istok-Zapada Publishing 2005, p. 17.
2. Law on Freedom of Religion in Kosovo No.02/L-31 promulgated by UNMIK in 2006 available at: http://www.assembly-kosova.org/common/docs/ligjet/2006_02-L31_en.pdf.
3. Blerim Latifi, *Kontrabanda e Sheriatit nen etiken e te drejtave te njeriut.* Latifi serves as a political advisor to the Head of Kosovo Parliament. Available at the following website: http://www.zemrashqiptare.net/news/id_24027/Blerim-Latifi:-Kontrabanda-e-sheriatit-n%C3%ABn-etiket%C3%ABn-e-t%C3%AB-drejtave-t%C3%AB-njeriut.html.
4. Ismail Hasani, Professor of Sociology, University of Prishtina. Statement available at the following website: http://www.gazetaexpress.com/lajme/politikanet-pro-dhe-kunder-fese-ne-shkolla-191999/?archive=1.
5. Article 3.7 of the Law on Pre-university education, No.04/L–032.
6. Administrative instruction 6/2010 on code of conduct and disciplinary measures for students of upper secondary schools, Ministry of Education, Science and Technology of the Republic of Kosovo.
7. Head imam of Kosovo, SabriBajgora, article available at: http://www.bajgora.com/index.php/artikuj/6-roli-i-fese-ne-edukimin-shkollor.
8. Main Human Rights Law Instruments.
9. M.TodsParker, *The Freedom to Manifest Religious Belief: An analysis of necessity clauses of ICCPR and ECHR,*Duke Journal of Comparative International law, Vol 17: 91, 2006.

10. Protestant Evangelical church available at: http://kishaprotestante.net/en/folio/kpec-teaching-subject-faith-kosovas-education-system/.
11. Report, Kosova Protestant Evangelical Church, May 15, 2009. See https://danutm.files.wordpress.com/2009/06/kpec-religious-freedom-report-09-05.pdf.
12. See: http://sq.radiovaticana.va/news/2016/04/19/q%C3%ABndrim_zyrtar_i_kish%C3%ABs_katolike_n%C3%AB_kosov%C3%AB_rreth_l%C3%ABnd%C3%ABs_feta/1223874.
13. Head imam of Kosovo, SabriBajgora, article available at: http://www.bajgora.com/index.php/artikuj/6-roli-i-fese-ne-edukimin-shkollor.
14. Curriculum, Ministarstvo Prosvete Naukei Tehnologije Republike Srbije. Following an aftermath of Kosovo conflict in 1999, a range of parallel structures was established by the Serbian state on the territory of Kosovo, including, in public administration, judiciary, security, health and educational institutions. Subsequently, all public schools in Serb enclaves in Kosovo use the curriculum of the Serbian Ministry of Education and Sports. The Ministry provides these schools with textbooks, diplomas and stamps.
15. The Universal Declaration of Human Rights, approved in the General Assembly of the United Nations dated 10.12.1948, Resolution 217 (Chapter III), Article 26, paragraph 3 states: "Parents have a fundamental right for their children to choose the kind of education."
16. Interview conducted with the history teacher from northern part of Kosovo. Interview conducted on December 7, 2016.

CONCLUSION

Education, as the most important tool for the development of an individual as well as for society, has to be a safe place where all can acquire basic skills, knowledge and values without prejudice of any kind.

The contributions in this book give us an insight into how education can be a tool in the hands of the political elite who deny opportunities to many to achieve the basic skills through education, skills which are essential to their further development as human beings. The overall functioning of the educational system in the Southeast has been compromised by overtly political influence and the politicization of its content. Such politicization of the learning process is jeopardizing the integrity and dignity of the entire educational system.

The main objective of the state in this context should be to prevent abuse and irregularities in the educational system and the protection of the system from all unwanted influence, above all political, and to provide conditions for a politicized education.

Unfortunately, the contributions in this volume show that even the government, which is responsible for the individual's realization of their right to education, actively participates in creating a grotesque form of politicization by allowing the use of questionable textbooks, or thus by supporting the structure, form and system of segregated schools, bringing education closer to the edge of a downfall.

© The Editor(s) (if applicable) and The Author(s) 2018
G. Ognjenović and J. Jozelić (eds.), *Education in Post-Conflict Transition*, Palgrave Studies in Religion, Politics, and Policy,
https://doi.org/10.1007/978-3-319-56605-4

What the contributions in this volume about religious education analyze is how the politicization of religion i.e. religion as instrument of
achieving a political goal, in the hands of the political elite seem to be
a perfect instrument for retaining the segregation achieved through the
war across the Yugoslav successor states. Educationalpolitics, in other
words, prolong this ethnic segregation as a 'normal state of affairs' until
today. Finally, examples of segregation in schools analyzed here only confirm that in the Southeast the educational system is a system of apartheid: confessional and religiousaffiliation being the form of existence and
a non-affiliation becoming an indicator of abnormality.

INDEX

© The Editor(s) (if applicable) and The Author(s) 2018
G. Ognjenović and J. Jozelić (eds.), *Education in Post-Conflict Transition*, Palgrave Studies in Religion, Politics, and Policy,
https://doi.org/10.1007/978-3-319-56605-4